mrscleanjeans'
housekeeping
with
KIDS

mrscleanjeans' housekeeping

with

KIDS

**Family Pickup Lines (and Household Routines)
That Work with Less Work from You**

by Tara Aronson

RODALE

© 2004 by Tara Aronson
Illustrations © 2004 by Michael Gellatly
Coins photograph © C Squared/Getty Images
Jacks photograph © C Squared/Getty Images
Boy sweeping photograph © Inc. Archive Holdings/Getty Images

Printed in the United States of America
Rodale Inc. makes every effort to use acid-free ∞, recycled paper ♻.

Photographs of Chris Jr., Lyndsay, and D. Payne Aronson provided courtesy of the author

Book design by Chris Rhoads

Library of Congress Cataloging-in-Publication Data

Aronson, Tara.
    Mrs. Clean Jeans' housekeeping with kids : family pickup lines (and household routines) that work with less work from you / Tara Aronson.
        p.   cm.
    Includes index.
    ISBN 1–57954–882–2 paperback
    1. Home economics.   I. Title.
TX147.A7597   2004
640—dc22   2003025442

Distributed to the book trade by St. Martin's Press

    4 6 8 10 9 7 5 3   paperback

WE **INSPIRE** AND **ENABLE** PEOPLE TO IMPROVE
THEIR LIVES AND THE WORLD AROUND THEM

FOR MORE OF OUR PRODUCTS

WWW.RODALESTORE.COM
(800) 848-4735

For Christopher—the love of my life, my best friend, my husband—with thanks for making the romantic dream begun on the beaches of St. Lucia a blessed family reality today. You're the inspiration behind my goal of making—and keeping—our house a loving, organized home. I thank God daily for His love, and for yours. May He continue to bless our union and our children—Chris Jr., Lyndsay, and D. Payne.

" . . . *But those who seek the Lord shall not lack any good thing.*"

PSALM 34:10

Acknowledgments

For Connie Ballard (also known as Mrs. Dirty Jeans), my dear friend, faithful confidante, and gifted and tireless editor for all things newspaper, Web site, and book for nearly a decade—I couldn't have done this without your input, your support, your dry wit and humor. Thank you, dear friend!

For Caroline Carney, of Book Deals Inc., my literary agent—thank you for taking a chance on me. Your faithful encouragement and prayers meant the world to me. Thanks for all your tireless work on my behalf. You're an awesome woman.

Thank you to a very special friend and tireless agent, Angelica Holiday. Your ideas, enthusiasm, and knowledge know no bounds. Thank you for coming along for the mrscleanjeans.com, mcjteens.com, and beyond Internet and television appearance ride.

For Ellen Phillips, my equally gifted and tireless editor at Rodale. It has indeed been an exciting ride with you at the helm! Thank you for believing in Mrs. Clean Jeans initially, and for your upbeat encouragement and tireless support during the writing and editing of this book.

Thanks too to Jennifer Bright Reich, project editor at Rodale. Your enthusiasm and great graphics ideas have been inspiring to me, and your insightful edits have made this a much better book. Thank you.

Kudos to book cover designer, Drew Frantzen. Thank you for creating the warm and wonderful visuals and cover for this book. Your creative talents are exceeded only by your dedication and vision for this project. People can—and do—judge a book by its cover. I'm most grateful you were instrumental in mine.

Thanks too to Chris Rhoads, who artfully arranged this book's interior graphics and photos. Your vision and simply elegant design are much appreciated.

And to my wonderfully quirky test subjects for all things home—my elder son Christopher Jr., daughter Lyndsay, and youngest son Payne—thank you for being the uniquely gifted individuals you are. Raising each of you is the greatest responsibility God has given me. And it is my greatest joy in life. Each day you teach me so much about what really matters in life and what making an imprint on eternity really means. Your mom couldn't love you any more.

Finally, heartfelt, humble thanks to my circle of girlfriends who prayed for this work's inspired completion—Norma Broudy, Lisa Bybee, Kelly Cicconi, Lou Mulford Greig, and Kim Selby. Your prayers are answered here.

Contents

Part III: Guests and Getting Around

Part IV: Cleaning Around the Year

introduction: housekeeping with kids

DONNA REED REALLY HAD IT GOOD.

She pranced about the house in a dress and a frilly apron. And all that she had to worry about was whether or not her floors sparkled.

Fast-forward to the 21st century. Today's mom only *wishes* that she had time to prance about *anywhere*—especially the house. On good days, she slips home for a few hours between carpools, volunteering at school, and errands, and she manages to single-handedly check a chore or three off her housecleaning list before dashing back out the door. On not-so-good days, she seriously considers giving up her firstborn child to have herself duplicated—or to pay for a full-time maid.

You'll see no hausfrau frills on today's mom. She's dressed for reality in blue jeans. And, unlike carefree Donna Reed, today's mom worries about virtually *everything*—including the floors, which are still covered with toast crumbs from breakfast. After all, most moms—myself included—wear many a daily hat: nutritionist, chauffeur, laundress, cleaning coordinator, event planner, hostess, master scheduler, errand runner, owie kisser, veterinarian, farmer, and more.

And then, of course, there are all of the other jobs—wife, friend, sister, and daughter—that she squeezes into her "free" time.

The solution? Get the entire family to pitch in at home. No kidding! It really is possible to integrate kids into (nearly) every aspect of cleaning and organizing every room in the home. Without starting World War III.

Really.

I know that a clean family household is no accident. I've also discovered (as most moms quickly do) that personal fulfillment isn't found in picking up someone else's dirty duds, but in spending time with loved ones. And since housecleaning (the cake) has a tendency to get in the way of family fun time (the icing), I created cleaning and organizing strategies that combine the two.

And now I offer my strategies to you. *Mrs. Clean Jeans' Housekeeping with Kids* is my simple system for cleaning and tidying every room of the house—together.

Firstborns everywhere are safe at last!

why involve the family?

Central to my housekeeping strategy is organizing the entire house—room by room—around the needs of every member of the family. After all, the reason most homes look war-torn is because rooms haven't been set up for daily living by parents and kids. To make matters worse, often one adult—usually Mom—has sole responsibility for masterminding all the details (which is why moms sometimes get that funny, shell-shocked look around 7 P.M.).

Besides being bad for Mom's long-term mental health, having one person holding all the scheduling, cleaning, and essential information cards leaves the family in a precarious position: Who will know where little Katie's soccer practice is this week, or how to run the wash without turning everything pink, or what project Johnny absolutely must turn in tomorrow if Mom gets hit by a bus?

Of course, Mom's demise would bring up other unpleasant dilemmas that I'm not qualified to provide solutions for. The point is: No Mom (or Dad) should be an island. Unless parents have a battle plan designed to guide the troops through the minefield of daily family life, they can't expect to survive the pre-college years with their sanity intact. Then once they devise their battle plan, it should not be top secret! The plan should be posted so everyone is in sync with what needs to be done when.

This book helps you (the generals) not only gain control of your home and keep it running smoothly, but it also shows you how to enlist the privates in the campaign. You'll find there will be room for every drawing, school paper, and test that arrives each day—and even the littlest privates will know where that is. The wild carpool routine will be tamed, the family plan for buffing surfaces will be in place, surprise visits from friends won't be dreaded, and even the most domestically challenged will be ready in a flash to host unexpected in-laws overnight.

In short: World War III will be averted, Mom won't be cranky any more, and the family will have a clean, happy, harmonious home to enjoy.

For example, here are three of my family's successful strategies for getting the kids to help clean:

The Marble Jar: This is a good system for encouraging long-term behavior change. I gave my daughter Lyndsay, 10, and my son Christopher, 11, each two pint-size jars. One was filled with marbles, and the other was empty. Each time Lyndsay or Christopher did a chore, we moved a marble into the empty jar. Every time Lyndsay or Christopher missed a chore, we returned a marble to the original jar. When the second jar was full,

each child received a really big reward. (Lyndsay worked on hers for almost an entire school year and was rewarded with her two cats. Christopher's tickets to the 49ers game took a bit longer to earn.)

Onesie: For my little guy, 3-year-old Payne, cleaning games work wonders. Yes, cleaning games. (No, that is not an oxymoron.) Here's how to play our favorite, which I call Onesie. Payne puts away one type of object, for example, everything that's blue, bigger than his hand, or round. When Payne was a baby, I simply had him put things into boxes or low plastic bins as we went. No, he really didn't help much, but he enjoyed it and became accustomed to the idea that he should help clean. Plus, games like these provide a great way to introduce Payne to educational concepts like colors, shapes, and sizes.

60 Minutes: On Saturdays, our whole family engages in a 60-minute, top-to-bottom cleaning routine. This is a round-the-room and through-the-home cleaning and organizing system, with a role for every family member. The tallest (my 6-foot-1 husband, Christopher) takes top duty, wiping down crown molding, cabinet tops, and hanging lamps, while the smallest (our 3-foot-3 three-year-old, Payne) tackles the close-to-the ground jobs, such as running his hand along the baseboards with a damp bobby sock. Meanwhile, our preteen son cruises around the room damp-mopping the floor, while our preschooler has happily moved on to getting old magazines ready for recycling. And me? I help our preteen daughter, Lyndsay, change the sheets on her top bunk. The goal of the day is to turn housework into teamwork, with each member of the family helping get it all done right—and fast.

let's get cleaning

All these rules and pickup games won't work for every family, of course. Families have children of different ages, different needs, and different tolerances for dirt and disorder. For that reason, I offer an arsenal of tips and strategies for parents to choose from.

These strategies and tips are time-tested: I've gleaned them from sources ranging from friends, my *San Francisco Chronicle* cleaning column "Coming Clean," my mrscleanjeans.com tip-sharing visitors, and the best source of all—from living with my own trio of angels, who often scratch their halos as well as their knees. It's all here for you to pick and choose from in *Mrs. Clean Jeans' Housekeeping with Kids*.

Bear in mind that the goal isn't a home that could pass a military white-glove inspection. You still probably won't have a picture-perfect home—at least not until the kids have homes of their own. But in the meantime, you'll have the next best thing: the tools to set up and run a clean, organized, stress-free home without nagging or tantrums. The goal is to take the stress—as well as the mess—out of your home for good. I hope that the time you spending reading this book will reward you with the basics you need to make your house a peaceful, well-kept home where everyone pitches in joyfully.

Tara Aronson, "Mrs. Clean Jeans"
mrscleanjeans.com

how to use this book:
a field guide

THIS BOOK COVERS EVERYTHING you need to know to put—and keep—your home and your family cleaning team on track. We'll talk about cleaning smarter and quicker with kids, organizing room-by-room, lightening the laundry load, corralling kids, and even preparing the minivan for calm carpools and relaxing weekend getaways.

For example, this book will show you how to:

• Make family participation in household cleaning and maintenance the rule rather than the exception

• Clean efficiently and quickly, even with a 2-year-old who's constantly underfoot

- Create fun storage for every family member's activities, so there's a place for everything and everything stays in place

- Get each family member to help lighten the laundry load

- Create a family calendar with everyone's appointments at your fingertips

- Design a homework center to ease the nightly study crunch

- Plan help-yourself menus for frantic nights

- Divvy up chores equably and get them done without nagging

- Convert your vehicle into a mobile home center

- Make your house a cozy, welcoming home

First, in chapter 1, I'll discuss why chores are important for children, and I'll offer tips on how to motivate them to take responsibility at home. For the rest of the book, I've broken down my cleaning and organizing strategies into separate rooms and activities, such as organizing or dealing with pets, and dedicated a chapter to each. Each chapter begins with a brief overview of the problems presented by that room or activity, followed by some or all of these six features:

1. **Clean House Rules:** These are the rules everyone in the home lives by to keep dirt and clutter under control. Far from draconian, these rules are fair and easy to understand and follow. (Take it out? You put it back. Eat off it? You put it in the dishwasher.) I will suggest Clean House Rules for each activity and room that will keep things clean and organized.

2. **A Home for Everything:** Here you'll find organizational solutions. The concept behind this is that everything in the house (from G. I. Joe outfits to cookbooks to C batteries) should have a designated home. I'll tell you how to determine what to trash (or donate) and what to stash (or store long-term). Then I'll show how to organize that stash. For each room, I'll suggest clever organizational ideas to contain kiddie clutter—as well as tried-and-true tips on how to involve the troops in the process.

3. **Chores by Age:** This section in each chapter lists the types of tasks kids can generally do around the house and at what ages they can do them.

4. **Dirty Little Secrets:** Check here for cleaning solutions. No matter how busy your family is, the regular purging of mildew, grime, dust, and dirt still needs to be done so you can stay healthy and teach your kids what

they need to know to take care of their own home someday. There's a role for everyone (tiny tykes to teens) in my top-to-bottom home-cleaning production that makes every family member—and your home—a star.

5. **Family Pickup Lines:** In each chapter, I'll share my motivational secrets. These are innovative ways to turn dreary cleaning routines into fun family activities and make cleaning and tidying a series of games to be enjoyed, not drudgery. Most kids really like to clean if the work is presented in an entertaining way. Look for these boxed tips sprinkled throughout each chapter.

6. **Penny Pinchers:** Be on the lookout for these sections that offer easy, innovative ways to save your family money.

After these separate room and activity chapters, you'll find a complete chore list, which shows what chores need to be done when. Some chores need to be done each day, others once a week, still others once a month, seasonally, or even yearly. In "Mrs. Clean Jeans' Housekeeping Routine," beginning on page 253, I'll give you my complete master chore list.

Now, assemble your cleaning team! Grab your husband, grab the kids, everybody grab your favorite cleaning tool, be it duster, mop, or broom. It's time to make your home sparkle!

Part I
Getting Started

Chapter 1

gearing up for a family (cleaning) affair

LET'S GET REAL HERE. A clean, tidy home usually isn't at the top of—okay, really even on—a kid's list of priorities.

Kids' lack of enthusiasm for cleaning is understandable. Do you know anyone who turns cartwheels at the prospect of mopping the crusty kitchen floor or taking out the smelly garbage? Me neither. But we grownups know that just because something doesn't make our Top 10 List doesn't mean we can chill out on it altogether. Some of life is just not fun.

So what's a clean-minded Mom or Dad to do when the playroom table needs a post-finger-painting wipe-down or the kitchen table has spaghetti splotches—and the culprit's less than eager to pitch in? Start by taking a deep breath, and wipe up the mess yourself—one last time.

If the kids are reluctant participants in your housecleaning routine, or if your requests to "pick up after yourself" are met with backtalk, dawdling, rolling eyes, or outright refusal, it's time to wrest control of the asylum from the inmates. And delegate chores to them.

Sure, our moms may have dusted and vacuumed every day (and without help from us). But we don't have to! It's a brave new world out there, and today's Mom knows the score: The only way to hit a cleaning home run is to draft a cleaning team from a family of volunteers.

Better still, involving the family in housekeeping will cut down on the amount of time we spend cleaning and increase the time we spend with our families. What could be better? (Yeah, I know, having a live-in housekeeper. But this is not that kind of book.)

the chore conundrum

Parents are all over the map on the issue of chores. At one extreme, parents post long chore lists that children must complete before any fun commences. Kids live here, too, they say, and they helped make the mess. We're building responsible adults. Kids should earn their keep.

At the other extreme are parents who don't expect kids to do anything at all around the house. Well, they explain, kids are so busy with all their activities. Kids are only kids once. It's easier to do it ourselves than to nag them into doing it. Or (and this is my favorite): That's what we have a maid for.

I take a moderate approach to chores. Even if you have a live-in housekeeper (not counting yourself), I believe that children should still do a reasonable amount of chores, based on their ages and homework loads. After all, keeping a house clean and running smoothly is the job of everyone who lives there—regardless of age and gender. (Hear that, Dads?)

Here are some of the reasons I think kids should have chores:

- Chores give children a sense of responsibility that follows through into other areas of their lives, especially school. If kids don't keep up with their belongings at home, they won't be responsible for them at school, either.

- Helping around the house teaches essential life skills. You won't be there to do the laundry or scrub the toilet for your son when he's in college, so he'd better learn to do it himself. As parents, preparing our kids for life is in our job description.

- Housekeeping gives kids a sense of ownership. Kids like to have things that are just theirs. That includes their rooms. If Mom is always rearranging their drawers, how can their rooms truly be their own?

- Helping to clean gives kids a sense of belonging. Kids like to help, under the right circumstances. And they like doing things with the rest of the family.

- Keeping things neat instills a love of order. A child with chores will grow up liking things in place. That predisposition will carry over into adulthood.

- Housekeeping gives kids a sense of pride of accomplishment. They'll learn to love that feeling.

- Giving children chores to do teaches them that no one is the family servant—not even Mom!

Those are just a few examples. There are many more. The point is: Take the time to bring up your child to be an independent, responsible adult. Yes, it's often easier to do chores yourself. But if you're interested in permanently turning down the volume in your home and cutting out the nagging, the negotiating, the drill-sergeant routine—or if you're simply tired of being a martyr—you'll be glad you chose housekeeping with kids. (And so will their future spouses.)

assigning chores by age

Getting kids to help with cleaning isn't easy, especially in the beginning. Besides, how much help can you realistically expect from a child?

The answer depends on the child's age. Below I've listed examples of chores that kids can generally do by certain ages. Your child may be capable of doing a chore sooner or later, depending on her level of concentration, fine-motor skills, or maturity. Once a child reaches a certain skill or age level, he can generally do the chores for his age group and those for the age groups below.

However, you'll want to be there the first time your child tackles a new task, regardless of age. Beginners need pointers for even the simplest jobs, such as washing dinner dishes by hand. What's second nature to us is a new experience for them. For example, you have to explain which dishes should be washed first and why, and you need to show them how to stack the freshly washed items in the dryer rack so that it doesn't go crashing to the floor. (Keep in mind that some of these chores need to be done each day, but others need to be done only once a week. We'll talk about these finer points and a complete age-by-age chore list in "Mrs. Clean Jeans' Housekeeping Routine" on page 253.)

Tasks for kids ages 2 and under:

• Get diaper

• Put toys in bins or drawers

• Put dirty clothes in the hamper if the top is low enough

• Turn off the TV if the button is within reach

• Wipe feet before coming inside

• Close cabinet doors

• Help set the table

• Turn on the dishwasher

Tasks for kids ages 3 to 5:

• Previous chores, plus:

• Pull comforter up over bed

• Place dirty dishes on the kitchen counter

• Put away toys and games and all their pieces in the proper boxes or bins

• Return books to bookshelves

• Dust low furniture

• Return CDs, DVDs, and videocassettes to their cases

• Sponge down the play table

• Help unload the dishwasher

• Water plants

• Remove clothes from the dryer

• Help fold laundry

• Take clean, folded clothes to his or her room

Tasks for kids ages 6 to 9:

• Previous chores, plus:

• Make the bed

• Feed pets

• Exercise pets

• Clean pets' bowls and cages

• Put away groceries

• Help make breakfast

• Set and clear table

• Do simple cooking tasks such as rinsing vegetables

• Put dishes in the dishwasher

• Wipe up spills

• Tidy bedroom

• Vacuum, with help, depending on machine's height and weight

• Sweep floors

• Empty wastebaskets

• Prepare recyclables for pickup

• Fold simple laundry items

• Match socks from dryer

• Hang up towel

- Do easy yard work such as weeding and pruning with small shears

- Rake leaves

- Help wash car

Tasks for kids ages 10 to 13:

- Previous chores, plus:

- Pour beverages for meals

- Help hand-wash dishes

- Make lunch for school

- Unload dishwasher

- Disinfect kitchen and bathroom countertops

- Do a surface cleaning of fridge

- Sort, wash, and fold laundry

- Change bed linens

- Clean bedroom

- Mop floors

- Clean the shower

- Clean windows

- Clean blinds

- Take trash containers to curb

- Wipe clean the car's dashboard and upholstery

- Help clean garage

- Shovel snow

Tasks for kids ages 14 to 17:

- Previous chores, plus:

- Clean toilet, sinks, and tubs

- Organize closet

- Prepare meals

- Mow lawn

divvying up the chores

So now you know what types of chores are appropriate for kids of different ages, but how many chores can they do? I've found a good rule of thumb for determining the number of chores that can be reasonably expected of a child is his or her age, divided by two and rounded up when needed. This number remains the same regardless of the number of chores that need to be tackled in a given week. The number of chores may be small, but some chores need to be done each day.

Using this system, an 8-year-old with six siblings would have the same number of chores as an 8-year-old only child. The point is not just to get the work done; the point is teach your child responsibility *and* to get some work done. After all, if you have only one child, it hardly seems fair to saddle her with the entire home's chores. If chores are to be successful, they must be both fun and fair. And your supervision and enforcement must be consistent.

These chore-divvying rules of thumb have worked for my family and many of my regular readers and Web site visitors. For example, Chris, our eldest at 11, gets six chores a week, 10-year-old Lyndsay gets five chores a week, and Payne, 3, gets just one.

Here's an important caveat: By chores, I don't mean making your bed, clearing your dishes from the table, or keeping your clothes on the hangers and off the floor. Those are essential tasks that are done—period. They are just a part of the routine of daily life, like brushing your teeth. We refer to them as "personal virtues" for which completion is reward enough. No cash or barter changes hands. Zilch. Nada. These tasks are so ingrained in our older two children's psyches that I can't tell you the last time I had to ask either one of them to make their beds.

What I mean by "chores" are all those other cleaning and organizing tasks that contribute to our family's comfort and our home's overall tidiness. These include tasks such as sweeping the floor, raking leaves, folding laundry, changing bed linens, and cleaning toilets.

our household routine

Here's how we divide the chores in my home. I've created a list of the Aronson family chores—all those things that could be done in a given week. (I say "could" because part of housekeeping with kids is adjusting your cleaning standards a bit when cleaning with wee ones.)

Sunday evenings, we gather around the kitchen table to discuss the week ahead and divvy up the chores. Chris chooses six chores; Lyndsay selects five; and we toss an easy chore Payne's way. Then we're set for the week. No whining; the kids chose their chores.

Our chore list includes:

Kitchen:

- Set table
- Clear table
- Load dishwasher
- Damp-mop floor
- Unload dishwasher
- Empty trash
- Sweep floor

Bathroom:

- Clean toilet, sink, and tub
- Buff shower doors
- Wash shower walls

General household:

- Vacuum rugs and carpets
- Clean windows and mirrors

- Vacuum upholstery and curtains
- Wash and fold laundry
- Change bed linens
- Polish silver

Outside:

- Sweep porches and walkways
- Mow lawn
- Weed garden
- Water flowers
- Clean garage

Okay, the mathematically inclined have probably already figured out that's 21 chores, with only 12 going to the kids. Who picks up the other 9? Mom and Dad, of course. And they don't get to choose! However, if a child does not do his or her chores, whines about them, or does not do them well, the next week he or she gets an extra chore. A bonus! This bonus system keeps them on track.

Conversely, if a kid is really motivated—as our son, Chris, often is, for example, to save enough between Nana's birthday checks to buy a laptop computer—there are big cleaning chores to volunteer for. These include seasonal chores such as spring cleaning his bedroom closet, wiping down the interior of all his clothing drawers, and raking leaves. (He'd shovel snow, too, but we're rarely in need of such help in Southern California.)

motivating kids to work

There are many ways to motivate kids to help out around the house. Often kids are so eager to please and help out that they need little motivation at all from their parents. At other times, serious incentives are required. These fall into two categories: cash and noncash.

cold, hard cash

The most obvious motivation to get kids to do chores is to pay them for it. You probably won't be surprised to learn that parents are almost as divided about paying for chores as they are about chores themselves.

The anti-allowance parents argue persuasively that kids shouldn't be paid to help out around the house; after all, it's their house, too. And being part of a family means giving your time and efforts to make the home a better place for everyone to live—no compensation required. Worse, they say, paying for chores gives kids the mistaken idea that there's a choice: "I'll skip my chores because I don't need the money this week."

The pro-pay parents argue, perhaps even more persuasively, that a tangible reward for kids' efforts motivates them to do extra jobs around the house. (In the interest of full disclosure I admit that I'm in their court.) And in the real world, they say, that's exactly how adults are rewarded or paid for their work. Having money to save or spend also provides an invaluable opportunity to learn important—and tough—money lessons early, while Mom and Dad are still around to talk with.

Here's an example. "Mom, please let me get those rare Pokemon cards," my son Chris pleaded several years back. "In a few years, they'll be worth a lot more than the $80 they're charging at the video store."

In spite of my repeated warnings that such trendy items often go out of style, causing any "value" to tank with it, Chris insisted on using his birthday money that he had saved up over the past two years to purchase two cards. I gave my reluctant blessing, seeing a lesson looming in the future.

the computerized chore chart

Here's a common scenario. The family meets, chores are assigned, and the next day there's a mix-up on whose turn it is to set the table. Solution: Create your own chore chart to keep track of who's doing what when.

You could just take a sheet of paper and write down who's supposed to do which chores. Or you could go more high-tech and create a computerized chore chart. It's quick and easy.

Using a basic spreadsheet program such as Microsoft Excel, simply type in the chores that need doing in the week ahead and which family member is doing them. Add check boxes next to each chore. After your child has completed a task, he can initial (teens), check (preteens), put a smiley face (younger kids), or you can affix a colorful sticker (toddlers).

If your kids can't read yet, cut and paste photos from magazines to represent the chores they need to do. A toy truck could represent playroom pickup, or clothes from a catalog could signify putting hers in the hamper or drawer.

Consider color-coding the chores and the names of the chore-doers. For example, Chris's column is blue, Lyndsay's column is pink, and Payne's is yellow. That makes it easier for each child to see his or her jobs.

Make sure you're setting up a *family* chore system, not a kid chore system. Put yourself and your significant other on the chart, too! For example, let them know that Mom will be doing the grocery shopping and laundry, and Dad will be mowing the lawn and separating the recyclables. Think like a kid here and you'll understand why:

Sure enough, we recently tossed out those "rare and valuable" Pokemon cards while spring cleaning his bedroom. Chris couldn't even give them away. The sheepish look on his face as he threw away the cards told me that he remembered our talk, regretting not having taken my advice. I never had to open my mouth.

On a more positive note, money-for-chores teaches the importance of saving and resisting impulse spending, and that it pays to work.

noncash motivators

Rewards for a job well done needn't be financial. Little ones can often be motivated in a big way with stickers and stamps that are placed on a simple chore chart you can create yourself.

Family chores = time with Mom and Dad

My chores = time away from Mom and Dad = punishment = something I should try desperately to wiggle my way out of

You could make a chart for each day or one for the whole week. Or you could have both, a chart for chores that need to be done each day and another for chores that need to be done once a week.

Daily Chore Chart --Monday

Family member	Chore (s)	Completed
Mom	Wash laundry	TA
	Prepare meals	
Dad	Load dishwasher	CA
	Unload dishwasher	
Jason (age 10)	Set table	✓
	Pour beverages for meals	✓
	Clear table	
	Load dishwasher	
	Make lunch for school	
Jane (age 5)	Make bed	☺
	Feed pets	
	Help make breakfast	
Johnny (age 3)	Put toys in bins	☺
	Put dirty clothes in hamper	

Here's an example of a daily chore chart. You'll see that of all the chores this family does each day, the 10-year-old has five chores, the 5-year-old has three chores, and the 3-year-old has two chores. Mom and Dad have the rest.

Weekly Chore Chart --June 1-7

Family member	Chore (s)	Completed
Mom	Clean toilet, sink, and tub	
	Clean windows and mirrors	
	Change bed linens	TA
	Damp mop floors	
	Sweep porches and walkways	TA
	Mow lawn	
Dad	Weed garden	
	Water flowers	
	Empty trash	CA
	Sweep floors	CA
	Clean shower	
	Vacuum rugs	
Jason (age 10)	Set table	✓
	Pour beverages for meals	✓
	Clear table	✓
	Load dishwasher	
	Make lunch for school	
Jane (age 5)	Make bed	☺
	Feed pets	
	Help make breakfast	
Johnny (age 3)	Put toys in bins	☺
	Put dirty clothes in hamper	

Here's an example of a weekly chore chart. This chart lists all of the chores this family does each week, even if some of them need to be done each day of the week. Even though there are more chores to be done, the 10-year-old still has five chores, the 5-year-old has three chores, and the 3-year-old has two chores. Mom and Dad have the rest.

(See "The Computerized Chore Chart" on page 18.)

If your kids complete the chores they need to, you can reward them with fun experiences, such as lunch at their favorite eatery (Mickey Ds, anyone?) or perhaps a new storybook from the library or local bookstore. For older children, cash-free alternatives include offering chunks of time with Mom or Dad, such as a father-son movie outing or dinner at your daughter's favorite restaurant. This is

the choose-a-chore chart

A friend of mine, Mary, adapted a common chore chart system for her family, which includes four children ages 3 through 13.

First, Mary created a chore chart out of a large piece of posterboard. She made a large table of index-card-size spaces. She listed her family members' names down the far left column with blank spaces in the columns to the right. In each blank space, Mary placed a piece of Velcro. Then Mary created a series of Velcro-backed index cards, each labeled with a different chore. The children designed symbols for each chore so that the non-readers could keep up.

On Sunday nights, the whole family gathers around the kitchen table to select their chores for the week. They take turns, choosing one chore at a time and then sticking their chore cards on the chore chart by their name.

The children have to choose as many chores as half their age. The 3-year-old gets one card; the 13-year-old gets six cards.

There are three types of chores: standing chores, weekly chores, and heavy-duty chores.

Standing chores are personal chores that you must do each week. Period. For example, making your bed and keeping your room tidy are personal chores. And in Mary's home if it's your pet, you feed it. You don't get a card for this; you just do it.

Weekly chores include cleaning the bathroom and washing the kitchen floor and emptying the dishwasher, setting and clearing the table, and helping prepare dinner each day.

Heavy-duty chores are harder jobs such as cleaning the garage, cleaning window tracks, raking leaves, and washing the car. The kids earn extra money for these chores. They can volunteer to do them in addition to their other chores to earn extra cash.

Each kid gets 25 cents per week per year of age as an allowance. The 3-year-old gets 75 cents; the 13-year-old gets $4.25. If they do not do their chores or if Mary or the nanny has to nag, they get only a percentage of their allowances—or none at all.

Mary has been using this system for five years. And she never nags.

probably overpayment for all but the biggest spring cleaning tasks, so you may want to give your child tickets for each small task. When he's collected 10 (or 20, or 50, your call), he can "cash" them in for a mutually agreed-upon treat.

make it easy, make it fast, make it fun

In addition to cash and noncash motivators, it will be easier to get your family to help out around the house if it's fun. And if cleaning is fun for the kids, they'll clean longer and do a better job, too. Really, it isn't all that hard to make housecleaning fun—or at least less unfun. Here are my best ideas. (You'll find dozens more tips sprinkled throughout the book in my "Family Pickup Lines" sections.)

Make it a family affair. The key to a successful family cleaning routine is that Mom and Dad join in. After all, if everyone is working, it's more fun.

Pump up the volume. Turn on upbeat music while you clean. Watch your kids howl while you do the Bump with the vacuum and the Macarena with the duster. You get the picture—a smiling group making short work of housework. Fill the house with positive energy, not grumbling.

We rotate the DJ selection in our home to keep the peace. One week Chris selects the tunes, and the next it's Lyndsay's turn. (Payne is a bit small yet.) Lyndsay loathes the Macarena, but Chris loves it. Lyndsay grooves to soulful '70s tunes, while Chris puts his hands over his ears. But knowing that every other week he or she gets to choose the tunes keeps them content.

Be Saturday morning players. This saved (or sunk)-by-the-lunch bell approach to getting it all done by lunchtime Saturday was designed for the revolving-door family whose weekly chores occasionally get sidetracked by tests, book reports, and science projects or meetings and business trips.

Whatever assigned chores are not accomplished during the week are due by noon Saturday. This creates a high-energy cleaning session as Saturday morning becomes a high-speed race to the noontime finish. (Mom note: *Never* volunteer to drive soccer carpool Saturday morning so this can really happen.)

Delegate pride. I call this system the "Room Monitor System." Each month, assign a different family member a different room as his or her point of pride. This means that before lights out, that family member has to give the room the once-over to make sure that it's in good shape. Assign the little ones the rooms that won't be used past their bedtimes, such as the dining room. At the end of the month, the family member who has kept the best room gets a special treat such as his or her choice of a family afternoon or night out.

Plan a Cinderella Saturday. When a big cleanup day is necessary, have the family don sweats and labor the day away dragging rags and pails, à la Cinderella. In the evening, with a wave of the fairy godmother's wand, the family dresses up and goes out to dinner and a movie, something everyone enjoys together. Looking forward to a magical family outing makes even the longest list of chores palatable, especially when they're done together.

it's never too late (or too early) to start

The best approach, of course, to housekeeping with kids is to train them while they're toddlers so they never imagine until later years that it's even *possible* to go to bed with toys on the floor. Picking up your own things should be as ingrained and habitual as brushing your teeth. Parents with older kids are going to have to work a littler harder here to get their children's attention, but it can be done.

getting your toddlers to clean

Start early. Introduce your toddler to the concept of cleaning up and putting away her things as soon as she is walking, out of

diapers at the latest. My youngest son began tossing his dirty jammies atop the laundry hamper in his room just after he turned a year old.

By the time he was 18 months old, Payne knew that the cars and trucks must be put away—along with the plastic mat "road" they race on—before the dinosaurs came out to play.

Today, at age 3, he automatically comes to me in the laundry room when he hears me opening the washer or dryer door. He loves grabbing chunks of soggy clothes and throwing them into the dryer. Something about the thud the soggy duds make landing in the dryer just floats his boat.

True, these small efforts aren't exactly a big help. You'll probably find yourself, as I did, redoing all the helpful cleaning young tots do for you. There's a good measure of truth in the old saying "cleaning with kids around is like shoveling the driveway while it's still snowing."

For example, I'm a big fan of those disposable floor mop wipes. And so is Payne. He figured out how the wet-mop leaves a snail-trail (and it's wet, oh goody!) while cleaning our kitchen floor. It has reduced him to tears on several occasions when I had to take it from him after 20 minutes of "cleaning." It took me an additional 20 minutes to clean up his cleaning up!

It's hard to be patient at times like these. But your patience will pay off in a big way: Your toddler won't grow up thinking Mommy (or Daddy) is the maid.

Invest the time now, and you'll be rewarded with a child who takes pride (if not joy) in carrying his share of the home-cleaning load. Neglect this lesson and your child will still be cute—for a while. Then she'll grow up and drive people crazy with her serve-me attitude toward life.

In short: Kids are born wired to clean. All we as parents have to do is encourage that tendency (even though it initially means tasks will take twice as long to complete). Kids love to help, so let's let 'em!

As soon as children reach ages 2 or 3, it's time to start using a more formal approach to chores, such as a chore chart and stickers. (See "The Computerized Chore Chart" on page 18.) The nightly ritual of placing blue and pink stars on Chris and Lyndsay's charts was the highlight of the day for these two. And today I'm thankful for the time it took to get them in the cleaning routine. For the most part, they're whine-free cleaners and helpers.

getting your older kids to clean

If helping out is a new concept in your home, you'll need to take the gradual approach with your school-age kids. Like grownups, they can get set in their ways. But you're in luck, even if chores have been few and far between up until now, because as long as they're still at home, you're the boss.

Keep in mind that it takes 21 days for a habit to form. So starting slow is essential for good cleaning habits to grab a toehold in your home. And that goes for you, too. Begin by creating a chore list with just one or two chores for each school-age kid. Initially give them responsibility for their own things—school papers, packing tomorrow's lunch, permission slips, making beds daily—and then graduate them to responsibilities throughout the home. A few weeks later, add a family Saturday clean-a-thon. By year's end, your eldest will be cleaning the bathroom, your youngest will be delighted to help sort laundry, and your new program of family housekeeping will be routine!

Give older kids some input in your new system. They're part of the overload-on-chores problem, right? So, make them part of the solution. For example, when you introduce the chore list or chore chart, talk with them about the best ways to set it up. Let them decide when they will do their chores. (Within reason, that is!)

calling a family meeting

Now that you've prepared yourself, it's time to get your family on board. Start your new housekeeping-with-kids routine off right by calling a family meeting.

Don't let the meeting part scare you: It can be as casual or as formal as you and your family like, no gavel or agenda required. Though ultra-organized folks like me would probably want to at least open the meeting with a brief overview of the topics to be covered and then tackle them in a preset order, it's probably not necessary.

What is required, however, is that your family meeting takes place on a day and time when every family member can attend. Saturday mornings or Sunday evenings work well for many families; your meeting time will depend on your schedule. Be flexible, and pick a time when everyone is relaxed. Here are some strategies for a successful family meeting:

Choose the location carefully. Hold your meeting in a place where the seating puts

make room for stepchildren

Of course, there may also be children that don't live at your home all the time. In today's blended families, many of us have "occasional" children. Maybe you share custody with your ex-spouse. Maybe you have the kids only every other weekend. Maybe you have your own resident kids, and then your husband's kids come every other week. How do you incorporate them into your family routine? Are they guests? How much work should a kid who comes every other weekend have to do during his special time with his dad? Should he really be expected to help clean a garage he had no part in messing up?

Yes and no. Of course, every situation is different. And what you set up will depend on the personalities of the kids and the frequency of their stays at your house. The main thing is to make them feel like part of the family, like they belong. But be fair. For example, the garage cleaning should be postponed to another day. But the kid should still live under the family's Clean House Rules and do whatever family activity (or chore) is going on at that time.

If possible, give the "visiting" child his or her own room. If he has to share with a resident child, conflict will inevitably rise. And he needs a place to call his own. If you absolutely don't have an extra bedroom, find some place, *any* place, that can be the kid's. At the very least, give him his own bureau and part of a closet.

If he has to sleep on the pullout couch, make sure he has total privacy. He needs to have a place to leave stuff and to feel confident that no one will mess with it.

every family member on relatively equal footing. Around the kitchen table would be better than having the kids sit on the living room rug while Mom and Dad talk from the sofa above them. The reason is simple: When you're starting any new system, especially one that involves every member of the home, it's essential to get everyone on the same page and make everyone feel a part of the process.

Sell your new plan. To make your new home-keeping routine successful from the start, you'll need to explain to your kids (and maybe your spouse, too) why sharing the load is good for them. And for you. Here are a couple of key selling points you could mention:

- The more the kids pitch in, the less Mom and Dad have to do, and the more free time everyone has to go to the movies, eat out at favorite restaurants, or take afternoons off and head to the beach.

- Chores teach kids salable skills. Babysitting and lawn-mowing are popular teen tasks. And who better to cut their teeth on than forgiving Mom and Dad?

Once your kids see what's in it for them, you'll find getting them to pitch in isn't the big deal it once was. It paid off at my home: Even 3-year-old Payne is tickled to be learning the ropes, much to his brother

and sister's chagrin at times. Payne regularly picks up stray pieces of paper (usually his sister's homework) from the kitchen counter and circular-files them in an earnest effort to help around the house.

Define the chores. Next, you'll need to explain what the chores are. Explain that there are some "personal virtues" such as making your bed in the morning that are expected to be completed by everyone and aren't on the chart. Go through your weekly chore list. (See "Mrs. Clean Jeans' Housekeeping Routine" on page 253.) You may even explain why each chore is on the list, such as we do the laundry once a week so too much doesn't pile up and become overwhelming. Detail each chore on the week's list, taking time to explain exactly what's expected of, say, doing the dishes. To you it might mean setting the table, clearing the table after dinner, and then helping you wash the dishes. To your 11-year-old daughter, however, it might mean waiting until you ask for her help. Or that she simply sets the table. Head off misunderstandings by being crystal clear about your cleaning expectations early on.

Divide up the chores. It would probably be helpful to bring a chore chart if you'll be using one so you can explain how you'll be keeping track of all housecleaning jobs.

Or, perhaps this would be a great time to ask the kids how they'd like to keep track of things. Some kids like the thought of earning stars by their name on the fridge; others prefer having a personal chart that they can consult and check off daily.

Explain how chores are to be divided up and when these chores are expected to be done. Perhaps you've chosen to write down each chore, place them all in a bag, and have each child draw his or her weekly task. If your daughter suggests laying them all out on the table, allowing each person to take turns choosing a chore he likes (or dislikes least), consider implementing her suggestion. If your son suggests, however, that because your daughter got to have a sleepover Friday night, she should be given *all* the week's chores, that probably shouldn't fly.

Discuss how the chore system will be enforced. No arm-twisting here, let the kids know you won't be "enforcing" these new chores. Instead, the entire family will be making a commitment to each other—and the shared home—to care for it as decided upon during the meeting. It's do-the-right-thing time. However, you may want to decide, as a family, what to do as a group with a chore no-show-er. Perhaps those who complete their chores get to decide where to go out to dinner Sunday night or which family movie to rent. Remember, the key to keeping it successful is keeping it positive.

Give the kids the floor, too. You'll want to hear their thoughts and concerns on the new system. Invite and accept reasonable ideas from the kids on your chore system.

Remember, it has to work for everyone, so really do what you can to make it work for them, too. Let everyone have a chance to hold court (or take the floor); everyone's involvement is essential. If yours is a family of talkers (and talk-overers), consider creating a gavel of sorts to signify who has the floor. For example, when Lyndsay has the dishwashing detergent bottle, she gets to speak. Uninterrupted.

Set ground rules. Consider setting a few ground rules at the outset, such as name calling is a no-no ("Chris never washes his dishes, Mom. He's such a slob!"), and when you state a problem ("Dad, you know I hate cleaning the bathroom!"), you must also suggest a solution ("But I *am* willing mop the floor, so maybe we could switch.").

Make it fun. This should be a fun time for your family. Serve popcorn and sodas. Or indulge in ice cream creations. Make it festive. So be sure to end your meeting on a high note. Family meetings are a great way to tackle all sorts of family dilemmas, not just the cleaning routine.

Plan to meet regularly to reward good efforts, discuss bad efforts, and consider reassigning chores. This is your family's system, and like any successful system, it needs regular retooling to stay relevant. After all, good systems are adaptable to changing schedules and needs. It's the secret to successful housekeeping with kids.

cleaning 101

So, now that you've got everyone on board, from the toddlers to the teens, you're ready to start housekeeping with kids. Here are some overall hints:

Don't have too many rules. Rather than a bunch of rules, just set a few important ones with catchy names. Post them on the fridge, and then enforce them. You'll find many more "Clean House Rules" in the chapters to come, but here are two of my favorites:

"When you put your towels in the hamper, I'll wash them."

"I feel your pain in not wanting to clean your cat's litter box, but you have to do it."

Lead by example. As the time-honored saying goes, it isn't what you say, it's what you do that will stick with your kids. If your papers, books, and CDs are neatly filed and stacked, your child just might think twice before he leaves his stuff on the floor. So do the right thing, Mom, whether the kids are around or not. After all, you may as well lead the way.

Limit chore time. An age-appropriate chore should take a child no more than 15 to 30 minutes a day, max.

Work together. Resist the temptation to assign too many chores that send your children off on their own. From a kid's point of view, cleaning his bedroom after school each day is downright banishment. Better still: Create a family cleanup time each day

> ## OUR CLEAN HOUSE RULES
>
> 1. We take good care of things.
> 2. If we open it, we close it.
> 3. If we turn it on, we turn it off.
> 4. When we take something out, we put it back.
> 5. We play with only four toys (or toy groups) at a time.
> 6. We leave a room as we found it—or better.
> 7. We clean up our messes.
> 8. We tidy up before lying down (in bed).
> 9. We never make needless work for others.
> 10. We ask for help when we don't know how to do something.
> 11. When we go to others' homes, we follow these same rules.

or once a week. Misery loves company, but the dirty jobs have to be done.

Don't nitpick. Don't be too picky about your child's cleaning results; he is, after all, a child. (Okay, you can press the perfection point a bit harder with your teens.) And whatever you do, don't let your son or daughter see you redoing a job. When a child feels successful at something, she's more likely to continue doing it.

Focus on the big picture. While one goal of housekeeping with kids is to help you take a load off, the more important goal is to teach your children the life skills they'll need to run a clean, organized, efficient home someday on their own.

Ensure success. Take the time to show your child how to succeed at a given task. For example, tell your teen about the wonders of bleach on white cotton polos and about its devastating effect on black Lycra running shorts before sending him off to the laundry room.

Break down big tasks. Don't tell your preschooler to clean up his room. That's too daunting. Say, "Let's put all the dinosaurs in the red tub." Then, when that task is complete, say, "Now let's put our crayons into the cup." You might not even get the room totally clean on the first attempt. The goal is to make kids feel good about what they did. Make the job small enough to do well.

Make helping easy for them. Whenever possible, set up your home with housecleaning with kids in mind. Stash a stool in the laundry room so even your littlest family member can help load the washer. Place breakfast dishes on a bottom shelf within reach of your 4-year-old so she can set the table herself.

Be patient. Make "good" good enough. Unless, of course, it's an older child trying to get away with sloppy work. They'll have no satisfaction in a job well done, an extremely important concept most of us want to instill in our kids before they head off on their own. In that case, you'll need to tell her the work just isn't up to par, and that she'll need to do it again, and again, if necessary, until she gets it (almost) perfect.

Praise often. Be effusive in your praise. Remember the last aced test proudly thrust in your hands after school? Our little ones clearly delight in our joy at the work of their hands.

mrs. clean jeans' housekeeping routine

If it's been a while since you actually considered the work to be done around the home daily, weekly, monthly, seasonally, and yearly, chances are you could use a cleaning primer. In just about every chapter of this book, you'll see a section called "Chores by Age." These sections list the chores for each room to clean or activity to be done that can be done by kids of different ages. But as you read these lists, you may wonder how often each of these chores need to be done. I've done all of the planning for you, at least to get you started. You'll find a guide to the frequency of chores you may want to consider tossing into the family housekeeping ring in the days, weeks, months, seasons, and even years ahead in chapter 13, "Mrs. Clean Jeans' Housekeeping Routine" on page 253.

Of course, your list will vary by where you live, how much (or how little) your family is home, and how meticulous you and the family intend to be with your housekeeping routine. But it's my hope that my housekeeping routine will give you lots of ideas to get you started.

truth and consequences

If, despite all of your planning and motivating efforts, your kids don't get the job done, you need to be ready with a combination of positive reinforcement and natural consequences. Here are several easy examples:

Add insult to injury. Give more chores to the rule-breaker whose duties aren't done; ditto for a child who keeps whining about her chores.

Take away privileges. Ground the scofflaw for the morning or the afternoon. Take away his TV privileges for the weekend. Call it the "no work, no play" rule.

Stand firm. Stand behind your rules. The advantage to having rules is that you don't have to reinvent the wheel every day. There are no arguments. Simply say, "You know the rule, and you're in violation, buddy! No exceptions."

Use natural consequences. This technique requires some restraint and patience. It means that you allow your kid to make a mistake and wait for him to experience the natural consequence of that mistake. (Of course, common sense must apply—don't let them do anything dangerous!) This technique is good for harmless things like putting off a chore for so long that a child has to miss a social event to complete the chore by its Saturday due date.

Don't get mad. Even if your kids don't do their chores or give you bad attitudes, it's wise to apply discipline but to keep your emotions in check. Avoid anger at all costs. It gives kids a license to misbehave and sends you tumbling back to square one.

On we go from here with the plans set up, chores divided, and—hopefully—your family cheerfully on board. But first, let's get organized.

Chapter 2

a home for everything

SHORTLY AFTER WE MOVED into our home in West Los Angeles several summers ago, our 12-year-old neighbor, Kelly, bopped over for an impromptu visit. Right out of Southern California central casting, this girl was blonde, blue-eyed, and brimming with fresh-from-the-volleyball-court energy. And, as I was soon to learn, as curious as our cats.

Delighted, Lyndsay invited the older girl inside. (It's very exciting to have a near-teenager visit when you're just shy of your eighth birthday.) It wasn't long before the pair wandered into the kitchen where I stood making dinner. I raised an eyebrow when the girls began peeking inside the cabinets and cupboards as Kelly was describing what used to be where in our recently renovated kitchen.

That's when Kelly screamed.

"Ohmygosh! Ohmygosh!" she repeated in that high-pitched holler only adolescent girls can make. Running to the nearby lower cabinets, she flung open the doors. "Here, too! Oh my gosh! You're so, so—so organized!"

Wow. Clearly, my penchant for seriously organizing our new kitchen (okay, everywhere else in our home, too) was a little extreme. My neatly filled, stacked, and labeled Tupperware containers and our pullout, serve-yourself kiddie breakfast drawer (stocked with labeled cereal containers and kid-size bowls and spoons) was frightening for small—and not so small—children.

Today, in my less hormonal state (I was pregnant with Payne when we moved in), I realize that my kitchen organizing was way over the top, even by my occupational hazard standards.

Then again, I probably should have gotten a clue that things were a bit too precise when my husband opened the pantry door the first time and blurted out, "What are we, the Stepford family?"

That pregnant period in my life is perhaps a perfect example of over-the-top organizing at its finest, or worst. (If you're pregnant and reading this, your nesting instinct is probably stirring.)

Today, I don't organize for perfection—I organize for life. As in, so I can have one, and so my family can, too. And being

able to find what we need at a moment's notice gives us more opportunity to live that life.

Most of us aspire to the middle-to-upper organizing ground: a living room uncluttered by papers, a kitchen counter free of mail or backpacks, and a clean dresser. Not perfect, mind you, but good enough to be cozy and livable. My goal for this chapter is to show you how to create organizing systems that work, without too much work from you. I call this having a home for everything.

Here are just some of the benefits to having a home for everything in your house:

- You will know where to look for everything.

- The rest of your family will know where to look.

- You will know where to return things.

- The rest of the family will know where to return things.

- You'll take the "But I don't know where it goes!" excuse out of the kids' playbook.

- You'll save money by not buying duplicates for things you already have.

In a house like ours, with "a lot of family" as my 3-year-old Payne is so very fond of saying, if there wasn't a designated place for everything, the place would look like a nuclear war zone by naptime.

finding the right home for everything

After nearly a decade of writing about cleaning and organizing—and slightly more than a decade's worth of mothering and all the on-the-job organizing training that entails—I've learned that organizing basically boils down to regularly doing three things: grouping similar things together; storing things in logical, convenient, and accessible places; and labeling everything. In a very organized fashion, let's go over each one in turn.

Group similar things together. It's so much easier to find things if they are in groups, not spread out all over the house. At least you'll know the general location to start looking for something. I know one woman who keeps some food in her kitchen, more in her coat closet, and still more in her basement. When she's looking for a box of rice, she has to search in three places! Instead, put all food in one area of your kitchen, pots and pans in one cabinet, towels in one closet, and all luggage together—you get the idea!

Store things in logical, convenient, and accessible places. Often, the reason things can't be found or are found but then aren't put away in the right place is that they are in the wrong place to begin with. If an item (say a telephone directory) was where it was needed (say, by the phone) it would be easy to know where to find it. And then anyone in the family would know the logical place to return it. But if the phone directory is stored above the microwave oven, 14 feet away from the phone, it's easy to forget its location because it's not logical.

If things aren't located logically, you will forget where you put them. Your kids, bless their sweet little hearts, will surely blame it on your age. And who needs them to bring that up again!

Here's the secret to finding a logical storing place for any item—put it where you use it! For example, store your keys by the door, keep your lint brush near your clothes, and stash your vases under the sink.

Another way to look at this is to organize your house in terms of activity centers. For example, if the kids always do their homework on the kitchen table, then keep a file, drawer, or basket nearby with all the supplies that they need to get the job done. If you like to read in bed, keep reading materials, eyeglasses, and a reading light in a basket by your bed. Try to arrange your life so that your necessities are at your fingertips and you don't have to spend what little free time you have jumping up and down to find things.

A challenge can arise when you have one item that is used in several locations. The solution? Buy two, three, or four of them. If you have only one pair of scissors and it's stored in the sewing basket in the upstairs closet, kids have to go get it for each art project and then walk back upstairs to return it. Oh, sure, *that* will happen! The scissors will never be returned. If you frequently use scissors in every room of the house, consider buying a pair of scissors for every room in the house. Such a purchase is well worth the expense if it saves you hours of time looking for the *&###!!! scissors. Time is money.

Along with storing things in logical places, they also need to be in convenient places. For example, put things you use often on eye-level shelves and in handy cabinets. Put things you rarely use on top shelves and in the back of closets. I know that sounds like a no-brainer, but before you laugh, think about where you put things. If your favorite spatula is thrown in a drawer with 23 other kitchen utensils, move it onto the counter, right next to the stove, perhaps in a pretty crock. (And resist the temptation to move the other 23 less-useful tools along with it!)

If things aren't located conveniently, you aren't going to return them to their proper resting place, and neither will the kids. It's just too inconvenient!

And lastly, storage places must be accessible, both to you and to your kids. If things aren't readily accessible, kids are going to use inappropriate things to do the job, such as a table knife for a screwdriver, and foul things up royally. For example, if you expect the kids to feed the dog, put the dog food on a shelf where they can reach it (preferably somewhere near the dish, but out of the dog's reach).

You owe it to yourself to make putting stuff away easy for your family.

Label everything. If everything is clearly marked, there are no excuses for not knowing where to find it and where to return it to. Portable electronic labelers, which are now affordable, thankfully, are an organized mom's dream. What bears marking? Label the locations for everything, including boxes, closet shelves, drawers, spare keys, the fuse box, and virtually anything else that someone might not immediately be able to figure out on their own, such as which switch is "on" and where you put the guest hand towels.

That way everyone in the home, including visiting friends, relatives, and babysitters, knows exactly where things are and where to return them.

Take Payne's closet, for example. Before I labeled where everything goes, I put things one way, his dad another, and the babysitter yet a third. This lack of a sys-

CLEAN HOUSE RULE
NUMBER ONE

Commit this Clean House Rule to memory (and maybe to the fridge door, too): Nothing Is Ever Left Homeless! Every member of the entire family will pick up after every activity. Nothing is ever left sitting out, away from its proper place. Dad's briefcase? It can't park overnight on the kitchen counter. Mom's purse gets tucked into the master bedroom, not hooked over a chair. The kids' backpacks are no longer allowed to linger haphazardly on the kitchen floor, ankle-spraining time bombs waiting to happen. Instead, each child must move his or her backpack into his or her room or to the place in the garage or front entry hall that you'll learn to create for them in the chapters ahead.

finding temporary homes for permanent stuff

So now, let's get real. The best-laid plans often go awry. Even if you have a logical, convenient, accessible, labeled place for every single one of your belongings, not everything is always going to be in place. (Unless you live on a movie set!)

There are going to be times when we aren't going put things away: when we're tired or cranky, when the kids are tired or cranky, or when we just want to get it out of the way. In those situations we usually:

1. Leave the item lying where it is, in plain sight

or

2. Stuff it somewhere, *anywhere,* to get it out of sight

With solution number 1, you have a messy house. If you have a lot of family members following this plan of action, you have a *very* messy house.

With solution number 2, you have a house where items are stuffed willy-nilly into the nearest drawer. The locations of

tem made Payne's closet an infuriating jumble to wade through when it was time to get dressed each morning. Solution: I labeled Payne's closet shelves to designate what goes where: "pajamas," "short-sleeve shirts," "swimwear and gear," etc. Now, if you can read, you can put things away correctly. (And for those who can't read, you can attach drawings or stickers to designate proper storage places.)

these items, of course, are promptly forgotten. You buy new items to replace the "lost" items. If you continue with this course of action, the new items will also be eventually stuffed willy-nilly into the nearest drawer, and the cycle will continue—until your home explodes.

We are in a recession, you know.

"So," you're probably asking yourself, "what would Mrs. Clean Jeans do?"

Glad you asked!

You need somewhere to stash stuff out of sight in places, temporarily, that you won't forget about. Here's my solution. Create a series of temporary holding areas in strategic areas of your home to contain receipts, mail, permission slips, and other important items until you have time to properly find a home for them.

I call these temporary storage places clutter-busters. Clutter-buster baskets provide a place to just stuff it. Out of sight, that is. Unlike "junk" drawers and black holes, clutter-buster baskets are not permanent dumping grounds because you will (yes, you will!) check them daily and distribute the contents. They offer a place to stash things only temporarily.

In our house, we have a wrought-iron stand that holds a set of wicker baskets (one for each member of the family) at the base of the stairs and near the entryway. When we don't have the time or inclination to put something away, we put it in our baskets. If we don't find something in its proper home, we know

to check our baskets. And if I find someone's stuff after I've kissed her night-night, I feel no guilt whatsoever stuffing whatever she left lying out into her basket. She can put it away in the morning.

I put the baskets near the entry for an important reason. Located there, they enable everyone to temporarily dump whatever they bring in from the car somewhere out of sight.

These temporary holding areas are so helpful, you'll want to have more than one. Other prime locations for basket clutter-busters are:

- Living rooms

- Dining rooms

- Family rooms

- Kitchens

- Offices

- By the garage door that leads inside

Two-story houses have a special need for clutter-busters: No one wants to run up and down stairs returning little stuff. Solution? Put baskets at the top and bottom of the steps to hold stuff that needs to go up or down, such as laundry, library books, and new shampoo from the grocery store. I make it a house rule that we all check the basket before going up- or downstairs empty-handed.

Mission accomplished.

lightening up

Before you can organize anything—
temporary or permanent—you'll need to
lighten up a bit on your belongings. The
prime cause for disorganization is that
you've got too much stuff.

You know what's coming: You need to go
through your stuff and toss what you don't
use, don't need, or don't want. And so will
your kids.

Many of us have stuff we never use and
don't need. We even have stuff we don't
like. And so do our kids. Don't be a pack
rat. And don't teach your kids to be rodent-

like, either. If you don't use it, get rid of it.
And help your kids to do the same.

This is not a Saturday-morning project.
Don't plan on purging the house of a year's
or a decade's worth of clutter in a morning.
Allot at least a half day per room.

Here's what you do: Pick a day. Pick a
room. Pile everything from the room in
the middle of the floor. (Really. Try it.
Trust me.) Look at each item individually
and critically, just as you would in a store.
Is this something you would buy? Is this
something you would be happy with if
someone gave it to you? If either answer is
no, well, it needs to go.

Here's an example of clutter-buster baskets.

You're probably feeling a little overwhelmed right now. (And perhaps a bit trapped by all the stuff in the middle of the room.) When you've got so much stuff, it's hard to even know where to begin!

Slowly but surely, go through everything in your home, piece by broken or frayed piece. If you decide to keep an item, great! Now put it away in its logical, convenient, accessible, and labeled place. If you decide you don't need it, you have a few options: throw it away, sell it or give it away, hold on to it, or store it. Gather four boxes or trash bags, one for each option, and start sorting stuff into them.

throw it away

Yuck. You hate it. It's no good to anyone. How did it get here?

Here are some good rules to live by: If you haven't used it, played with it, or worn it in six months; if it's missing many of the essential pieces; or if it's broken, it goes.

Once you have a pile of throw-aways, grab the kids and go through the to-be-trashed stash, separating plastic, paper, glass, cardboard—whatever is recycled in your community. Then take each pile to its final resting place (at least as far as your family is concerned).

sell it or give it away

Yuck. You hate it. She hates it. But *somebody* might like it.

Decide whether you're the garage-sale type. If so, carefully pack up all the items you'd like to include in a future sale in plastic bins (transparent ones are better for remembering what's there), boxes, or bags that you will, of course, label "Garage Sale." If you prefer to donate the items, neatly fold or place them in bags or boxes, label them, and call the recipient to arrange pickup or drop-off. Stash them in your garage or basement in the meantime.

hold on to it

Hmmm. Forgot you had it. Everyone else did, too. You want it, but you haven't used it in 10 years.

Oh well, put it away for another year and think about it again. But find a more convenient place for it this time to increase the chances that you might actually use it.

Take the time to figure out where each item should go—and put it there. You may move things a couple of times until you find a space that's the right size for these items. In a bedroom, for example, you might try assign one drawer to stationery items, or one part of the closet shelf to games. Then you might move the games to under the bed, where the kids can reach them more easily. It's trial and error.

But take your time. The better you organize things, the easier it will be to stay organized. It took you a long time to get this messy, so don't expect to clean up your family's act in one weekend.

For these items (and for those you want to place in long-term storage), the next step is a touch more complicated and a bit more work. If you want to do it right—not necessarily fast—that is. And having tried both ways, I'm here to tell you it's just a lot easier for everyone in the house if you do it right the first time. Otherwise, you end up stuffing stuff in places you can't remember and in ways you shouldn't, such as putting heavy items on top of a box of extra glasses from the kitchen.

store it

You don't use it now, and neither do the kids. But maybe some day you could use it. And it would be too expensive to replace, or it has sentimental value.

For things you really don't use but can't part with, either, the solution is to find a safe place to store it long term. Few of us are blessed with an overabundance of storage, so we've got to develop a system that maximizes what we do have. And if that system is going to work, the whole family has to be in on it. This will help everyone down the road. For example, next winter, your husband will be able to find the Christmas lights and your son will be able to grab his snowboard at the first sign of the first flake of the first snow of the season.

When we moved into this house, I was most excited about the extra bedroom, the larger closets, and the bigger garage. "Storage!" I thought to myself. "I'll never have to worry about storage again."

what goes in what closet?

If you're blessed with a home with lots of closets, they're ideal storage sites for things that you use a lot but need neatly tucked away. Here's how I allocate my closets:

Parents': seasonal clothing or shoes, sweaters, sweatsuits, gift-wrapping supplies, photos, and scrapbooks

Child's: board games, dress-up clothes, school projects, and papers

Guest room: Sewing supplies, craft supplies, assorted baskets, off-season clothes, formal clothes, and those extra gifts you buy throughout the year

Study: Old tax receipts, canceled checks, and files

Entry: Boots, wine cases, backpacks, and a basket for hats, gloves, and scarves

Linen: Sheets and towels, naturally, but also medical supplies and extra toiletries

Utility: Vacuum cleaner, tools, light bulbs, and batteries

Boy, was I mistaken. I have stuff I see only when I move. Stuff from college, from when I was a SINK—single income, no kids. (I don't remember a minute of it, though I'm sure I had some good times in my tiny loft in Boston.) Now that I think about it, I didn't have enough storage space then either. And it was just me and my high school stuff.

Fact is, *nobody* has enough storage. Just look at the growth of the storage warehouse industry. Time was there wasn't such a thing. Or at least if there was, we'd never heard of it. Now, it seems

develop a long-term storage plan

I borrowed this idea from a friend who borrowed it from another friend. We've all added our own touches to it over the years, and you'll need to adapt it to your needs as well. This method can work whether you have an attic, a loft in the garage, boxes stacked against the walls of the basement, or a rental storage unit. You can even track boxes stored in various closets this way. You'll need sturdy boxes or plastic bins, a permanent marker, and paper to make a storage map and list. Here's how it works:

1. Divide your stuff into large categories, such as dishes, holiday, kids' clothes, paperwork, etc.

2. Put the items into boxes, with each category in its own box or boxes. For example, you might have three dish boxes, four holiday boxes, five kids' clothes boxes, and two paperwork boxes.

3. Label each box by category, such as Dishes, Holidays, Kids' Clothes, etc., on five sides in large letters with a permanent marker. (That's every side except the bottom!) Then assign each box in each category a number. For example, Dishes 1, Dishes 2, Holiday 1, and Holiday 2.

4. Divide your storage space into as many parts as you have categories. (You don't have to actually divide them, just mentally imagine your attic divided into four parts, for example.)

5. Assign one area of your storage space for each category. For example, holiday decorations go in the southeast corner of the basement.

6. On your paper, sketch your storage area, divide it up into the category areas, and label them.

7. On the same page or another page, list each box (Dishes 1, Holiday 1) and its contents (Christmas tree lights, Christmas wreath, etc.). If you add more boxes to a category, you can just add a number (Holiday 5, Holiday 6).

Take note on your list of how many boxes you have in each category. That way, when you there's at least one storage warehouse in every neighborhood of every city.

The problem with storage is that once you store something, it's much harder to keep track of. You need a written plan to keep from forgetting what you stored where. And you need to tell the rest of the family where you put that written plan. You'll need to realize, as I have, that garages and basements are not designed to be the repositories of a lifetime's accumulations. You need to keep stuff there that you actually intend to use at some time. Sell, give away, or toss the rest.

retrieve things, you'll know if you have them all. After Christmas last year, we found one box of decorations we never even unpacked. (We wondered where the Santa hats were.)

Now, when you want to find a special Christmas decoration, all you have to do is consult your list (it's in Holiday 4) and your map. (Holiday is near the southeast corner of the basement.) And so can your family!

Box	Contents
Dishes 1	Blue glass dishes
Dishes 2	Grandma's china
Dishes 3	Christmas dishes
Holiday 1	Valentine's Day decorations
Holiday 2	Easter decorations
Holiday 3	Christmas wreaths
Holiday 4	Christmas decorations
Kids' Clothes 1	3 month–6 month clothes
Kids' Clothes 2	12 month–18 month clothes
Kids' Clothes 3	2–3 years-old clothes
Kids' Clothes 4	4–5 years-old clothes
Kids' Clothes 5	6–7 years-old clothes
Paperwork 1	Old tax paperwork
Paperwork 2	Miscellaneous paperwork

Storage List

Here's an example of a storage list.

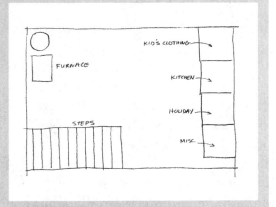

Here's an example of a storage map.

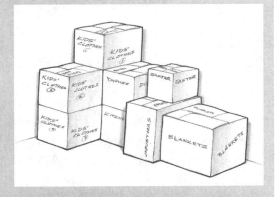

And here's what the corresponding storage area would look like.

Trust me, even though you *think* that you'll use that fold-up table or those unmatched glasses in your second home some day, you won't. By then you'll be able to afford new, stylish stuff.

organizing with kids

If it's your child's stuff that's in chaos, she needs to help make the decisions about what stays and what goes. If your child is too little to make these decisions, you can make them for her. If you're not sure, create a holding zone in which to stash ignored toys and books where she won't find them. If she hasn't missed an item in a month or two, it's fair game for donation or disposal. Just cart it away in a black garbage bag so she can't see it go and decide she knew it was missing.

If kids are actually involved, it can be challenging. You try to chuck that one-armed Barbie or that dented dump truck, and suddenly your child can't live without it. How do you lose the excess and keep the peace?

Here are some great ways to get your kids to pare down their belongings:

Help needy kids. Go through books and toys together with your child. Have your child choose some things that are still in good shape to give to needy kids. Call it "Playing Santa."

Have a garage sale. If you hold a garage sale, let your child buy one new item with the proceeds from selling some old ones. Or let your kid hold her own garage sale and keep the proceeds. But explain to her that if she sells her baseball mitt, Mom and Dad aren't buying a new one.

Give kids time. If your child isn't ready to part with a toy, let him store it for six months. If he hasn't missed it, you toss it.

Organize clothes. Let even the littlest one decide what goes in each drawer. Label the drawers with stickers to remind him what goes where. Make him responsible for putting clean, folded clothes away, and challenge him to keep it neat and tidy.

Recycle it. See whether pieces from one game or activity can supplement another or go into the craft box.

Remember it. Let each child have a memory box for extra-special toys, clothes, and papers. They get to select what goes in the box each year. But, each year they also have to clean out last year's memory box so that all past years' stuff fits into one box. This means you always have only two boxes per child. One for the current year, and one for previous years. You may want to create a secret memory box to save some of the stuff your kid throws out but *you* can't part with, you old softie you. I keep three large boxes (one for each child) tied with ribbon underneath our bed. I secret-file sweet notes and aced tests in these memory boxes.

WHAT GOES WHERE? It's

easy to turn organizing into a game, especially for kids under age five. And it's good for their fine-motor skills.

Give your kids a pile of things to organize and empty shoe boxes or bins and ask them to separate the items into different boxes and bins. Or give your son a sectioned container and let him organize his toy cars or marbles. Along the same lines, I bet your little girl has quite a jewelry collection that has outgrown her jewelry box. Try this: Buy Plexiglas drawer sectionals and put them in her vanity drawer for her earrings, rings, bracelets, and necklaces. If she has lots of necklaces, install hooks on the inside of the cabinet door under the sink and hang them there.

finding time for everything

Remember the futurists' predictions about living in the 21st century? Computers would handle our jobs. Robots would do our dirty work. We would be the new leisure class.

While many of these predictions have come true, we're busier than ever. Whatever time technical innovations have saved us we have more than filled with extracurricular activities.

To keep some semblance of order in our hectic lives, we must organize our time as efficiently as we do our possessions. Here are some coping mechanisms.

make a family calendar

Everyone in the family has activities. In order to get everyone to those activities (and to know where everyone is), post a family calendar above or near the phone.

List all activities (from your 3-year-old's play dates to Dad's board meetings) on the calendar. The kids should also write important school information such as tests, project due dates, and special events on the calendar. Before anyone in the family commits to anything, they should check that calendar.

Sit down with the family each Sunday evening and look at the upcoming week. Use the calendar to make an intelligent game plan. Consider these questions:

- Can it all be done? If your son has piano and football on the same day, something has to give. Make the decision now and cancel one activity.

- Should it all be done? If your daughter has her biology final on Thursday, perhaps she should skip swim team Wednesday night. This is the time to discuss it, not Wednesday night.

- Which errands can be combined? Can you do the grocery shopping while your son is at the tutor's?

- Do you need to arrange carpools? Can your friend take your daughter to play practice this week with her kids so you can get your son to the tutor's?

- When are you going to eat? Depending on your extracurricular activities, some dinners will be early, some will be late, and still others will be eaten on the run. Plan your menus and make your game plan now.

establish routines

Don't reinvent the wheel every day. Develop a schedule or routine and stick to it. When the days are hectic, routines ground you and ensure that at least the important things get done. For example, kids should have certain set times for homework and play time as well as firm bath and bed times.

Weekly routines are also important. For example, you might designate Saturday morning as housecleaning time. Unless it's an emergency, your kids and husband know not to schedule anything for that time. Likewise, Saturday afternoons might be golf time for Dad. And then Sunday afternoons might be gardening time for Mom, when Dad knows he's in charge of the kids.

The more routines you set up, the more smoothly life will run, and the better everyone can plan their lives without inconveniencing the rest of the family.

eliminate morning madness

Simplify your mornings. Try to do as many things as you can the night before. I know nights are busy and you're tired, but mornings are crazy, too.

Each night, do the following:

- Give kids baths.

- Sign off on homework and school papers.

- Pack lunches.

- Pack up backpacks and station them near the door. (If there's something that needs to be given to the teacher, I tie a ribbon to the child's backpack as a reminder.)

- Lay out school clothes, including shoes, socks, and hair bands.

- Tape the Out-the-Door Checklist for School Days on the kitchen door. (See "The Out-the-Door Checklist for School Days" on the opposite page.)

- Go over tomorrow's pickup arrangements and after-school activities.

the out-the-door checklist for school days

The mornings go by so fast, it's easy for kids to forget important things for school. I create Out-the-Door Checklists and go through them once each morning. They may change from day to day depending on your kids' schedules. I type one up on the computer for each day of the week, then amend them when activities change. Here's what's on mine:

Do you have?

_____ Books

_____ Assignments

_____ Backpack

_____ Signed papers

_____ Lunch

_____ Gym clothes

_____ Extracurricular equipment (swimsuit for swim team, piano books, riding clothes, track shoes, dance outfits)

_____ A way home?

- Have the kids set the table for breakfast. Put out boxes of cereal, bowls, and spoons.

- Put out vitamins and medications.

- Make sure kids set their alarm clocks. It encourages them to be responsible for their own schedules.

In the morning, do the following:

- Everyone gets up on time.

- Get kids to make their beds and get dressed before breakfast.

- Set a timer to go off 10 minutes before out-the-door time to give kids a chance to brush their teeth and grab their lunches from the fridge.

- Minimize distractions: no TV, last-minute homework, or cramming for tests.

- Set this rule: If the kids miss the bus or the carpool, they're at your mercy. If you're heading out in 10 minutes, they'll be only a little late. If you're 45 minutes from departing, well, they'll have a lot of makeup work for that unexcused (and you'll need to make that clear to the office when they arrive) tardy. Trust me: This worked like a charm for my older son, a notoriously slow mover in the morning.

Part II
All Around
the House

Chapter 3

lightening the laundry load

GOT KIDS? THEN YOU'VE GOT LAUNDRY. Piles and piles of it.

A recent survey found that the average American family washes seven loads of laundry each week.

My response to that: Who's doing their *other* seven loads?

With school uniforms, sports clothes, play clothes, Mom and Dad clothes, and everyone's bed linens and towels, our house often resembles a Laundromat, with both machines humming and a half-dozen or so loads waiting for their turn.

We want to keep our kids in clean clothes and looking somewhat presentable, but that takes lots of work. And the more kids (three for us), and the more activities the kids are in (jazz, baseball, basketball, golf, and biking for ours), the more overwhelming the laundry becomes.

And then there are the stains: chewing gum, chocolate, crayons, fruit juice, and grass, to name a few. And heaven forbid that one, or all, of these drips, drops, or smears are defacing favorite duds! Just try to get your kid to hand over his favorite pair of jeans for an hour so you can wash it before it stiffens.

All the new fabrics just compound the problem. Microfiber. Spandex. Hemp. Who's ever heard of hemp? (Okay, if you have, you don't have to tell the kids.) And why does your teenager have a shirt made out of it? (Because it's a natural fiber, three times stronger than cotton and naturally resistant to mold and mildew.) And how on earth do you wash it? (Machine, warm, tumble dry low.)

It's hard enough to keep up with the laundry load, let alone the latest fabrics and their special care. As a result, the laundry basket eternally runneth over, and

PENNY PINCHER

CUT YOUR DRY-CLEANING BILL   If the label
reads "Dry Clean," not "Dry Clean Only," it may be hand-washable. If the garment is simply constructed with no sewn-in shoulder pads, lining, or delicate trim; has no sequins or beads glued to the fabric; and is not open-weave or loosely woven, give it a try. Hand-wash only please, with a gentle fabric wash.

PENNY PINCHER

THE SCRUNCH-AND-RELEASE TEST   If "iron" is a four-letter word in your household, use the Scrunch-and-Release Test before buying a new article of clothing. Grip some of the fabric in your hand for a few seconds, then release it to see if it wrinkles or bounces back. If it's wrinkled, walk—or run—away.

no one ever seems to have the right thing to wear. You feel like you're on an ever-accelerating Laundromat treadmill.

Think it's time to throw in the towel? Not a chance. I'm too tough for that. And you are, too. Consider this chapter Laundry 101, with a 21st century twist: a little help from the kids.

What can kids do to help? At what age can they do it? How can we teach them?

I've quizzed everyone I know for laundry solutions that work in their homes—friends, family, acquaintances, and even people I've met standing in line who actually were buying more groceries than I was. (I figured they must have even more laundry and even more kids!)

Some suggested I get a maid. (Yeah, some day.) Others recommended I throw everything in together and run the machine on cold. (So what if Dad's Jockey shorts are a little pink. Who's gonna see?) Still others suggested dividing up the laundry into appropriate baskets with directions neatly laid on top (cold wash, dry flat; warm wash, tumble dry medium). Each kid has to do at least one load of clothes a week. Just pick a day. That way, everyone knows how to wash, and laundry left by the machine gets done, with no bleeding, stretching, or fading. (But then you've got piles of laundry waiting for some kid to be struck by the urge to wash.)

Still another friend suggested I try her approach: She makes her daughters (ages 11 and 14) totally responsible for their own laundry. If they don't wash it and put it away, their laundry just doesn't get done. When the children don't get around to the laundry and complain that they have nothing clean to wear to school, my friend is sympathetic but unmoved. "Oh, how terrible that must be for you," she says. It's their problem.

That hands-off approach may not work for your family, but your kids should still help. After all, you're crunched for time as it is. Why should responsibility for everyone's dirty duds land in your laundry basket? You can't do it all *and* do all the laundry. So, if you want to make those soccer games, school plays, weekly play dates, etc., you're just going to have to learn how to delegate the laundry chores.

I have, and what a blessing it has been. I've lightened my load by bringing each kid in on a level he or she can handle.

CLEAN HOUSE LAUNDRY RULES

1. If it's not dirty and it doesn't smell, don't put it in the hamper. Wear it!

2. If it's not in the hamper on laundry day, it won't get washed.

3. If it's turned inside out (unless neatly on purpose), it doesn't get washed.

4. If socks aren't clothespinned together, prepare to play "find the mate" from the "homeless" sock basket next time you need a sock. Or two.

5. Anything left in pockets belongs to the laundress. Payday!

What can a 3-year-old do? What should your 10-year-old do? What on earth can that teenager with a Walkman growing out of his ears do? Lots, as it turns out.

Start by creating a functional laundry room. Then rally the kids for a Mom- or Dad-led laundry lesson. And let it be known that from then on, keeping clothes clean is a family affair. It's worked in my home, and it can work in yours, too. Choose from the tips and strategies below, keeping in mind your family's personalities and schedules.

Just do it.

a home for everything

Laundry areas come in all shapes and sizes, ranging from tiny closets to full-size laundry rooms. Many older homes have small laundry areas, but it seems like lately architects and builders are finally getting with the family program, and newer homes often have separate laundry rooms.

But the great news is the wash-for-success setup is a no-brainer, regardless of whether or not you have a specific room for laundry.

Here's what you need on your laundry shelf:

- Detergent

- Gentle fabric wash such as Woolite for delicates

- Net bags for washing delicates, such as men's dress socks, women's lingerie, washable sweaters, and everyone's swimsuits

- Chlorine bleach

- Color-safe bleach

- Stain pretreater

- Fabric softener

- Dryer sheets

- Stain-buster chart (See "Treating Stains" on page 61.)

- Starch

Nearby, you should have:

- Iron

- Distilled water

- Ironing board (Those fold-up boards truly are a godsend for the overworked space-challenged laundry area.)

- Dryer rack on which to hang sweaters and delicates

- Collapsible three-section laundry basket for sorting dirty duds and carrying clean, folded clothes to their various homes

- Laundry baskets

- Trash can for laundry lint

- Small basket for wash-day finds, such as hair bands, coins, and buttons (You still get first dibs on "keepers," however.)

- Hangers

- Basket for stained "special attention" clothes

- Basket for "homeless socks"

- Basket for clothes to go to the dry cleaner

- Basket for items that need mending

doing laundry with kids

Now that your laundry area is set up, it's time to go over the laundry basics with your kids. (And your spouse too, if he needs a refresher course.) These are the basic concepts any kid will need to succeed in the world of dirty laundry. The whole process can be broken down into three major steps: getting the dirty clothes to the machine, washing and folding the clothes, and putting the clean clothes away. Let's talk about each step in turn.

getting the dirty clothes to the machine

Of course, you have to get the dirty duds off the child, into the laundry basket or hamper, and finally, into the laundry room before any laundering can occur.

Here's how to make it easy for the entire family to get their clothes to the machine, regardless of the school-to-practice or gym-to-work rush they happen to be in:

Place laundry baskets strategically. Provide laundry bins for each bathroom and/or bedroom for garments needing standard laundering, such as school uniforms and play clothes. Then, position

Here's an example of a well-organized, if tiny, laundry area.

a "special attention" or "stain" basket on the washing machine for clothes sporting visible drips, drops, or smudges of everything from finger paints to Cross pen leaks. (Less-visible everyday splotches usually come out quite well if you wash as directed with an enzyme-containing laundry detergent and bleach if safe for the fabric.) And last, place a "dry cleaning" basket in one of the bathrooms for those items labeled "Dry Clean Only."

End the search for sockmates. Here is my favorite pre-laundry trick for shaving time off the laundering process and removing the "Whose sock is it, anyway?" question.

A few months ago, frustrated to the breaking point by complaints from the troops about getting mismatched or some else's socks, I instituted the "Clipped Sock Rule." If dirty socks aren't clipped together with their mates, they go out of

the dirt on detergents

The everyday detergent should be a tough, all-fabric cleaner that does as well on a baby's burp cloths and leaky-diaper stains as it does on his big brother's collared polo shirts. Powders generally outperform liquids, but it's a preference thing.

How much detergent should you use? The answer varies by load. When reading the product directions, keep in mind that, because laundering conditions differ from home to home and from load to load, package recommendations should be considered only a starting point for determining proper amounts. The amount of detergent you use will depend on water hardness (the harder the water, the more detergent needed), the amount of soil (more soil requires more detergent), and the

water temperature (cooler water requires more detergent). The hotter the water, the more effective the detergent will be. When using cold water for washing, increase the amount of detergent to one-and-a-half to two times the recommended amount.

Detergent works by loosening dirt and gunk from fabrics. Then it holds the removed dirt in the wash water until it can be rinsed away. If you use too little detergent, clothes can become dull and dingy, white items may turn gray or yellowed, body soils are left on cuffs and collars, and lint isn't held in the water until it is rinsed away; instead, it's redeposited on clothes. You might also notice greasy-looking stains because, if you regularly use too little detergent, it allows gunk to build up on the outer tub of the washer. These soils then wash off and redeposit on other loads. Ick. Err the other way.

the dryer directly into the "homeless sock" basket. No whining allowed.

Before they put their socks into the laundry basket, each family member clips each pair of socks together with a clothespin. To make identifying the clipped sock pairs easy, I picked up an industrial-size clothespin bag, the kind that comes with four colors of clothespins. Then I assigned each of us a color: Dad is green, Lyndsay is blue, I'm yellow, and Chris is red. (Payne's tiny socks are pretty easy to distinguish from the rest of ours. And he couldn't reach the "homeless sock" basket on top of the dryer, anyway. Too short. So he gets a pass. For now.)

I'm happy to report that the socks stay clipped together through the wash and dry! What a difference a clip makes! The tedious matching of socks is history. We have no more complaints about missing socks or misdelivered pairs.

Be creative. Just about every kid has a favorite item that she's always wearing, making laundering it on a regular basis a bit tricky.

If this describes a child in your home, you may want to forgo the power struggles and instead go back to the store you purchased it from to get a second item just like the first. I know of which I speak. Payne has become so attached to his blue Pottery Barn Kids fleece blanket that he's dubbed it "Night-Night" (pronounced Ny-Ny). I now have two others in his closet. The spares come in handy in case of emergency

FAMILY PICKUP LINES
COLORFASTNESS TEST

How can you teach your kids what it means for an item to be "colorfast"? Do the cotton swab test. Have your child place the inner seam of a shirt or sweater on a paper towel, then soak a cotton swab with cool water, and press down firmly on the seam. If no color "magically" appears on the swab, it's colorfast and safe for her to wash.

(Can't find Ny-Ny!) and for when I need to give the favorite a spin in some really hot water to kill all the germs he's picked up while dragging it along the floor.

Try reasoning (or mild threats) with older kids. Tell your daughter that if said item doesn't make it to the basket on laundry day, it will be out of commission for an entire week.

Or, you can get really tough and tell your son that he can only wear said item X days a week. More, and it disappears. This is a good time to explain the importance of washing clothes to keep them looking (and smelling) fresh.

Whatever you choose, choose something. Continually fighting and begging a kid to hand his treasured article over so you can wash it isn't doing either of you any good. He's learning that if he resists strongly enough, he won't have to do something. Even something that's good for his health. And that's probably not the message you're meaning to send.

washing and folding the clothes

So now the clothes are coming off bodies and going into baskets as directed (and not onto the floor). This is good. But someone needs to run the machines. And it can't always be you. This is not so good. Especially if your family has gotten used to your being the resident laundress.

PENNY PINCHER

LOWERING YOUR WASHER'S ENERGY USE

Try these simple changes to lower your laundry bills.

- Keep your hot-water heater set at 120°F. Every 10-degree reduction in water temperature will cut the cost of washing clothes by up to 13 percent.
- Really dirty duds? Use the presoak or soak cycle. You'll avoid two washings and save energy.
- Don't use too much detergent. Over-sudsing causes your machine to work harder and use more energy.
- Don't overwash clothes. Delicate clothes don't need as long a wash cycle as dirty play clothes.
- If your machine is more than 10 years old, it's time to replace it with an Energy Star–rated appliance. Many of the newer machines use up to half the water and two-thirds less energy. Your pocketbook will thank you.

FAMILY PICKUP LINES

HOOP DREAMS Installing a basketball hoop over the hamper really works up enthusiasm for neatness. Be sure, however, that you have adequately covered Laundry Clean House Rule Number 1 (If it's not dirty and it doesn't smell, don't put it in the hamper) so that the hamper is not full of clean clothes.

If you have older kids, they can alternate doing laundry for the family. If you don't have older kids, the parents are stuck with this job. If you *only* have older kids, everyone in the house could do his or her laundry. What a concept! The problem with this solution is that you'll have more small loads. The benefit of this solution is that you'll be teaching your kids responsibility while ditching some of your own. (In a healthy way for your kids, of course.)

Here is my very simple step-by-step approach to getting clothes clean. Share it with your kids. Consider posting a photocopy of these instructions in your laundry area.

1. Treat spills fast. Immediately rinse or blot away spills on your clothes to prevent stains from setting. (Dampen a clean white rag and dab at the stain. You'll see color transfer to the rag. That's how you'll know it's working.) Then wash the clothes as soon as you can.

Have your kids red-flag stains and spots by clipping a clothespin to a chocolate smudge or by tying a grass-stained jeans leg in a loose knot before dumping the garment into the clothes hamper.

2. Before washing stained garments, pre-treat or presoak the spot, according to the product directions.

3. Sort laundry by color, amount of soil, wash cycle needed, and water temperature required. (Read fabric care labels before you wash. Your clothes will last longer if you care for them as recommended.) Also sort lint givers, like towels, from lint takers, like corduroy. Separate delicates from heavy clothes such as jeans. One more thing: Don't wash heavily soiled clothes such as gardening duds with your fine linens.

Also, you may want to run an empty load (with bleach) after washing sneakers or the dog's bed to decontaminate the machine.

4. To keep snags and lint to a minimum, zip zippers, button buttons, brush away lint, and empty pockets before tossing clothes into the hamper. Melted crayons overlooked during this process are no fun to tackle. (See "Treating Stains" on page 61.) Hard objects such as pins and yo-yos can bang around in the washer and tear your clothes.

5. Select the water temperature. Generally use hot for whites or very dirty or greasy clothes, warm for most loads, and cold for delicates or dark or bright colors that could run. (See "Dirty Little Secrets" on page 63 for more

set a washing schedule

A friend of mine, Kathy, has one daughter, age 10. Instead of doing one big wash on one day of the week, Kathy does one specific wash each day. Her husband and daughter know that:

- Mondays are towel days.
- Tuesdays are linen days.
- Wednesdays are undies/delicates days.
- Thursdays are darks days.
- Fridays are whites days.
- Saturdays are warm wash days.
- Sundays no laundry is done. (Yippee!)

Laundry is a part of this family's daily routine. Hubby and daughter deliver the appropriate items to the washing machine each night. Kathy runs the load and puts the folded laundry on the table. Her spouse and daughter pick it up in the evening and put it away, and then they deliver clothes for the next day.

specifics.) Always select "cold" for the rinse-water temperature. It saves energy and is just as effective.

6. Turn the machine on to fill the tub with water.

7. Add detergent and laundry boosters, such as color-safe bleach, bleach, and/or fabric softener (for fluffier clothes), according to the package directions. If you don't have a special dispenser for the boosters, just pour them into the wash water once the machine is filled. If your clothing is heavily soiled, if you're washing a large load, or if you're using cold water, add extra detergent.

8. Dump in the clothes. If you have to stuff them in, you've got too much stuff. The machine should be no more than about two-thirds full. The clothes need to tumble around to get clean. Unsure? Watch for rollover of small items such as socks when the machine is washing. They should sink and reappear later. If they don't, they're too cramped for their own good. And yours.

9. After clothes have been washed, check wet garments for remaining stains, and re-treat as needed before drying. If you dry stained clothes in the dryer, the heat will set the stains.

10. Once the clothes are clean, you can usually just put the load from the

DIRTY LITTLE SECRETS
THE CLEAN JEAN (JACKET)

This first generation of the 21st century has claimed the 1960s staple outerwear, the denim jacket, as their own. Here's how to keep your kid's jacket from looking like it's your grandmother's relic from her flower power days:

• Wash dark denim separately the first time. The dye transfers readily to its fellow bathers.

• Wash denim inside out in warm or cool water to prevent fading (unless you want fading, of course). Keep denim away from detergents with bleach for the same reason.

• Avoid frequent tumble-drying and dry-cleaning. Heat may damage fibers, and dry-cleaning may cause discoloration. When necessary, tumble dry while dryer drum is cool and use delicate settings.

• Don't try to spot-clean denim. Instead, wash the whole jacket so you don't create a faded area where your spot or spill was.

• Iron the jacket while it is still damp.

washer right into the dryer. Keep in mind, though, that it's best to dry loads of clothes that are similar in fiber content and weight. Heavier stuff, such as towels and sweatshirts, require more heat and time in the dryer than lighter clothes, such as gym shorts and swimsuits. Dry only full loads. Tumbling a handful of garments prolongs the drying time by reducing the tumbling. Don't overstuff the dryer, either. Overloading causes wrinkles and increases drying time, too.

11. Set the heat and time for the most delicate item in the load. Don't use a high or regular setting for all clothes. Read the label. Fibers that don't absorb lots of water, such as microfibers, nylon, and acrylic, dry faster and need a lower temperature setting than other fabrics do.

12. Keep your eye on the drying time. Drying a load for too long can cause shrinkage and buildup of static electricity. Over-drying can ruin clothes, and it also wastes energy. (And we know how Dad hates that.) Leave clothes in the dryer just long enough to remove wrinkles and moisture. Some fabrics, such as Spandex and linen, will be damaged or shrink when dried with too much heat.

13. Fold clothes right away. The longer they sit in the dryer, the more wrinkled they become.

14. Clean the lint screen. A clogged lint screen can make dryers run a long time. That wastes energy and money and causes wear and tear on your favorite clothes. Plus, it's a fire hazard.

You may need to show kids how to do the laundry several times—and then supervise them doing it several more times—before letting them go it alone.

FAMILY PICKUP LINES

SORTING FOR PRESCHOOLERS
Use laundry as a sorting game for younger kids. Start by having your tot sort the dark colors into the following piles: blacks, blues, and browns. Then have him sort the lights: light blues, pinks, and yellows. Finish with a whites-only pile. In addition to making your laundry routine more fun and involving the kids, this game also helps them learn colors.

getting the clean clothes put away

So far, so good. You've set up your home with laundry baskets in logical places. The family is dumping dirty duds where they belong. Everyone is taking turns bringing down the laundry baskets, running the machines, and folding the clothes.

But who's going to wave the wand to put the clothes back into their appointed drawers and closets? If you're fresh out of fairies, here are tips for helping clean clothes get put away.

Make each family member responsible. Each person fetches his or her laundry basket and puts his or her own clothes away. A Clean House Rule: Any baskets left unclaimed for more than 24 hours (without a school or sleepover excuse) will be removed from sight for one week (into the garage or a closet). Once your

FAMILY PICKUP LINES

JELLY ROLLING Teach your
youngest child still developing her coordination
skills to "jelly roll" rather than fold her clothes.
Rolling is a simple skill that kids ages 3 to 6
can manage on their own. Now even the
youngest family member can put her clothes
away and keep them tidy. By age 6, they're
ready for the fold-and-go lesson.

daughter has to live without her favorite
jeans or your son has to go to practice
without his uniform, the problem is
unlikely to arise again anytime soon.

Make it easy. To simplify the process,
make emptying the dryer and folding and
sorting clothes by room a weekly chore for
one child. The sorter also has the
responsibility of looking out for tears or
missing buttons and placing those
garments in a special mending basket.

Those with large families (like ours) may
have several adults doing the laundry, at
least when the children are very young. In
our home, it's Mom, Dad, and now and
then the babysitter or Grandma when
she's visiting. And with three kids, it can
almost seem overwhelming to sort out
what belongs to whom. Especially for our
older two, who are only 12 months apart
in age.

The solution? I mark the labels on kids'
clothing with a permanent clothing marker
with dots. One dot for the oldest, two dots
for the second child, three dots for the
third child . . . you get the picture. Then,
whenever a question arises about
ownership, it's simply connect-the-dots-to-
the-kids time. Change of ownership due to
growth spurts poses no problem, just add a
dot. (Older children rarely shrink so you'll
not have to worry about erasing dots.)

troubleshooting

Be cautious as you go forth doing laundry
with kids. Mixing water, soap, dirt, and
kids can be a recipe for disaster. Here are
some solutions to kids' common laundry
problems:

Sweater shrinking. Soak the shrunken
sweater in a sinkful of warm water and
two tablespoons of baby shampoo, which
relaxes natural fibers such as wool, for 15
minutes. Remove the sweater from the
water, and roll it in a towel to reduce
moisture. Pin the sweater to a large
corkboard, and stretch it to size. Return
every few hours to restretch and repin the
sweater until it's dry.

Graying or yellowing of fabrics. For
clothes that come out of the washer gray
or yellow, rewash the item before it dries,
using more detergent.

Color bleeding. Guess they forgot to sort
properly. But all is not lost, especially if
the overly colored shirt or pants haven't
been tossed in the dryer. Wash again, in
the hottest water safe for the fabric, as

many times as necessary to rinse out the transferred color. I know about this one. It's a challenge I've successfully tackled in my own home.

Fabric pilling. Many synthetic clothes shed small fibers that ball up and cling to the clothes. Remove these pills with a fuzz-removing device sold in drug and gadget stores. To prevent future pilling, use a fabric softener in the washer or dryer to lubricate fibers. And remind Junior that overloading can make pilling worse. Some clothing manufacturers suggest washing clothes inside out because it limits abrasion on the "good" side of the fabric, reducing pilling, and extends the life of fabrics such as corduroy. Use this strategy to keep school names on uniforms crisp and sharp.

treating stains

Stains are such a common problem that I'm giving them their own special section. Try these no-fail techniques (and my Homemade Stain Solutions) next time the kids show up with a splattered sweatshirt. Or dress. Or jeans. Or . . .

First, be patient. Zapping a drip, drop, or splat without zapping the fabric itself requires a gentle touch and the patience to repeat a treatment until the blight is lifted. Try these techniques and then wash the garment as usual. (See "Homemade Stain

HOMEMADE STAIN SOLUTIONS
Try these recipes for homemade stain busters:

Household ammonia mix: Mix one part of ammonia to eight parts of water.

Enzyme laundry detergent mix: Add one teaspoon of a laundry detergent that contains enzymes to one cup of water.

Hand dishwashing liquid mix: Add one teaspoon of commercial dishwashing liquid to one cup of water.

Hydrogen peroxide: No change required here! Just use 3 percent, undiluted.

Fels-Naptha paste: Shave off slices of Fels-Naptha bar soap. Add one part of shavings to ten parts of water. Work the mixture into a paste.

WD-40: Use full strength, undiluted.

After treating stains, always wash clothes in the hottest water safe for the fabric, using chlorine bleach or color-safe bleach, depending on the label's instructions.

Solutions" on this page for the ingredients mentioned here.)

Chewing gum: Rub the gummy spot with ice to harden it. Scrape away as much of the gum as possible with a dull knife. Saturate what remains with a prewash stain remover.

Chocolate: Treat the spot with an enzyme laundry detergent mix; allow to sit for 30 minutes. If a ring or a slight stain remains, feather the edges or spotty areas with a cloth dampened with hydrogen peroxide. Rinse thoroughly with clear, cool water.

Crayon: Place the garment on paper towels, crayoned side up. Spray the crayon-smudged or melted-on area with WD-40. Let stand 10 minutes. Turn the garment over and spray the underside as

well. Allow to sit another 10 minutes. Using paper towels, blot on some hand dishwashing liquid mix, replacing the towels as they absorb the waxy colors. If crayons melted onto your dryer drum, too, spray a soft cloth with WD-40. Wipe clean.

Grass: Soak or prewash the garment in your washer, or in a sink or bucket, along with a laundry detergent that contains

LAUNDRY CHORES BY AGE

Here are some laundry chores and the ages by which most kids are able to do them. Once a child reaches a certain skill or age level, he can generally do the chores for his age group and those for the age groups below. Of course, some of these chores need to be done each day, others once a week, and still others once a month or even less frequently. Use your best judgment for what gets done when, and see "Mrs. Clean Jeans' Housekeeping Routine" on page 253 for guidelines.

AGES 2 AND UNDER:
- Put dirty clothes in hamper if the top is low enough

AGES 3 TO 5:
- Previous chores, plus:
- Remove clothes from the dryer
- Help fold laundry (See "Family Pickup Lines" on page 60.)
- Take clean, folded clothes to his or her room

- Air-tumble throw pillows in dryer

AGES 6 TO 9:
- Previous chores, plus:
- Decide which clothes are dirty and which can be reworn
- Take hampers to the laundry room
- Fold simple laundry items
- Match socks from dryer

AGES 10 TO 13:
- Previous chores, plus:
- Sort, wash, and fold laundry
- Change bed linens
- Wash washable curtains

AGES 14 TO 17:
- Previous chores, plus:
- Clean the dryer exhaust vent
- Sew on buttons and mend torn clothes (This could be a heavy-duty chore for extra pay or privileges.)
- Remove dust ruffle from beds to wash or dry-clean

DIRTY LITTLE SECRETS

CARING FOR HOT NEW FABRICS AND SOME OLD FAVORITES, TOO

It's new, it's so cool it's hot, but how do I take care of it after I get it home? For the kids' new stuff and your old favorites, it pays to know your fibers.

FABRIC	WASH	BLEACH	DRY	IRON	STORAGE
*Acetate	Warm	Color-safe	Drip	Inside out, cool iron	Cool dry place, away from sunlight
*Cashmere	Cool	No	Flat	No	Cool dry place, away from sunlight
Cotton	Cool to hot	Color-safe	Drip	While damp	When fully dry, cool dry place, away from sunlight
*Hemp	Warm	No	Drip	Damp inside out, low	Cool dry place, hang in old dry-cleaning bags to prevent wrinkling
*Linen	Warm	No	Drip	Damp inside out, low	Cool dry place, hang in old dry-cleaning bags to prevent wrinkling
*Microfiber	Cool	Color-safe	Drip	Warm	Cool dry place, away from sunlight
*Rayon	Cool	No	Drip	Inside out, steam iron	Cool dry place, away from sunlight
*Silk	Cold	No	Drip	Cool	Cool dry place, sealed against insects, light, and air
*Spandex	Cool	No	Drip	Low	Cool dry place
*Wool	Cold	No	Flat	Wool setting	Cool dry place. Cedar chests are ideal, or store with cedar chips

Generally speaking, whites, very dirty or greasy clothes, and sturdy, colorfast fabrics that retain their dye can be washed in hot water.

Light colors that won't run, regular and sturdy fabrics, towels, jeans, cottons, sheets, sturdy playwear, school uniforms, 100 percent manmade fibers, blends of natural and manmade fibers, and moderately soiled stuff are best washed in warm water.

Dark or bright colors that may run or fade; delicate fabrics including washable silk, Spandex swimsuits, and active wear; and delicate lingerie should be washed in cold water. Cold water will also minimize the shrinking of washable woolens. It's also okay for lightly soiled clothes. Always use cold water for clothes stained with blood, wine, or coffee. Warm water could set these stains.

*Use machine's gentle or delicate cycle or hand-wash these fabrics.

fabric care symbols

Federal Trade Commission regulations require a garment to have a sewn-in label with proper care instructions. They will be either solely symbols or symbols and words. Clothing care labels tell you all you need to know in written or symbol form about how to wash, dry, and iron your favorite volleyball uniform or church dress. Read your clothing care label; it's the secret to successful laundry.

Here's how to decipher what you see.

SYMBOL	CARE INSTRUCTIONS
	Hand-wash
	Machine wash (number of dots indicates wash water temperature: one dot, cold; two dots, warm; three dots, hot)
	Machine wash, permanent press/wrinkle resistant cycle
	Machine wash, delicate/gentle cycle
	Do not wash (in general, anything with an "x" over it is a "do not")
	Chlorine bleach okay
	Only non-chlorine bleach
	No chlorine bleach
	Tumble dry (one dot, low heat; two dots, medium heat; three dots, high heat)
	Line dry or hang dry
	Dry flat
	Iron (one dot, low, 110°C/230°F; two dots, warm, 150°C/300°F; and three dots, high, 200°C/390°F)
	Dry-clean

enzymes. Apply an ammonia solution to remove any lingering greenery.

Ice cream: Apply the enzyme laundry detergent mix directly onto the smudge. Let sit for 30 minutes. Rinse thoroughly with cool, clear water.

Ink: Pull the stained area of the fabric taut over a clear jam or jelly jar. Slowly drip isopropyl rubbing alcohol onto the spot until it lightens substantially. The liquid will dissolve the ink from the fabric and send it dripping colorfully into the jar.

Ketchup: Apply Fels-Naptha paste, followed by ammonia and vinegar mixes if needed. This also works for spaghetti sauce, mayonnaise, and salad dressings.

Wine: Generously sprinkle salt on the site of the stain to keep additional liquid from saturating the surface. Sponge or soak the stain immediately in cool water for 30 minutes. Apply a dishwashing liquid solution, continuing to blot until no more stain is coming off on your paper towel or rag. Use this technique for soft-drink and fruit-drink spills, too.

Chapter 4

kitchen sync

THE KITCHEN IS THE HEART OF THE HOME. And all too often its arteries get clogged with kid stuff and parent stuff, not to mention big bodies, little bodies, and animal bodies everywhere. It's the room where:

- Mom and Dad cook
- The family eats
- The pets eat
- Older kids do homework
- Younger kids do artwork
- Slacker kids watch TV
- Dad enjoys a drink while reading his mail (and getting in Mom's way)
- And it's where the whole family dumps whatever they're carrying onto the kitchen table—or the first counter they encounter.

The kitchen is the room where everyone congregates, and, consequently, it's usually one of the messiest rooms in the house. Yet it's also the place where we gather at the end of each day (as often as we can, anyway) to break bread, wind down, and refuel.

It's these activities especially that require an elevated level of cleanliness.

Unfortunately, the kitchen is also often one of the dirtiest rooms in the house. Because the kitchen is usually the family entry point—as it is in our home via the garage and small hallway—it's the first place we track in and deposit a day's worth of dirt. In other words, the floor's a mess. And the kitchen sink isn't any better. Sure, it looks pretty good. But that seemingly clean place where we rinse vegetables and meats has been called one of the most germ-laden areas of the home. In fact, according to some studies, you'd do better to eat off the toilet. Researchers at the University of Arizona studied 14 areas in the kitchen and bath for germ count. The top 5 germiest areas were in the kitchen. Ready for this? The toilet seat came up dead last on the germ scale.

Ugh.

Oh, yes. And about those science experiments closer to home, in the fridge? The mold is getting out of control. It's tough to keep up with expiration dates. And it's even tougher to make sure everyone's handling stuff properly to prevent cross-contamination that can lead to major tummyaches. Worse, it can be difficult to work together as a team in one room without being in each other's way. And that leads to cranky moms and dads and little ones being even more constantly underfoot.

Don't fight it; organize it and clean it!

CLEAN HOUSE RULES FOR A CLEANER, CALMER KITCHEN

1. Never put anything on the kitchen counter or table as you come in the door. These are forbidden zones.

2. Always take shoes off at the door and hang up coats and backpacks.

3. Eat only in the kitchen and dining room.

4. Always clean up behind yourself.

5. Always put dishes into the dishwasher, not the sink.

6. Wipe down counters after use.

7. Close cabinet doors that you open.

8. Ask to be excused from the table.

9. Ask before snacking or having dessert.

10. If you eat and can reach the counter, bus your own plate.

CLEAN HOUSE RULES FOR A SAFER, SANER KITCHEN

1. Don't touch anything that will go into someone's mouth until your hands are washed with soap.

2. Don't cook anything without help unless you are old enough to have a driver's license learner's permit.

3. Always read the entire recipe before you begin cooking to make sure that you have all the ingredients.

4. Always turn pot handles away from yourself. Put boiling stuff on the back burners only.

5. Always use oven mitts or potholders when handling hot stuff from the oven or stove.

6. Work slowly when chopping or using knives, giving tasks your full attention. Never pick up knives by their blades.

7. Do not run or play with knives or sharp objects in your hands.

8. Don't put hands in a bowl that has a running mixer inside. Ditto for blenders.

9. Always make sure the base is tightened and the lid is securely on the blender before turning it on.

10. Always clean up after a cooking adventure, and before you eat the results.

a home for everything

To get the most out of your kitchen, first consider all the activities your family does there. Then reorganize the space to accommodate those activities.

Well, duh. That seems obvious, doesn't it? But often we just put things away in the closest place that we can find at the time, without really giving it a second thought. So think about it. What are your garnishing tools doing in the top drawer on the kitchen island? How often do you use those things? Shouldn't they be at the back of the bottom drawer with the cake decorating tips? And where is the paring knife you use every day? Oh! *That's* in the back of the bottom drawer!

I've organized my kitchen into eight activity centers: the coming-home center, the communications center, the congregation center, the cooking center, the food storage center, the pet feeding center, the recycling center, and the study hall. Let's take a peek at each of them in turn.

coming-home center

Most clutter happens as kids come in from school and adults come home from shopping or work. We're tired, we're hungry. Sometimes we're cranky, too.

As a result, we all dump whatever we're carrying—books, newspapers, mail, shoes, shopping bags, coats, papers for Mom to sign, soccer balls, briefcases, etc.—on the first solid surface inside the door (often the kitchen counter or table). We're just happy to be home at last, where we can take a load off.

The solution to coming-home clutter? Declare the kitchen a "no dumping" zone and enforce that rule. No one, including you and your spouse, is allowed to dump stuff on the kitchen table or counters. Not even for a minute. Instead, establish a clutter-catchall loading and unloading zone outside the garage or kitchen door where you and the troops tromp in. (Yellow paint is not required.)

There, you'll create convenient places to stash this stuff. This is where the family will remove muddy shoes and hang up outerwear. Hang decorative hooks in pewter or gold near an entry door to give kids a quick place to hang up coats by themselves rather than throwing them onto the floor. Install a low shelf for depositing backpacks, lunch boxes, papers to be signed, and the rest of the daily

A well-organized entryway with lots of convenient storage encourages neatness.

clutter, to be sifted through and emptied later, once tummies are full. Put up hooks for backpacks, car keys, umbrellas, dog leashes, and doggie bags. Hang a clean, dry (old) towel for drying Poochie off on rainy or snowy days. Also position coat racks for coats, cubbies for mail and newspapers, baskets for gloves, and tubs for sports equipment and lunch boxes nearby. Why should all this stuff be mucking up your kitchen?

communications center

The kitchen is often the room where we answer the phone and take messages. It's also where we leave messages for each other. Some families post messages on the refrigerator. Others use a bulletin board. Still others just leave notes on the counter by the phone.

Choose whatever method works best for your family. Just make sure everyone answering the phone and writing down messages knows the established place to leave them.

Our phone sits on a peninsula cook station with scant room for stuff. Instead of a junk drawer full of jumbled pens and pencils, our home has a funky holder we saw in a magazine. It's an aluminum test-tube holder that keeps each pen, pencil, and marker individually visible and accessible. (A coffee mug works well, too!)

Also in our communications center, we keep a mini-pad of paper in its own small stand and an ongoing grocery list. Messages taken are stationed in a prominent place so they're the first thing any of us see when we come home.

You can create your own communications center by simply grouping the following items together:

- Telephone and answering machine
- Notepad or notebook
- Pencils and pens
- Family calendar or Phoneside Binder (see page 72)

The goal is to organize your time as well as your stuff. By placing all the communications basics together, you'll be the picture of relaxed organization when the phone rings with a last-minute carpool emergency. With all the day's family commitments at your fingertips, a notepad on which to jot down details, and a pen with which to write, you can easily reply, "But of course, darling, I'd be delighted to help." No time wasted running up and down stairs, or scrounging for the school phone book so you can find your daughter's friend's mom's name.

The communications center is also a good place to post weekly menus so you can tell what to buy at the store, how much to buy, what time you'll need to be home to cook it, and how many people you're expecting. Not only will you be free of every-other-day trips to the market, but Dad will be happy. He'll know what to avoid for lunch each day so he doesn't end up with chicken for lunch and dinner. If only moms had such weighty problems!

In your communications center, it's helpful to have a Phoneside Binder to keep track of the family's activities and information. Time is on your side with this handy scheduler. Instead of keeping practice and game schedules and team rosters in individual files upstairs at your desk, simply place them all in a three-ring binder that is easy enough for even the youngest (reading) family member to use. Simply inscribe each tab with a family member's name, and include all his or her sports and social commitments for the week, month, or season. Keep the binder next to the kitchen phone. Every family member has a tab, so when the phone rings and you're asked a schedule question, you're the picture of relaxed organization.

Another feature of a communications center could be an ongoing shopping list. Simply place a notepad or hang a corkboard or dry-erase board nearby, and encourage family members to list food and nonfood items that need to be purchased at the store. For the not-quite-writing set, create a "more, please" station. Simply hang a paper or plastic bag on a drawer pull or place one on a shelf. When a child drinks the last box of juice or uses the last paper towel, she places the empty box or roll in the bag, telling Mom to stock up.

congregation center

No, I'm not anticipating that you'll be preaching here (though if my kids are any indication, kids often require a moral lecture), but whether you like it or not, company always gravitates toward the kitchen. You can put the chips and guacamole on the coffee table, and guests still wander into the kitchen to watch you burn the appetizers. Relax and go with the flow. If you're entertaining, go ahead and put some munchies on the kitchen counter as well as the living room table. And for unexpected guests at other times of the day, keep your kitchen visitor-friendly: Arrange a little lazy Susan with a basket of fine teas, sugar swizzle sticks, and biscotti. Now you're ready for drop-in neighbors.

cooking center

Cooking can be subdivided into smaller sub-activities. Organize the cooking area into activity centers. (Well, actually these are activity centers within the overall cooking activity center. Isn't this fun?) Such a plan not only saves steps, but it also enables two people to work at once without falling all over each other, which is good for a night of Twister among tipsy newlyweds but bad for married-with-children types packing butcher knives. Organize your cooking area into these groups:

Cooking (as in the actual heating of food): Around the range, put all things needed for cooking. Pots and pans go in the cabinets directly underneath. Hang hot pads by the range. Put a jar of utensils on top of the range, but include only those utensils you use at least once a week.

Slicing and dicing: Near the sink, create a workstation with all the paraphernalia you need to wash, peel, and chop foods, including knives, butcher block, peelers, scrub brushes, bowls, etc.

Food preparing: Here's where you would group scrapers, colanders, mixing bowls and spoons, whisks, measuring cups and spoons, blenders, and your food processor. Try to contain them all in one cabinet.

Baking: Arrange all the things you'll need for baking in one cabinet. Then organize the items inside plastic storage containers for grouping like items. I put our collection of cake and ice cream sprinkles and candy toppings in a big plastic box. When it's time to frost cupcakes for class, Chris and Lyndsay know right where to go.

Nearby, in a second see-through container, they'll find baking soda, baking powder, and sugars, everything they'd need to make cupcakes. (Except the flour. To chill out any wiggly creatures that might make a home here, I put my flour inside a zip-close bag that calls the freezer its home.) You don't have to be so finicky. But you should at least place your opened sugars (brown, powdered, and regular) and flours in airtight plastic containers or

This is what my family's snacking center looks like. We keep it on the countertop, so it's really accessible.

Organizing breakfast foods and dishes in a convenient serve-yourself drawer makes breakfast a snap.

zip-close bags to close in freshness and contents and close out nasty bugs that love to cozy up, then divide and multiply there.

Snacking: Make kids more independent and let them fix their own breakfasts, lunches, and snacks. In an accessible low cabinet (away—far away—from the stove), station snack foods for the kids: peanut butter, bread, jelly, raisins, cereal bars, cereal, chips, and zip-close bags. This is also a good spot for storing lunch boxes. Grouping these items makes it easy for kids to pack their own lunches.

Our pullout breakfast drawer was instituted when Chris and Lyndsay were 3 and 4 years old. We'd leave a small cup of milk on the lowest shelf in the fridge. In the morning, they'd pour their cereal and add milk with no help required from Mom and Dad, who were rewarded for their creativity with an extra hour of sleep on Saturday mornings.

Coffee drinking: In the cabinet above the coffeemaker, store filters, flavorings, grinder, beans, sugar, teas, and all the stuff you need to perk up your mornings. That way you can enjoy your first cup without having to search around with your eyes half open.

Storing dishes: Oh, yeah. You eat in the kitchen, too! So you'll need to make room for your daily dishes, your serving dishes, glasses, and utensils in here, as well. Put them all in one area, please, and as close to the sink and/or dishwasher as you can get them to minimize the time spent putting clean dishes away.

food storage center

Of course, food takes up a large amount of your kitchen. Food storage breaks down into three categories: food that goes in the pantry, cool foods that require refrigeration, and frozen foods that go in the freezer. Let's go over each now.

the pantry

No pantry? No problem. If you don't have a built-in pantry, just assign some cabinets to the task. Ideally, choose a few large cabinets close to your refrigerator and stove. Most kitchens have a lot of cabinets and drawers, but they are usually a chaotic mess. You buy marinara sauce, just to find three jars hidden behind the olive oil. The solution? Organize your storage so you know what you have and where you have it.

- Group foods by type. Don't just stuff items into the first open space you see; instead, stock foodstuff in the same place each time, grouping like items. In my pantry, I put crackers, chips, and other snack foods on the highest shelf not easily in reach; cereal and other breakfast items on the second shelf; pasta, pasta sauces, and boxed pasta and rice mixes on the third shelf; canned vegetables and fruit on the fourth; and soups and canned beans

on the bottom. This way, I can tell at a glance what I have and what I need to buy. If there's no oatmeal on the second shelf, I know there is no oatmeal in the house.

- Put rarely used items on the tallest shelves and in the back of cabinets. Put your family's favorite foods in the middle, at eye level. Heavy items such as cans go near the bottom.

- Use lazy Susans, pullout shelving, and wire racks to maximize storage space.

- Repackage shelf hogs. Get rid of half-empty cartons of cereal and place the cereal in smaller, airtight plastic containers. Then label them with the contents and the expiration date. Unlike wine, foods don't get better with age!

- Place drawer liners in drawers to keep contents from slipping and sliding around. You'll be rewarded when you carefully divide everything up, using varying sizes of containers to house your stuff, and the stuff actually stays that way. This also makes it easy for you to wipe off the dust that naturally settles there.

- Finally, store bulk purchases—you know, the 17 boxes of pasta, 40 cans of chicken noodle soup, and 100 rolls of paper towels you got for a steal at the club store—in the garage or downstairs in the basement. Call this your overflow pantry, and replenish your kitchen supply as needed.

the refrigerator

Used correctly, your refrigerator will keep food safe from spoilage and bacteria. Used incorrectly, it could cause big trouble. Your refrigerator could make you sick. Essentially, no food benefits from storage. You want to eat everything as fresh as you can. But since we can't all tromp out to the garden to harvest produce for each meal, here are some guidelines for making your fridge function at its best.

- To keep food from spoiling in the refrigerator, the temperature needs to be between 34° and 40°F. You can't depend on the little gauge (1–5) in the refrigerator. Buy a refrigerator thermometer.

- Some parts of your refrigerator are colder than others. The meat compartment at the bottom is designed to store meat, so put meat there. Not only is this the coldest area, but if a package leaks, it won't contaminate other foods.

- The door is the warmest part of the refrigerator. This is the best place for nonperishables (sodas)—*not* perishables like eggs.

- Don't put hot food in the refrigerator. Bring it to room temperature before refrigerating it. Hot food can cause refrigerator temperatures to drop.

- On the other hand, don't leave food out too long either. Refrigerate

how long do foods keep?

Refrigerating foods helps keep them fresh, but they still won't last forever. Here are some examples of how long it's safe to keep some foods:

FOOD	SHELF LIFE
Eggs	3 weeks
Hot dogs	1 week opened; 2 weeks unopened
Meats, deli	5 days; 3 to 5 days for prepackaged deli meats once opened
Meats, fish, or poultry	2 days cooked; 1 to 2 days uncooked
Meats, other	3 to 5 days
Milk	5 to 7 days
Pies	1 to 2 days
Sour cream	4 weeks
Vegetables, cooked	3 to 4 days
Vegetables, fresh	Ranges from 2 days for soft veggies like asparagus or okra to 2 weeks for hard vegetables like radishes or carrots

Best advice: When in doubt, throw it away. A little thriftiness is not worth a tummyache, or worse.

prepared food within two hours of cooking (one hour in the summer).

• Don't overload the refrigerator. Parties are a dangerous time because you cram a lot of food into the refrigerator, and then you're continually opening the door. Turn the temperature down during these occasions to keep the food cold.

• Cover foods tightly. Leave meats in their original packaging to prevent spreading bacteria.

• Don't store breads, cookies, or most types of cakes in the refrigerator; they will become stale.

• Tell your family not to stand gazing slackjawed into the open refrigerator while they decide what they want to eat.

• If you lose power, do not open your refrigerator or freezer. If the door is not opened, food should keep 8 hours in the refrigerator and 48 hours in the freezer.

freeze-frame foods: what's safe, what's not

Be sure to properly package steak, fish, burgers, and chicken if you plan to marinate and freeze them. Use bags or containers designed for freezers, or wrap food in foil or plastic bag. Always make the fitting as airtight as possible around the item you're freezing. Do not freeze meats in their supermarket wraps. These wraps are designed to breathe. Remember, proper packaging prevents that icky freezer burn. It looks gross but if you cut away the dry ("burned") areas, it's usually safe to eat. Date your packages and use the oldest first.

Here are the general guidelines for frozen foods:

FOOD	FREEZER SHELF LIFE
Breads	2 months
Butter	9 months
Chicken	6 months
Fish and shellfish	6 months
French fries	6 months
Fruits	4 months
Ground beef	2 months
Guacamole	3 months
Ice cream	2 months
Pancakes and waffles	2 months
TV dinners and breakfast entrees	3 months
Vegetables	8 months

Note that it is unsafe to freeze foods in cans or glass and previously frozen meats, fish, or chicken products.

Finally, remember to check your freezer temperature regularly to make sure it's between 0° and 5°F.

the freezer

Freezing food will keep it from spoiling, but quality will still deteriorate over time. Use frozen foods as soon as possible, and follow these guidelines:

- Don't refreeze foods.
- Mark the date on foods when you put them in the freezer.
- Don't rely on the little freezer gauge (1–5). Buy a thermometer instead. The freezer should be kept at 0° to 5°F.
- Freeze only fresh foods.
- Wrap foods tightly.

pet feeding center

Hey! You're not the only one chowing down in here. And, yes, you can feed the pooch in the kitchen without letting the whole place go to the dogs.

Stash the less-than-fragrant dog or cat food dish out of the way of (foot) traffic lanes. Try to locate the food nearby. We keep Chloe and Cocoa's (Lyndsay's calico cat sisters rescued from the streets of West Hollywood) trio of bowls—two food dishes and one big water dish—underneath an inconspicuous corner table. The food is tucked into a nearby cabinet out of sight, but within reach when cats need chow.

recycling center

Under the sink, keep plastic tubs for recycling aluminum, glass, and plastic. Let the kids do this. They'll love it. They'll even like taking it out to the garage. Really. And while you're at it, start a composting pail (with a tight-fitting lid) with non-meat table scraps. You can add this to your composting pile or worm bin. (Another great kid project.) Maybe keep your dishwashing detergent here, too.

While we're thinking about the sink, let's talk about what not to keep under there. Do not store poisons, such as cleaners and bleach, under the sink. It's a bad idea with those little ones in your home. This is not one of those times that you want to have logical stuff (like drain cleaner) handy. Homes with kids should have cleaners and other dangerous brews stored up high and out of reach in the garage.

study hall

Many a mom, including me, likes her kids to do their homework in the kitchen so she can answer kiddie questions while they work. If your kids study here, too, keep all supplies close at hand, so the kids aren't continually jumping up and down (and prolonging the whole homework process) for erasers, compasses, protractors, dictionaries, etc. Empty a cabinet and create a little office supply center with notebook paper, construction paper, folders, pencils, pens, rulers, calculators, markers, crayons, and whatever else your kids use. Leave room

deciphering the food label

When it comes to food freshness, it's a confusing food world out there in groceryland. What does the "sell by" date on the organic milk carton really mean? How long is it good after the "sell by" date? Why doesn't the butter have one? And do I really have to use by the "use by" date?

There ought to be a law. But there isn't—at least not on all products in all states. In fact, U.S. federal law requires expiration dates only on infant formulas and baby food. They are voluntary for the rest of the food chain. Worse, your grocer isn't required to take dated stuff off the shelves. Icky.

Because all labeling isn't created equal, how can you tell what's good and what's allowed bacteria a toehold? Here's a look at sell-date wording, and what it means:

Best If Used By (or Before) and Use By dates: The date you see is the last day the baker or farmer who created/baked/squeezed the product is willing to guarantee its freshness on. You can also look at it as the day the item begins to go bad. Most foods are still edible after this date if they're stored properly, but no guarantees here, Mom. You'll find calendar dates on perishables such as dairy products, eggs, meat, and chicken. Choose the freshest you can find (the date furthest in the future) digging your way to the very back of the display. It's worth searching for.

Sell By or Pull dates: After this date, the grocer is advised by the manufacturer to remove the item from the shelf. The item may still be eaten if it hasn't been around longer than the recommended storage time.

Expiration date: Don't push it, Dad. When this date has come and gone, so should the food inside the dated label. This is one you can take to the (food) bank. It's as firm as food dating gets. Choose the item with the date furthest in the future so it will last longer in your fridge. Exception to the rule: eggs. Their expiration date is the last day a store can sell them as fresh. Buy eggs before the expiration date, and use within one month.

Closed, Coded, or Pack dates: This tells you when shelf-stable stuff such as cereal or canned tuna was packed or boxed. And no, they are not easy to read, by design. These dates are really more of a manufacturer's code to help them (not you) to rotate their products or track them in the event of a recall. (There's a scary thought.) Some of these dates are coded by month (M), day (D), and year (Y); others use an encrypted type code. If you can read the date, choose the product made most recently. Unsure? Plan to keep canned goods in the pantry no longer than one year. The same rule applies to cake mixes, too. Some contain oils that may become rancid over time.

The exception to this rule: Canned olives and packaged pickles and peppers should be used within three months.

to store ongoing projects, such as term papers and note cards.

Although younger kids don't do homework, they do artwork. For younger kids, like my Payne, I've found that since the kitchen is the room best suited to cleaning up messes, it's the perfect place for our art center. I use a cleaning-supply caddy as a portable home for coloring books, paper, markers, crayons, and a three-ring binder with zip-close clear plastic cases for stickers and pipe cleaners. You could also use a storage tower with see-through drawers for art supplies.

To manage the flow of art in this busy room, date each day's efforts, tuck them in file folders (a different color for each child), and then in a kitchen drawer. Pick the best artwork every few weeks and transfer it to a treasure box: a lidded plastic bin or sturdy cardboard box that can be tucked under your bed or stored on a closet shelf. Include school photos, teacher's notes, and other special papers. You'll have a trove of memories by year's end, which you can transfer to a scrapbook if you're so inclined. Oh, yeah, that would be on one of those slow days.

cleaning with kids: the kitchen

It's a real challenge to keep the kitchen clean, and yet it's so important. Germs are

A well-organized kitchen can save hours of frustration and make cooking and cleanup easy.

everywhere. These nasty little interlopers stow away in your handbag or briefcase and hitchhike home on raw meats and vegetables. Since you can't see them, how can you beat them? You must know where the biggest, germiest bugs lurk, and how to zap them.

As I mentioned before, in one study, the top five germiest places in the home were in the kitchen: sponges and dishcloths, the sink drain area, the sink faucet handle, cutting boards, and the refrigerator handle. Here's a look at how to debug these top five hot spots, and the other major kitchen areas needing cleaning.

Sponges and dishcloths: Not only are sponges and dishcloths great breeding grounds for germs, but when you use them to wipe up countertops and other surfaces they are perfect germ spreaders. Disinfect them each and every day. You can simply wash them in the clothes washer (in a separate load from undies, please!), run them through the dishwasher, or microwave them for a few seconds to kill germs.

The sink drain area: Disinfect sinks each day. You can actually disinfect your sink, sponges, and dishcloths all at once. Here's how: Fill the kitchen sink with a basic disinfecting solution (¾ cup of bleach to 1 gallon of warm water). Soak sponges and dishcloths for five minutes, and then let the bleachy water run down the drain. This sanitizes the sponges and disinfects the sink and drain area in one easy step.

Sink faucet handle: Wipe down the faucet handle daily with a disposable

---

DIRTY LITTLE SECRETS

OVEN SPILLS A holiday pie or cheesy lasagna meltdown can turn your oven into a smoky, burnt, ooze-encrusted mess. Plus, the gunk becomes an instant fire hazard. The solution? Tackle the gooey drips as soon as they happen. Cover the spill with a thick layer of salt as soon as it drops on the oven floor, while the goop is still hot and soft. Continue cooking. When the oven cools, the spills will harden and can be easily lifted away with a plastic spatula.

Old scorched-food blights can be removed by rubbing with a small pumice stone. This technique will leave a sandy residue that is easily brushed away. Wipe clean with a damp sponge.

---

disinfecting wipe, or spray it with a combination cleaner/disinfectant.

Cutting board: For cutting boards and other porous surfaces, mix 3 tablespoons of liquid bleach with 1 gallon of water. Apply to the surface. Keep the surface wet for two minutes. Rinse with water and let dry.

Refrigerator handle: For fridge handles and other hard, nonporous surfaces, mix 1 tablespoon of liquid bleach with 1 gallon of water. Apply to the surface. Keep the surface wet for two minutes. Allow to air-dry. Do not rinse.

Countertops: From toast to cereal and beyond! These crumby culprits and all sorts of other drips, smudges, and dirt on countertops are ubiquitous in any household where Buzz Lightyear and SpongeBob fans reside. Here's a simple solution to the Hansel and Gretel syndrome: Park a travel-size pack of baby wipes counterside. This does double duty: It serves as a reminder for kids to clean up, plus it provides a quick and easy way to do so. Now, post-meal surface wipe-downs are a snap, even if you can't reach the sink for the sponge. Floor and counter crumbs stick to the wipe's damp surface, and the wipe is tossed after use, making it easy enough for your 2-year-old to master.

Each week, do a more thorough countertop cleaning. Take everything off of your counters and wipe them down with a nonabrasive, disinfectant cleaner. Let the counters dry, and then put everything back.

The refrigerator: Wipe up any spills in your refrigerator immediately to keep bacteria from growing. Wash first with warm, soapy water, then disinfect with a solution of 1 teaspoon of bleach in 1 quart of water. Each week, do a more thorough cleaning and toss out old foods. Check expiration dates of foods and condiments you keep, rotating so that the oldest of any item (milk, for example) is front and center when little hands are searching.

Every few weeks, do a major cleaning. First, unplug the fridge for safety. Then remove all food. Dissolve 4 teaspoons of baking soda in 1 quart of water. With a soft, clean cloth, wash all interior surfaces, including the top, bottom, drawers, and walls. Pay special attention to corners and crevices. Then, rinse all surfaces with warm water. Dry with a soft, clean cloth. Don't forget to plug the fridge back in!

Other kitchen chores: In addition to cleaning, there are other housekeeping chores in the kitchen. For those, such as setting and clearing the table, eliminate the "I did it last time" excuse by assigning permanent rotations that are easy to remember. In our home, Chris sets the table on even days of the month, while Lyndsay sets it on odd days.

cleaning kitchen floors

Floors are a potluck of dirt, grunge, and grime. Keeping today's fabulous flooring materials—linoleum, vinyl, hardwood,

FAMILY PICKUP LINES

WHISTLE WHILE YOU WORK
Set the kids up in an assembly line. The youngest one clears the table and passes the items to the next one, who scrapes the plates at the sink and hands them to the oldest, who loads the dishwasher. (If you only have one kid, Mom and Dad can take their places on the line.) Each evening, a different child gets to pick the song to whistle. The goal is to finish the dishes before the end of the song. Non-whistlers may hum or sing.

KITCHEN CHORES BY AGE

At what age can a child set and clear the table? When can a kid take out the garbage? Kitchen patrol isn't anyone's favorite chore, but it beats cleaning the bathroom hands-down. You could always give your kids the option of scrubbing the toilet if they're not in mood to rinse dishes and put them in the dishwasher. This quick guide will help you divvy up the KP chores. Once a child reaches a certain skill or age level, he can generally do the chores for his age group and those for the age groups below. Of course, some of these chores need to be done each day, others once a week, and still others once a month or even less frequently. Use your best judgment for what gets done when, and see "Mrs. Clean Jeans' Housekeeping Routine" on page 253 for guidelines.

AGES 2 AND UNDER:

- Wipe feet before coming inside
- Close cabinet doors and drawers
- Turn on the dishwasher
- Help set the table

AGES 3 TO 5:

- Previous chores, plus:
- Place dirty dishes on the kitchen counter
- Sponge down the play table
- Help unload the dishwasher

AGES 6 TO 9:

- Previous chores, plus:
- Help make breakfast
- Do simple cooking tasks such as rinsing vegetables
- Set and clear the table
- Put dishes into the dishwasher
- Wipe up spills
- Wipe kitchen table, chairs, high chair, counters, and cooktop or range
- Wipe down interior of the microwave
- Feed pets
- Sweep or vacuum kitchen floor and damp-mop any spills
- Bring groceries in from the car
- Put away groceries
- Empty and wipe wastebaskets clean, using disinfecting wipes
- Take out trash and recycling; remove compostable material

AGES 10 TO 13:

- Previous chores, plus:
- Pour beverages for meals
- Help hand-wash dishes
- Make lunch for school
- Unload the dishwasher
- Disinfect kitchen countertops
- Do a surface cleaning of fridge (This would include a lesson on reading package expiration dates.)
- Mop floors and dry- or damp-mop wood floors
- Clean windows

AGES 14 TO 17:

- Previous chores, plus:
- Prepare meals
- Clean and disinfect sink
- Clean coffeemaker thoroughly
- Organize pantry
- Scrub or strip and wax floors

KITCHEN OIL WELLS All is
definitely not well if you've got a puddle of cooking oil on your kitchen floor. Don't try to clean it up with soap and water; it'll become an even more slippery mess. Instead, have the kids sprinkle the puddle with a very generous amount of salt. If you run out, pour flour on the spill and mix it in. Allow the salt to soak up the slippery stuff for several minutes. Then sweep up the salt. Clean the remaining film of oil with a few drops of dishwashing liquid squirted on damp paper towels. (This technique works wonders for dropped eggs, too!)

laminate, stone, tile, terrazzo, and concrete—sparkling like new requires a special cleaning regimen. That's why they warrant a special section here.

Using the right cleaners for the job is critical in keeping these specialty surfaces shining safely. But which cleaning product is right for your kitchen floor? Consult my list below.

Linoleum: Keeping linoleum really clean requires little more than regular damp-mopping (use very little water, which can make the surface brittle) or dry dust-mopping to rid the surface of grit and dust before it is ground in.

Each week, deep-clean with a neutral-pH cleaner, such as a little dishwashing detergent dissolved in lukewarm water.

To keep floors shiny and lustrous, each year apply a wax such as carnauba wax to seal and protect the surface. Areas that get heavy use should be stripped and rewaxed as needed. For heavy-wear areas, you may need to wax once a month.

A few cleaning don'ts: hot water, strong soaps, solvents, or anything abrasive.

Vinyl: Vinyl floors require only regular sweeping and damp-mopping with water for general cleaning. But for those grimy jobs, a cleaner with a surfactant will provide more uniform cleaning and drying. For regular cleanings, a water-based, neutral cleaner, such as Spic and Span pine cleaner, is sufficient.

In general, stay away from anything soapy, such as mop-and-shine products. They can leave a soapy, tacky residue that actually attracts dirt. Instead, use ammonia and water, which also works well for a cork floor with a urethane finish.

Other vinyl don'ts: detergents, abrasive cleaners, paste wax, and highly abrasive scrubbing tools.

One of vinyl's most vexing cleaning challenges is keeping daily dirt out of surface crevices. Since these tiny particles can quickly become ground in, vacuum your floor regularly rather than sweeping it with a broom. The reason? A vacuum pulls the dirt away from the floor, while a broom drags dirt across the floor, increasing the risk that smaller particles will be left behind.

Hardwood: Hardwood floors are a tough challenge in high-traffic kitchens. Still, whether yours are oak, maple, ash, or beech, cleaning them is as safe and simple as it gets.

For hardwood floors in the kitchen, wiping up spills promptly is key because standing water can damage a hardwood floor's finish. The only other major consideration—and this goes for any room in the house with hardwood floors—is to try to keep the floor clear of dirt, sand, and grit, which can act like sandpaper and scratch a floor's finish.

Once-a-week cleaning with a broom, vacuum or dust mop is all most floors require. If your floors get a lot of use, and if they don't have a urethane finish, damp-mop once a week with a neutral-pH wood-cleaning product. Wring the mop almost dry before mopping.

Laminate: Keep laminate floors luxurious by regularly vacuuming, dust-mopping, or wiping them with a damp (not wet) cloth. When the dirt and grime get tough, as they so often do in the kitchen, those who don't mind a bit of scrubbing will find that a solution of vinegar and water works well for general cleaning. To remove tough spots or stains, buff the blemish with acetone nail-polish remover, and then wipe it clean with a damp cloth.

No-nos include allowing water or a cleaning solution to stand on or below the surface of your floor, and using soap-based detergents or mop-and-shine products (they'll leave a dull film on your floor), wax, polish, abrasive cleaners, steel wool, or scouring pads that will scratch the surface of your floor.

Stone: You need to wipe down natural stone floors daily. Even with the modern sealers on the market today, stone floors are vulnerable to staining from water and oil-based liquids.

Daily wipe-downs may seem cumbersome, but if you're prepared for the job with a water-only mop hanging in a nearby closet, it takes just minutes for a shine that lasts the whole day.

Tile: Tile presents a tough cleaning dilemma: How do you get it really clean without marring the shiny surface? Start with a cleaning routine designed to keep grime from building up and prevent the need for big-gun cleaners. Regularly vacuum and damp-mop, and clean up spills as they happen. For deeper general cleaning, use a neutral-pH cleaner without surfactants (which can leave a residue on tile floors), such as Armstrong Once 'n Done, for tough grease-cutting action. Make sure your cleaner has a built-in reinforcing sealer.

Terrazzo: This polished natural stone also benefits from regular sweeping and damp-mopping, using water and mild detergent. Since this surface stains easily and the polished finish tends to wear quickly, professional products tend to be the safest cleaning bet.

Concrete: This may be the ideal kitchen flooring. All that you need to do is sweep, vacuum, or damp-mop regularly.

Chapter 5

boffo bathrooms

AT ABOUT THE AGE OF 2½, our youngest son, Payne, hit the major milestone that every parent dreams of: Bye-bye diaper time!

One day, I'm powdering his velvety bottom on the changing station in his room, the next I'm teaching the tyke how to aim and let the stream flow standing up. (It's a messy Mommy moment.)

My joy at having all three kids potty-trained was immediately tempered, however, by this frightening realization: Our bathrooms were going to get really nasty in the weeks and months ahead as our little guy refined his aim.

After all, bathrooms need to be hygienic, *because* of kids and *in spite* of them. Good hygiene is especially important with babies in the home, who love nothing more than to crawl about in the most

the busy bathroom schedule

It's a parent's paradox: You can't get your school-age kid into the bath or shower, and you can't get your toddler or teenager out. What's a water-conscious mom or dad to do? Start by setting a time limit (and a timer) for older kids and toddlers. Ten minutes is plenty for most kids, unless they've tackled a quarterback (teens) or a Quarter Pounder (toddlers).

For those school-age kids who find every excuse in the book not to bathe, consider investing in a shower radio. Perhaps it will encourage them to whistle while they work. With the soap and shampoo, that is.

People who live in homes with only one bathroom and more than two people have an additional challenge—they can run into huge traffic jams as everyone tries to use the space at once. Timing is of the essence for a successful co-bathroom experience. Especially if the children in question are of opposite sexes. Warning: The problem only intensifies as the kids enter their teen years.

One family I know copes by designating specific bathroom times for each child on school mornings or at other high-traffic times of the day. For example, one kid gets the room from 6:30 A.M. to 7:00 A.M. Another child reports for duty from 7:00 to 7:30.

Firm rules are necessary here. Our family favorite: If you snooze (during your allotted time), you lose. No whining allowed.

unsavory of areas (like around the toilet bowl while an older sister is on the potty). In our home, this lovely exploration moment was often followed by a lengthy finger-sucking session.

I only had to observe this stomach-turning sight once before deciding that really clean bathrooms were my newfound priority. Yet I didn't want to scare the poor kids out of their gourds with shouts of "Don't touch that!" every time they ventured into a bathroom to do their business.

And to complicate matters further, the challenges presented by this tiny room go well beyond keeping it clean. The smallest room in the house is often the busiest and the most space-challenged.

It's where kids, Mom, and Dad go potty, bathe, dress, and perform their basic grooming routine to start each day. It's the place where we dump junk from our pockets and stash spare earrings and hairbands. It's where we clog the counters with too many jars, candles, and other space hogs in a well-meaning attempt to brighten up a usually drab room.

Most bathrooms are also woefully short of storage space. And, of course, most of the stuff we use in the bathroom needs to be kept close at hand. That means everyone who uses the bathroom needs to be ultra-neat to keep the small space from becoming a big clutter klatch.

And the fact that bathrooms are often shared spaces just compounds the problems. Husband and wife fight over sink space. Siblings fight over shower time. Everyone's stuff gets all mixed together as everyone tries to beat the clock out the door each morning.

Since ultra-organized kids is an oxymoron, the key to keeping bathrooms clean and harmonious is to create simple organizing systems and cleaning routines. Relax—it's as easy as washing your hands.

a home for everything

Because the biggest challenge of the bathroom is that a lot of people need to share it and it's a small space, keeping it all organized and neat goes a long way toward keeping it clean.

Like we did in the kitchen, we'll divide the bathroom into activity centers—the sink area, the medicine cabinet, the tub and shower area, the toilet area, the dressing area, and storage areas—and conquer each in turn.

CLEAN HOUSE RULES FOR THE BATHROOM

1. Don't hog the bathroom.
2. Brush your teeth for two full minutes.
3. Put the toilet seat and lid down and flush.
4. Clean the sink and counter after you use it.

salvaging the sink area

The counter space around the sink is precious real estate. And the space in the cabinet under the sink is limited, too. Most families have far too many potions and lotions here, and far too little space.

Since most bathrooms don't have much storage room, you'll need to use what you have to maximum effect.

Let's start with the counter area around the sink. Look critically at what you have sitting here. If it isn't used often—several times a day—get ready to move it somewhere else. Certainly, get rid of anything that's just decorative and serves no useful function for you or the kids. Come on—I *know* you can do it! Keeping bathroom counter clutter to a minimum will help you and the kids maximize time spent here in the morning's mad dash.

Added benefit: It gets Mom and Dad to bed sooner at night.

Get rid of anything that doesn't truly belong on the counter. Then, get a few attractive containers to organize what's left, such as Q-Tips, cotton balls, spare change, and that day's jewelry. Keep those to a minimum, too.

One thing that *does* belong on your bathroom counter is soap. Supply the sink with a pump bottle of liquid soap that's easy (and fun!) for little hands to use. Liquid soap is much less messy than traditional bar soap.

To make the soap and water handy, an essential piece of bathroom furniture (if you have small kids) is a stepstool. It allows little ones to step up to the sink for hand washing.

Consider installing a paper-cup dispenser in the bathroom on or near the sink counter. Using disposable paper cups instead of reusable plastic cups prevents spreading colds and other viruses among family members. Some germs can thrive for days on rinseable cups.

Now let's work on the cabinet under the sink, along with drawers if you're

don't be taken in by antibacterial soaps

What good moms we are. We go the extra mile to protect our families from germs. Some of us even buy liquid antibacterial soap to keep the bad bugs away.

Unfortunately, we were led astray.

The latest research from the Infectious Diseases Society of America (there really is one) shows that antibacterial soap does not kill bacteria any better than ordinary soap. Worse still, there are lingering concerns about it promoting a new generation of drug-resistant "super bugs."

What's a concerned mom to do now?

Here's the scoop on what really makes a difference in your home—and what doesn't.

You see, the antibacterial soaps, which contain the antimicrobial agent triclosan, do work in theory. The problem is, you would have to wash your hands for several minutes for triclosan to be effective. Just try keeping your kids at the sink that long. You're lucky if their hands even get wet.

Here's the rub. Some triclosan does stay on bath and kitchen surfaces for a while, but not in strengths sufficient to kill the little bugs. However, it's enough to possibly make them drug-resistant.

A better choice: Use the waterless alcohol-based gels that work by drying up the bacteria instead. Best of all, your kids don't even have to get their hands wet!

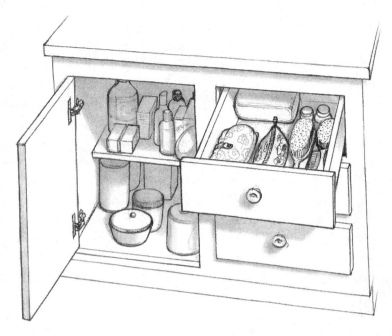

Adding under-sink shelving and organizing similar objects in convenient kits really cuts down on bathroom clutter.

lucky enough to have them. Start by dividing, paring down what you and the kids really don't need, and organizing the rest so that you free up precious under-sink and drawer space. (You'll probably want to do this when you're alone, or at least at night when the rest of the family is fast asleep!) This will require a bit of concentration to get the dirty job done right—and fast.

First, empty the contents of every drawer and cabinet in your bathroom. Toss what you can. (Do you really need to keep those six bottles of hair gel you tried and didn't like?) Next, sort what's left into two piles or boxes: one for frequently used items

and a second for seldom-used items. Place the second box outside the bathroom door: You'll need to find a place to store these non-essentials later. (Perhaps they can go in the back of the linen closet or on the top shelf of a child's closet.)

Under the sink (if you have a cabinet, that is) is the place for a space-saving plastic drawer unit. These are sold in container stores in different heights and widths. You may be able to fit two or three drawer units under your sink. They're great places to stash:

- Makeup kits

- Kids' hair accessories

- Extra shampoo and products

- Contact lens kit

- Toiletry kit

- Shaving kit

- Sewing kit

- Manicure/pedicure kit

This is also the space for that cumbersome blow dryer and untamable cord, hairspray and styling gels, and extra bath soap, toilet paper, and tissue boxes.

Your vanity drawers are where you should stash daily jewelry and toiletries for easy reach as you're cleaning up for bed each night. Kids' stuff, too. Teach the kids to organize their daily-use items, such as jewelry, combs, brushes, toothpaste, and toothbrush, in the place that's easiest to reach and use. And provide them with places to stash stuff at night, too.

Drawer dividers are basic components of an organized bathroom, and they should be considered essential in both your bathroom and the kids'. They keep things from being a jumble. You can buy dividers for this purpose, or just use little cardboard jewelry gift boxes to keep like items together. For the hair accessories drawer, for example, you could have one basket for combs and brushes, another for barrettes, a third for hair ties and elastic bands, a fourth for headbands, and a fifth for scrunchies.

If possible, keep toothpaste and braces supplies, hair supplies, and face medications in separate drawers. Plan to keep brushes, mirrors, and other frequently used accessories in the top drawer for easy access. If there are no built-in drawers, no worries, the plastic drawer units I mentioned earlier (hidden in cabinets beneath the sink), will do in a pinch.

The vanity cabinet in the kids' bath is the place to hang long necklaces and bracelets on hooks inside the cabinet door. It's also a handy location for a basket with blow dryer, brush, gels, and hairspray. It can also store those other fun gadgets you want to have on hand for the kids but have a tough time finding space for: hot curlers, straightening irons, and crimpers.

To keep all Lyndsay's headbands out of drawers and off the floor, I hang them on a ring-shaped towel holder. She can see her options at a glance, and it frees up precious drawer space.

One very important note: The bathroom cabinet or counter is *not* the place to store medications. Be sure to keep all medications on top shelves or in a medicine cabinet, out of a small child's reach.

sharing sink space

If you have more than one kid, you know that sharing space can be challenging. Siblings sharing anything, let alone a small space like the bathroom, can easily lead to World War III if you don't have a battle plan for keeping each kid's stuff separate. So you'll have an extra step here, creating separate areas for each kid.

Divide and conquer. Start by dividing and assigning separate areas: his sink, her sink, his drawers, her drawers, etc. Then grab the troops and have them lend a hand in organizing their areas.

Color their world. Plastic caddies, in different vibrant colors, are the perfect solution if drawer, sink, or shelf space is at a premium. Have each child choose a color and place personal shampoo and grooming supplies inside the caddy. You can keep the caddies in another area out of sight, perhaps in each kid's room.

Keep the peace by assigning a color for everything from toothbrushes to towels for each family member. Not only will this reduce sibling squabbles, it will also help solve the mystery of who "forgot" to hang up his towel.

Create kids' kits. Divide each kid's toiletries in her own toiletry bag. Include toothpaste, floss, cleansers, contact lenses and glasses, and manicure supplies.

Start off sparkling. Once you've tossed what you can and organized what's left, clean up goopy cough syrup or other spills on shelves to give your counter and cabinet a healthy new appearance. Wipe down shelves, drawers, and counters before you return items to their new homes in clutter-busting groups, containers, or bags.

mastering the medicine cabinet

You'll be amazed at what you'll find in your medicine cabinet. (And maybe a bit scared, too.) Really give thought to what you store here. Try to reserve that precious, accessible medicine-cabinet space for items you use most frequently, not the Pepto-Bismol you only take on New Year's Day. Otherwise, you're wasting your most convenient storage space. You'll be surprised at the number of items you can store elsewhere.

As you're looking at each item in your cabinet, check the labels carefully. Many of us treat medications much too casually. Some medicine labels specify storage in a cool dark place, *not* the bathroom, due to its inherent humidity. Light, heat, or humidity may damage medications. Humid bathrooms are not the ticket for these. Consider placing these medicines in a secure drawer the kids can't reach in your bedroom closet, or on a high shelf in a hall closet.

Also, as you're going through the medicine cabinet, look carefully at expiration dates. Toss what's expired or no longer used. Expired medicines and vitamins lose their potency. (Ditto for sunscreens, by the way.) Discard medications where children cannot find them. Do not toss them casually into the bathroom wastebasket. Flush them down the toilet or put them at the bottom of the trash can when you take it outside on garbage pickup day.

Store medications in their original containers. Don't repackage them as you would food. It's important that you have the medication's original label so you can check dosages, expiration dates, and other safety information.

Heed this very important tip: Post the Poison Center Hotline number on your medicine cabinet door: (800) 222-1222.

tidying the tub and shower area

Bath essentials have a tendency to overrun a tub or shower, especially when women are involved. Add a kid or three and things can really get messy. The key to keeping Barbies from overrunning the tub and Mom's scented body scrubs, facial cleansers, shampoo, and conditioner from drowning the shower in stuff is to divide and conquer.

Plastic dispensers in the shower for soap and shampoo eliminate a bottle or three. Racks or hooks for washcloths and the essential post-scrub wipedown of shower and tub surfaces keep these items from cluttering tight spaces. And a suction-cup net or plastic tray across the tub keeps toddlers' bath toys tidy.

taming the toilet area

The toilet area is pretty easy to organize—there's not much to it. (Now cleanliness, that's another story. More on that later on page 105.) The toilet itself being fixed in place, you don't have much to find a home for here.

If you have a potty chair for little ones, for cleanliness you'll want to keep the potty chair away from the big-person potty. You don't want your little one grabbing onto the big potty while sitting down, getting up, or whiling away the time on the pot.

And, of course, you wouldn't want a big person tripping over the little potty and making a big mess if it should be full. By keeping the two separate, on opposing walls, say, you'll find it easier to keep each cleaner.

And for the little guy learning to aim? A target worked aiming wonders to help Payne learn exactly where that stream is supposed to go and to give him a little more motivation, as well. (I created a target by floating a small square of toilet paper right on top of the water before Payne had to go. Get creative—it should be flushable, however, so no one has to get his or her hand dirty.)

Keep extra rolls of toilet paper next to the toilet. I keep mine in a covered woven basket stashed between the wall and the porcelain potty so hands in need of a washing don't go wandering and contaminate cabinets beneath the sink and other surfaces. This is also a good place to keep a bowl or a basket of sanitary supplies or individually wrapped hand wipes.

Station a magazine or book rack near the potty to keep big and little hands occupied.

decking out the dressing area

Since we not only bathe and pamper in the bathroom but often dress there as well, it makes sense to carve out an area for clothing and make a hamper part of the decor. This is an especially good idea for kids' baths: It's the rare child indeed who needn't be reminded to deposit his peeled-off dirty duds into the dirty clothes hamper. Skip a nagging step by placing a small hamper near the tub or shower so kids taking off clothes can bypass the floor for the hamper.

Clothing hooks are a good investment for both grownups' and kids' bathrooms. If you've ever set the sheer top you were planning to wear on a wet counter (or worse, a dirty one), you know why.

A chair or stool is a nice accessory as well. It creates a relaxing nook on which to sit to put on socks or apply makeup. And it's a great place for kids to sit while doing their hair, or having Mom or Dad do it for them.

spiffing up storage areas

No matter how luxurious your bathroom is, the under-the-sink cabinet and medicine chest probably don't offer enough storage space. Make the most of every inch of bathroom space with one or more of these accessories. They can dramatically increase your bathroom's storage power.

- Use a wicker or wrought-iron wine rack to store rolled washcloths and towels. This is not only a way to put extra storage and spare towels at the ready, but rolled towels can also provide a colorful accent, especially in a child's bathroom. Coordinate the towels to your decor.

- Add over- and above-toilet shelving. Put wooden shelves along one wall or buy an over-the-commode unit with shelves. Here you can place those little knickknacks you can't live without and a small clock to keep you and the kids on schedule in the morning.

- Near-sink shelving. If you're really short on space, single shelves hung near the sink provide perfect resting spots for soap, toothbrushes, and other daily essentials.

- Towel bars with built-in shelving over the top. You can hang used towels on the bar and stack fresh replacements

A well-organized bathroom is easier to clean, more hygienic, and more inviting.

on the shelves for easy use. Or forgo the traditional towel bars altogether in favor of antique or whimsical drawer pulls. You'll find these at flea markets or garage sales for a song. Connect them to the wall with screws. Two or three together give a collected look. Hang a towel through each of the pulls for a finished look.

- Wicker storage units are a good choice for baths because they withstand humidity well. And most pieces come with drawers for more bathroom-stuff storage for you and the kids.

- Even antiques can add storage to bathrooms. Need to recycle a few pieces from the other rooms in your home? An antique armoire, cupboard, chest, or table gives a bathroom more space as well as a delightfully elegant touch.

cleaning with kids: the bathroom

I'll admit it, my kids don't stay clean. And I wouldn't have it any other way. Childhood is a contact sport—one I've always believed is best played by diving in.

For my oldest son, a day at school invariably leaves him with that fresh-off-the-recess yard sheen of sweaty brown. Daughter Lyndsay's come-home look is usually more of an "I wrestled with the glue gun and lost." And preschooler Payne brings in the worst kind of kid mess on his hands and face: germs from shared crayons and toys and grime from lengthy spins around the playground.

While I don't complain when my kids arrive, I do make sure they pop into the nearest bathroom and take a layer or two of life's leftovers off of their hands before grabbing an after-school snack. Keeping sanitizers or wipes close at hand makes quick cleanups at the half-bath by the front door a cinch.

Good hygiene is essential to keeping any room clean, especially the bathroom. There are many things a bathroom should have that we'll discuss in a minute. And there's one thing it shouldn't that we'll get out of the way first thing: carpeting.

You can't sanitize a carpet. And, as I've learned with my boys during the toilet-and-aim-training years, flooring sanitization is quite essential and must be done on a regular basis. Another problem with bathroom carpets is that they don't dry easily. Combine playful kids in a bathtub with a carpeted floor and what do you have? A recipe for mold and mildew.

So, if you have carpet in your bath, rip it out and get rid of it as soon as possible!

Consider putting in tile, vinyl flooring, or any hard surface that will weather regular applications of chlorine bleach and a good scrubbing. Whew, now that I got that off my chest, let's move on to cleaning the bathroom.

If you know the secrets, daily bathroom cleaning will take less time than brushing your teeth!

In general, every surface in your bathroom, with the exception of the mirror(s), can be cleaned with a single disinfectant cleaner. Disinfecting wipes stashed under the sink are the perfect way to quick-clean almost any surface in this busy room. Don't forget light switches and doorknobs.

Keep the bathroom smelling fresh between cleanings by placing a scented fabric softener sheet in the wastepaper basket. Or, put a dab of fragrance on a light bulb. When the light is on, the heat releases the fresh scent.

essential supplies

Before you start cleaning, gather your arsenal of cleaning supplies. (These products should all be stored out of reach of little hands, naturally.)

- Tub of disposable disinfecting wipes

- Tub of disposable glass and window wipes for mirrors and fixtures

- Ready-mop with disposable wet floor wipes

- All-purpose nonabrasive cleaner

- Scrub brush with a good grip for scouring tub and tile

- Household squeegee (hung in the shower)

- Toilet brush with caddy (choose an enclosed caddy that you can fill with an all-purpose cleaning solution to keep the brush fresh)

Now, we'll cover cleaning each area of the bathroom in detail. Grab the kids!

the sink area

To keep your sink area cleaner and reduce soap slime, choose liquid soap in a pump instead of bar soap. Wipe the sink down each day, several times a day. In fact, if you use the sink, wipe it clean before leaving. Every time. Kids who always wipe away the toothpaste blobs and stray counter hairs after using the bathroom are the kids who get invited back to friends' homes. Make this one rule that sticks in *your* home.

Similarly, after applying your makeup or brushing your teeth, use a tissue or your hand and running water to remove any

This bathroom dressing and storage area uses every inch of space. And it looks great!

DIRTY LITTLE SECRETS

TOWELS   If you care for your new

towels right, they'll keep you and your kids wrapped in post-bubble-bath softness and comfort for at least five years. And they'll look color-correct, too. That's right, a good-quality towel, properly laundered, can arrive with your newborn and stick around until he starts kindergarten and look little worse for wear. The expected life span of a good- to best-quality towel is five to ten years. (Best-quality towels are those made from premium fibers, such as Supima or Egyptian cotton.) Here's the care and feeding routine:

Wash new towels before using. Don't just put that new towel on the bathroom hook or towel bar! Get it primed for softness and absorbency before the first use. Many manufacturers add a finish that creates a sleek, soft feel, but in truth this actually diminishes the towel's absorbency. While these chemicals will rinse out with a few washes, you're often left with a scratchy, rough towel. To get the fluffiness and absorbency you crave, first soak or wash the towel in cold water without detergent or fabric softener. Then tumble dry low. And only then, into the bathroom they go!

Wash towels separately. This is both for the towels' longevity and that of your family's clothes. Towels can cover co-washed clothes with lint. And clothes with zippers, hooks, and buttons can pull loops out of terrycloth towels

and snag others. Further separate dark-colored towels from their lighter cousins. This will keep both light and dark colors intact.

Read the label's washing directions. If the fiber wears best in cool-water washings, the label will tell you this. Otherwise, warm is best. Extra-hot water can fade colors and reduce the softness the kids love. (And hey, who are we kidding here? Moms and Dads love it, too!)

Unless the towel or washcloth has come into contact with an ill family member (thereby requiring a stronger laundry detergent and possibly chlorine bleach), choose a gentle laundry detergent to protect both the fibers and the color during weekly washings. Use only half the recommended amount of detergent to keep towels absorbent and soft. Wash towels at least once a week, every three to four days if needed. Wash towel sets together so any color fading is uniform.

Dry right. Tumble-dry towels on a low setting and remove the towels while they're still slightly damp. Excessive heat wears down towel fibers. If they're hot (not warm) to the touch, you've overdried them.

Skip the silicone softeners. Some fabric softeners contain water-repellent silicone, the death knell for towel absorbency.

Let them hang out. Between bathing, hang towels loosely on the towel rod or on hooks to allow quick air-drying. This will keep mold at bay, meaning your towels stay fresh longer and need fewer washings (a double plus: less work for you and less machine time for the towels).

traces of your having been there. This includes hair, girls. I swipe it with a sink-side tissue. Then into the trash it goes. Ditto for counter surfaces.

For quick bathroom cleanups that even the youngest family member can help with when time is short, grab a baby wipe from the kid's room down the hall. Give the shower, tub, and sink fixtures the once-over, and then toss. Your bathroom will sparkle, and so will you.

Each week, disinfect the sink, counter, light switches, and doorknobs with a disinfectant cleaner; wipe clean and shine

decorating your bathroom

While we don't normally talk about decorating in this book, in the bathroom it's relevant because space is at such a premium that your decorations must be functional as well.

If you want the kids to spend enough time in the bathroom to follow the cleaning rules, make it a place that's fun as well as functional. And make kids a part of the decorating process. Give the room a theme you can live with, and let the kids choose the colors. Make it fun!

My friend Allison let her preteen daughter go wild in her bathroom, or at least tropical. She painted the three walls and trim in zany fluorescent colors: chartreuse, teal, and aqua. The towels, washcloths, and rug are in eye-popping oranges, yellows, and limes. The tropical shower curtain pulls all the wacko colors together, and fish accessories on the vanity complete the look. Here are some bathroom decorating ideas I think your kids will love.

- Use child-safe decorations to make the bathroom safe for wet little ones. Add nonskid rugs, slip-resistant tub decals, and plastic cups for post-brush rinsing. With safety secured, move on to the playful decor.

- Choose kid-friendly accessory themes. Kids don't want their bathrooms to have a spa look—that island-of-tranquility bit is *not* their thing. This is the place for color and fun, a place where a child can make his or her own imprint.

- Choose a theme. Consider a ducky bucket for hairbrushes and accessories, along with ducky soap dispensers and shower curtains for your toddler. An older daughter might choose tiny ceramic flowerpots (self-decorated, of course) to contain her cotton balls and Q-Tips. Let them help you choose a look they'll love. For a less cluttered look, choose coordinating containers for toothbrush, soap, and tissues.

- Give the bathroom a facelift. A new coat of paint is the quickest, cheapest, and arguably most dramatic way to give new life to an old bathroom. Don't forget the switch plate, toilet paper holder, and the like. Accent the bath in a mirrors and chrome fixtures with a glass cleaner; and empty and wipe wastebaskets clean with a disinfecting wipe.

Keep bathroom floors clean and hair- and dirt-free with a disposable wet mop cloth. Several include disinfectants, which is a good choice for this room.

Keep the package under the sink, and at day's end, wipe up tracked-in dirt so tomorrow's shower will have you emerging on an (almost) squeaky clean floor.

Each week, give your bathroom floor a good mopping.

contrasting color for a stylish flair. Seal with a clear waterproof coating. Good, calming color choices (blues and greens) can help make mad morning dashes feel less stressful.

• Bring in fresh replacements. Soft, thirsty, fluffy new towels in a hot new color or seasonal hue will provide not only the update you're looking for, but a luxurious treat for your hands and body as well.

• Replace the shower curtain. Fresh, clean colors and styles will appeal to your sense of cleanliness and loveliness, and if they coordinate with the linens, it'll help give the tired bathroom a complete new look. (If your bathroom's *really* small, however, a clear curtain is the best choice.)

• Replace the shower curtain hooks, too, with something snazzier. We have silver dolphins holding up the curtain in Payne and Lyndsay's shared bath. Chris's hooks are antique silver.

• Add a new reflection. Why stop at just one bathroom mirror? Brighten up the smallest bathroom by bringing in a new looking glass. This tried-and-true decorating trick makes the room seem larger by reflecting light. Add some serious pizzazz by framing your mirror (if it's one of those basic mirrors that you adhere to the wall above the sink). Cut your choice of molding to fit, and then paint it your favorite color or brush on an elegant gold or silver. Glue the molding in place with liquid glue.

• Replace old, mismatched fixtures with new, personality-plus styles. Drawer pulls and cabinet handles come in myriad colors and styles. I used a pewter bat-and-ball drawer pull for son Chris's bathroom. You can buy pulls in whatever sport, color, or animal (the possibilities are endless) your child likes to make a jazzy statement on a shoestring. Replace rusted, old, or unsightly faucet and light fixtures. While this is not an inexpensive option, it does make a world of difference. And while you're at it, consider a new showerhead or new faucet and handles for the sink.

• Add light. It opens up a small space and adds interest. A recessed spotlight is a low-profile option. Wall sconces are an elegant choice for half-baths and guest baths.

• Make it bloom. Add a small decorative bud vase and fill it with a flower fresh from the garden.

BATHROOM CHORES BY AGE

The bathroom is one of the dirtiest and most-used rooms in the house. And it's the least fun to clean. The good news is, kids are able to do many, many chores to help out. Here's a list of which tasks kids can generally do by which age. Once a child reaches a certain skill or age level, he can generally do the chores for his age group and those for the age groups below. Of course, some of these chores need to be done each day, others once a week, and still others once a month or even less frequently. Use your best judgment for what gets done when, and see "Mrs. Clean Jeans' Housekeeping Routine" on page 253 for guidelines.

AGES 2 AND UNDER:
- Put the seat down on the toilet and flush
- Put dirty clothes in the hamper if the top is low enough
- Help rinse out the tub
- Hang up towel (on hook)
- Put tub toys in bins or drawers

AGES 3 TO 5:
- Previous chores, plus:
- Put tub toys in the proper nets or bins
- Rinse out the sink after use

AGES 6 TO 9:
- Previous chores, plus:
- Rinse out the tub
- Wipe up spills
- Squeegee the shower
- Hang up towel (on towel rack)
- Sweep or vacuum floor and damp-mop any spills
- Wipe smudges from walls and door
- Empty and wipe wastebasket clean, using disinfecting wipes
- Wash inside and outside of cabinets

AGES 10 TO 13:
- Previous chores, plus:
- Disinfect bathroom countertop
- Wipe chrome fixtures and mirrors clean and polish them
- Clean the shower
- Mop the floor and dry- or damp-mop wood floor
- Clean windows
- Clean blinds
- Put out fresh towels and soap
- Disinfect light switches and doorknobs

AGES 14 TO 17:
- Previous chores, plus:
- Clean toilets, sinks, and tubs
- Wipe down walls
- Clean shower curtain
- Disinfect the sink and drain
- Clean lights and light fixtures

the tub and shower area

To keep your tub clean, rinse it out after each bath. You know the drill, Mom. After the bath water drains, swish around some fresh water to loosen and remove any soil or soap residue. Toddlers can help, and school-age kids can learn to do this simple cleaning trick by themselves in no time. Grimy tub rings? Not in your house.

After kids' baths, air-dry tub toys. Group toys in a tub net to allow them to drain and keep mold and mildew in check. Or shake water from the toys and place them on the tub edge to dry. Better still, store bath toys in a dishpan under the vanity. Take a minute to squeeze water out of the washcloth and hang it on the tub spout or a bathroom hook.

Each week, get the kids to help clean the bathroom. They'll love to make fizz fun by cleaning the sink and tub with baking soda and vinegar. Kids love the fizzing, and it gets the sink and tub sparkling clean. Older kids can scour the tub each week to keep it spotless.

Deep-cleaning weekly must-dos include disinfecting the toilet, tub, shower, sinks, and drains. One trick I used to make toilet disinfecting a more frequent but much less cumbersome chore is to use an enclosed toilet-brush caddy that I fill with water and a half-cup of bleach and place beside our toilet. That way, I can swoosh the bowl with a disinfected brush daily.

I choose cleaners based on how well—and quickly—they work. Which means for me bleach is an absolute must-have for weekly potty-room disinfecting. Bleach-containing toilet and tub/shower cleaners are my top choice. My newest faves include Clorox Disinfecting Wipes for cleaning sinks, light switches, handles, knobs and countertops; Clorox or Swiffer-brand (type) ready-mop products that you just put the mop/wipe on and then toss it; and Soft Scrub with bleach for disinfecting and cleaning tub, shower, and all bath tile.

Here's the easiest way to keep your shower area clean. Squeegee shower surfaces before toweling off. It takes just 30 seconds or so to wipe away any soap or shampoo. Any kid old enough to shower alone is old enough to wage war against the dreaded Shower Scum Monster.

The added benefit to in-shower cleaning is that any soap scum left over from a kid still learning the clean rules (or your significantly preoccupied significant other) is steamed loose during the shower, which makes it a cinch to send soapy residue down the drain.

Each week, scour the tiles and grout around your shower to keep mold and mildew at bay. Don't forget to clean your shower curtain. Send washable curtains and liner for a spin in the machine with bleach to remove mold and mildew. Before rehanging, soak in a salt-water solution to prevent mildew. Clean plastic with a

THE POTTY

THE POTTY If your family is flush with reasons not to deal with the weekly toilet tune-up, tell them to have a seat and relax. Today's disinfecting cleaners make this once-tedious task a breeze. These steps even work on a toilet that's been neglected for a while. This is a job for teens and adults in your home, as the cleaners are strong, and when used incorrectly they can damage surfaces—and kids.

1. Wearing rubber or latex gloves to protect your hands, spray a disinfecting toilet-bowl cleaner around the inside of the bowl and under the rim. Or, you can clean with chlorine bleach alone by pouring one-quarter cup of bleach into the bowl; it both whitens and disinfects. (To avoid creating hazardous fumes, don't combine bleach with any bowl cleaner or any other product. Be sure to teach your teens this important cleaning-safety rule.)

2. Allow either product to sit for 10 full minutes to fully annihilate germs, bacteria, and viruses. While the disinfectant is doing its job in the bowl, you can begin cleaning the seat and lid (both sides) and the rest of the toilet surface, including around the hinges and the base, which is especially necessary if you have little boys learning to aim. Spray on a nonabrasive disinfectant (a separate product from the toilet bowl cleaner). Allow this cleaner to chill and kill germs for 10 minutes, too.

3. Moving back to the bowl, swish the cleaner around the bowl, underneath the rim, and as far into the trap as possible, using a long-handled toilet brush. Then flush the toilet to rinse.

4. Turning your attention back to the seat area, wipe the seat and the outside of the bowl clean and dry with paper towels. They're the simplest: no rinsing needed, and no chance of spreading germs if you toss them. Don't forget to dry the hinge areas and bumpers.

5. Each week, pour 1 cup of baking soda into the bowl to keep it fresh. And finally, once a month pour a half-gallon of white vinegar into the bowl to keep it ring-free. Let it soak overnight before flushing.

laundry pre-wash spray. Simply spray along the top, letting it run down to cover the curtain. Allow to sit for a few minutes, then rinse.

Teach your kids to hang up their towels after showering or bathing. Everyone. No towels are allowed to be wadded on the floor. Younger children can fold towels in half and sling them over the towel rack. If even that's too much of a struggle, consider replacing racks with hooks or pegs in the kids' bathroom. Even toddlers can hang up towels then. This is essential because, as you know, a wadded-up towel gets mildew-smelling much quicker than one allowed to air-dry quickly on a towel rack or peg. And whether they smell or not, bring in fresh replacement towels every three days.

the toilet area

To keep your bowl clean, pour a half-cup or so of bleach into the potty each morning or evening and let it sit. This will help keep harmful germs in check. (*Never* combine bleach with toilet bowl cleanser! The two combined release dangerous fumes. And, of course, store your bleach out of the reach of little hands. If you have pets, make sure the lid is down to avoid accidents.) Each day, also wipe the toilet seat and rim with a disposable disinfecting wipe. (I keep bleach-containing disposable wipes near

the kids' potty for quick spot-cleaning during the potty-training process. These wipes are a godsend when a child gets the stomach flu and things get messy there.)

Teach your kids to flush. Period. This is one rule you'll want your kids to follow, especially when they're visiting at friends' homes. This rule can be broken only during seven-year droughts.

A well-mannered boy always puts the seat down after using the toilet. And a clean-minded child, regardless of gender, always puts down the toilet lid prior to flushing. Besides being much more pleasant to look at, a closed potty when flushed doesn't send stirred-up, ahem, upleasantries spiraling into the air where they can land on your sink, counter, or toothbrush. Ugh.

Chapter 6

making living
areas livable

LIVING AREAS ARE NOT LIMITED to just living rooms or even dens or family rooms. Living areas are *any* rooms where the family congregates, such as:

Great rooms: In many homes, the living area is a living room/dining room combination. Those are ideal because they give families room to spread out so each member can do his or her own thing.

Living rooms and family rooms: Some homes have a separate living room and family room. In these cases, you could have the best of both worlds: Live in one room and entertain in the other. Be sure, however, that the room you're living in is large enough to accommodate your family's needs.

Basements and garages: Some families have transformed these underutilized spaces into family or rec rooms.

Formal dining rooms: These are generally not living areas. These are entertaining areas. If you have a formal dining room, consider whether you have enough actual living space to dedicate a whole room to 10 or 12 meals a year. Or could you make better use of the room in some other way? Whatever you decide is fine, but make a conscious decision instead of following some builder's arbitrary floor plan that may not meet your family's needs.

Generally, for a family, the more living areas, the better. You need one large area where you can all congregate, but you also need places where you can get away from each other. After all, it's the rare family that doesn't occasionally have "issues" that are best resolved by a little space.

In today's increasingly open home designs, most rooms are visually connected, anyway. You can watch *American Idol* in the living room with your preteen, while your teen surfs the Net in the den, Dad reads the paper at the kitchen counter, and your toddler does his best to demolish all three rooms simultaneously. Now *that's* togetherness.

Our previous home in San Francisco was designed and built by my husband's great-grandmother (lot of moxy, that side of the family) in the early 1920s. Naturally, it included a formal living room and a formal dining room. The problem was that with little ones underfoot, our

"formal" entertaining was limited (dare I say nonexistent?).

We had two perfectly good rooms and a full house of big and little bodies. Yet that formal duo of perfectly good rooms (I dare not think of the square footage) sat undisturbed and gathering dust until Christmas and Easter rolled around.

As we began preparing for our move to West Los Angeles in 1999, I vowed not to let an inch of usable space linger for the sake of formalities. And being the mildly neurotic nesting-focused pregnant person I was at the time, I spent far too much time figuring out how to make those same rooms in our new home just the opposite: livable luxuries. After all, given where I was coming from, the gift of two more usable rooms sure seemed like a luxury! And I was bound and determined to make it so.

Looking back, the time spent on these rooms was worth every pregnant pause. Today, our home has a lovely living room that's really lived in. And I've traded a formal dining room for a fun family nook.

That lovely 1970s-era disco chandelier in the small (the Realtor called it "cozy") formal dining room? Gone. Instead, the room is distinguished by a sturdy new built-in desk that doubles as a kiddie entertainment center, with room for a computer and shelves above it for games, DVDs, videos, and school books. At the right-hand side of the desk, there are a half-dozen assorted-depth drawers with colorful pulls. The desk runs the entire wall, providing plenty of surface space for kid stuff, with room to spare on the end for the essential wide-screen TV and DVD player for our favorite family films.

Bye-bye formal dining, hel-lo family room!

The living room presented a bigger challenge: to keep it an area suitable for grownup entertaining without giving it a "do not touch" feel. The answer was surprisingly simple. By adding a few more laid-back furniture pieces and creating cozy nooks for relaxing, reading, and sharing a pre-dinner cocktail, the Aronson living room soon lived up to its name.

a home for everything

Living areas present a special set of organizational challenges. These rooms are generally highly visible, so you want something that's company-ready yet family-friendly at the same time. (Dream on, right?) Here are just a few of the issues to consider in your living areas:

How do you keep a family room presentable with minimal fuss?

How do you create family-friendly storage in living areas?

Here's what our reading nook looks like. It's very rare to see it empty like this, though!

make space work harder

My friend Susan has an ideal floor plan for her family (a husband, a preteen, and a kindergartner). Her kitchen abuts their family room, which opens up onto a huge deck. There's a dining room off to the left of the kitchen that has a huge "window" into the kitchen. The "living room," which they use as a music/reading room, is about 20 feet away, just across the foyer. Susan's husband cooks (lucky her) while she gardens on the deck and the kindergartner watches cartoons in the den. The preteen can practice her piano or do her homework on the dining room table and still be connected to the rest of the family.

The point is: Susan's family uses all of their available space. In some families, that living room would have never been used because it's a bit off the beaten path. By assigning it a function, Susan and her family incorporate it into their daily routine. They read there, play games, play piano, or just enjoy some quiet time away from the bustle of the family room.

How do you make formal rooms feel warm and welcoming?

How do you keep various types of surfaces clean with kids and pets all over them all the time?

Actually, keeping living areas presentable ties in closely to the problem of minimal storage. Living areas are usually set up for sitting, not living. You have your basic sofa, chair, end table, and coffee table. Note that none of these pieces of furniture usually has storage. Where do you put the remote? Magazines? Newspapers? Paperwork? Headsets? Game Boys? Sewing? Games? Videos? Books? Glasses? Tissues?

You get the drift.

Most families just carry the stuff they need or are working on into the living room, and then leave it there (of course!). You—and your guests—will find abandoned items on the coffee table, beside the chair, and on the floor. This is precisely what you don't want.

Solution? Give the family a place to put their things so they can keep them where they use them. That means you've got to get creative and figure out how to incorporate some storage areas into the room.

Here are some ways to create more storage, from least to most expensive:

- Incorporate attractive baskets into your décor.

- Choose furniture with hidden storage, such as ottomans, benches, etc.

- Choose furniture with built-in storage such as armoires, hutches, and bookshelves, as well as coffee tables or end tables with baskets, shelves, or drawers.

- Invest in custom-designed storage units.

- Buy or build wall units.

Fortunately, furniture designers are on to the problem, so there's a lot of furniture available today with storage capabilities.

Once you've arranged some storage, now you have to decide what goes where—and how to keep it there. Look at your room(s) in terms of the activities you'll be doing there, write down what items you need for those activities, and then start intelligently planning where you'll put them. Here are a few examples:

Reading: Store books, newspapers, or magazines in baskets, on shelves under coffee tables or end tables, on bookshelves, or in attractive magazine racks.

Music: CD towers or holders are one option. Racks on a bookshelf are another. Some wall units have CD racks built in.

TV: The problem is not so much where to put the TV as where to keep the remote and the TV book. If you watch TV a lot, just leave them on a tabletop. If you try to limit your kids' viewing (or if you have a toddler who might dip the remote in the toilet), stash it out of sight. But always put it in the same place, or you'll miss your favorite show while you're searching under sofa cushions for the pesky thing.

Sewing: Even if you don't sew, per se, you probably mend and stitch on buttons. If you keep your sewing kit handy in a cabinet in the entertainment center or hutch, you'll be much more likely to actually do those minor repairs. If you sew a lot, keep your basket right by your special chair.

Correspondence: I find that the perfect time to write thank-you notes is while the kids are immersed in some TV show. I keep my address book, note cards, stationery, pens, and stamps in the top drawer of an end table. Then I have no excuse for not sending out my notes in a timely fashion. (It's also a good time to write Christmas cards or to put photos in albums.)

Toys and games: Many wooden toy chests are attractive enough to grace your living room. (Make sure, however, that any chest you use for toys has supports that will hold the hinged lid open in any position. Many children have been injured by lids crashing down on their arms, heads, and hands.) Benches with storage underneath are another option, and they can neatly camouflage an entire battalion

CLEAN HOUSE LIVING AREA RULES

1. Have only one toy or toy set out at one time.

2. Keep your feet off the furniture.

3. Don't eat in the living room or family room.

4. Don't use loud voices.

5. Watch TV only with parental okay.

6. Put everything away before you leave the room.

of G.I. Joes. Otherwise, group toys by type (LEGOs, Barbies, Beanie Babies, coloring, drawing) in plastic containers, and stack them neatly on shelves or in cabinets. Allow little ones to pull out only one container at a time.

Napping: The only accessories you need here can be stored in plain sight—afghans and pillows.

In addition to these organizational groups, I also give each member of my family a personal place to stash stuff. Each family member has a drawer in the living room to hold the items they just can't live without at the moment: lanyard materials, Game Boy, favorite novel, Walkman, etc. Whenever they get a free minute, their stuff is within easy reach.

It's helpful to locate these personal places beside each person's favorite spot to relax. You know what I mean: People tend to gravitate to the same spots to sit. This territorial thing is natural; don't fight it (unless kids are fighting over it). Instead, give each person some personal space. Dad might call that big recliner his resting place, so put the remote and TV book nearby. Mom likes to snuggle up in the love seat, so keep her sewing basket next to it.

You'll see this family room has a place for everything—and everyone.

toddler safety

As every parent knows, most living areas aren't set up for kids under the age of three. Think about all the times that your heart stops when your youngest is pulling porcelain figurines off the table at Grandma's house. Or how you have to hover over the little tyke when visiting friends, hissing "No! Don't touch!"

You obviously can't do that kind of supervision in your own home. It's not fair to you or the kid. Here are a few tips for childproofing your living areas:

• Most kids seem to get in trouble when the phone rings, so invest in a cordless phone and follow your tyke around as you talk.

• Put breakable, fragile objects out of reach.

• Cover any sharp corners on furniture or hearths with foam protectors.

• Put safety caps on electrical outlets.

• Put gates around staircases.

• Before you buy houseplants, check to make sure they are not poisonous. (Toxic or not, keep all plants out of reach of toddlers. If they don't eat the leaves, they'll empty out all the dirt.)

• Put safety latches on any cabinets you don't want the kids plundering.

• Move furniture away from walls with windows or other hazards.

• Secure furniture, such as hutches, that children may try to climb. Earthquake braces work very nicely to keep furniture from tipping over.

• Remove area rugs that could trip up kids just learning to walk.

• If you have cords on your shades or blinds, tie them high enough that kids can't get their necks caught in them. Most companies now make childproof cords without loops on the ends.

Most important of all, remember that parental supervision is the best childproofing.

decorating living areas

The goal of any living area is to make it a warm, welcoming place. It's so ironic, but usually living rooms are the deadest rooms in the house. The kids are afraid to go in there because Mom will yell at them to be careful of that rug or not to bang up against that table. Dad doesn't go in there because there's no TV and Mom won't let him prop his feet up on the coffee table. Mom doesn't go in there because she wants to be with the rest of the family, and they are all cowering in the den.

I've been blaming us moms too much. There's another reason why families avoid the living room, and it has nothing to do with having to be tidy or careful.

Some living rooms are just too tidy! It's really okay to want to keep one room nice for company, if you've got one extra room. But if keeping that room nice means scrunching six people into a matchbox-size family room, you need to rethink your priorities. There are ways, believe it or not, to actually use a room and not destroy it. Really.

Living areas should be rooms you actually *live in*, not the front-parlor type room my husband Christopher's great-grandmother surely had in mind—you know, the one that's psychologically cordoned off with velvet ropes. Actually, I don't really believe you should even have a front-parlor type room that's off limits to any member of the family. Modern families should use all the possible space they have available. And if you don't need the space, well, maybe you've got too large a house. Why are you paying to heat that room, anyway?

reclaiming the great room

Along the same lines, walk in any newer-style home and you'll find a gorgeous living/dining room combination with comfortable sofas, vaulted ceilings, and even a TV. One thing is missing—the family. And where are they? Huddled in a dark, cramped 10-by-14-foot TV room, fighting over the one old lumpy loveseat.

Why are they there? It's cozy. Yes, it's dark, it's dingy, and it's crowded. But it's cozy.

I wonder whether architects ever think about who will be living in those "great rooms." Giraffes? Yes, vaulted ceilings are very impressive, but they just don't satisfy that cocooning instinct. And neither do great rooms the size of an assembly hall.

Before you go throwing up partitions in your living room, however, there is an easier way to bring great rooms down to scale: Create little "rooms" within the larger one. Make small intimate areas with furniture placement. Pull the couches and chairs off the wall, anchor them with an area rug, add a table or two, and voilà! You've got a little room within the big room. Put a couple of chairs over by the fireplace, connect them with another rug, and add a table with a lamp. Voilà, room number two.

You can also visually divide a room with activity areas. Set up a small table and a couple of chairs in one corner for games, crafts, and puzzles. Put a skirt on the table and you can tuck the games out of sight underneath. Make a little reading corner with a cozy chair, afghan, table, light, and a shelf or drawer for books, papers, and glasses. Create a play area in another corner with a stain-resistant rug under a chest of toys.

Place a cozy overstuffed chair next to the piano and station a book and/or sewing alongside in a basket. Now you can be an audience for your daughter's daily piano practice. Often kids don't mind practicing as much when they have company (and/or an audience). You can work on your sewing, reading, or correspondence so you can multitask as usual.

Other tricks? Soft, indirect lighting makes a room feel warmer. Avoid stark white paint on walls; go for warmer tones. If your kids are past the toddler stage, add some life and more visual settings with large potted plants. The next time you're buying furniture, consider recliners or swivel rockers instead of couches and loveseats. Big fat chairs are cozy, plus they're easier to arrange in small informal groupings.

Finally, don't forget that living rooms are real rooms and need all the accessories necessary in other rooms. You wouldn't believe how many people don't have wastebaskets in living rooms. If you want to keep the room tidy, encourage, don't discourage, kids to throw away trash. By the same token, if you've got little ones, hide a roll of paper towels and some wipes somewhere in the room for those inevitable messes. And if you don't want your dog on the furniture, place a pillow or dog bed on the floor for him so he can be with the rest of the family.

coexisting with kids and furnishings

So, now that you have some decorating direction, you may be asking, can kids and nice things peacefully coexist?

The answer is: sometimes. Don't make yourself crazy. Don't turn into the evil mom, either. If you turn your kids and pets loose on a pristine living room full of family heirlooms, you're setting the whole family up for disaster. Kids will break things. They will spill things. They are kids. This is their learning period.

Realize that if those heirlooms have been in your family for hundreds of years, they will probably survive quite nicely in a box until your kids leave home. But your kids will only be kids a few years at most. Enjoy the kids now and the heirlooms later. You really *can* have it all, but perhaps not simultaneously.

But that doesn't mean that you have to live in a hovel until your youngest goes to college. You can still have nice things. Just choose and position them wisely. Here are some tips:

- Choose kid- and pet-friendly furnishings with tough, stain-resistant upholstery. This will not be your White Period.

- Establish firm rules about protecting what you *do* have. No feet on the furniture. No food outside the dining room. Crafts only in the kitchen. Just because a room is kid-friendly doesn't mean it has to look like the playground or school cafeteria.

- Consider *where* you put things. You might want to relocate your precious

Oriental rug to the dining room or your bedroom for the next few years. Or put it in an area of the room where the kids are unlikely to congregate.

- If you're buying sofas or chairs anytime soon, consider leather. Leather is much easier to care for if you have kids. (And usually where there are kids, there are pets.) You spill on leather, you wipe it up. You spill on chenille, you'd better catch it fast. Leather is also more rip resistant. And it looks better longer. Enough advertising for the leather industry . . .

- If you already have the sofas and chairs that you will go through early parenthood with, invest in slipcovers. They are trendy now and they actually look nice. Buy washable ones.

- Put out only what you truly love. Living rooms are infamous final resting places for knickknacks, tchotchkes, whatnots, and other decorative junk. Clutter is clutter, whether it's collectible Hummel figurines or garage-sale finds. Everyone has treasures, of course, and they do give a room personality and interest. But when you've got so much stuff that your eye cannot focus on any one thing, Mama, you gotta cut back.

- Organize items in eye-pleasing groupings of two or three objects. This works best if the items have a similar

kids' space

My friend Suzi had an only child. She created a little world for her child as soon as the kid could sit in a chair. Suzi simply bought her a pint-size table and chair and parked it in front of the TV in the den. The kid spent most of her life there. It was her special place. She would put her blankie on her chair and place her bunny on the other chair for company. She watched her favorite videos at her table. She ate her snacks at her table. She colored. She did crafts. She had tea parties.

It's amazing the scope of activities that can occur in a square yard of space. The point is that this space was hers and hers alone. Suzi's daughter was master of her tabletop universe. And since her mess was confined to one tiny area (a plastic mat beneath the table completed the picture), Mom was happy, too. Suzi's daughter sat at that table until her legs just got too long at around age 7. She still misses it.

So does her mom.

theme or if they provide contrasting textures, shapes, or colors.

- Don't pack every inch of surface space. Items stand out when they have room to stand out.

- If you've got a lot of stuff that you really like, try rotating collections. Having fewer objects on display is not only more attractive, it makes dusting infinitely easier. (They don't call them dust catchers for nothing.) And rotating collections will keep your living areas looking fresh.

formal dining rooms

Talk about the final frontier! I know one couple who has never *ever* eaten in their formal dining room. Not once. Are there chairs and a table in there? You bet. Are there people? Only to clean once a week. Another friend scrimped and saved to buy the dining room set (with matching hutch) of her dreams. You never see the table, though, because it's always under a load of laundry. And the chairs are along the wall to make room for the ironing board. Guess what kind of room she really needed?

A lot of people have formal dining rooms only because the house plans labeled a room that way. Do they need a formal dining room? Probably not. Do they use it? Maybe on holidays.

If you want a formal dining room, that's fine and dandy. Good for you. You can entertain in style. But think about your lifestyle for a second. Is another room doing double duty? Are the kids fighting over counter space to do homework in the kitchen? Are the little ones always

Tucking in an inconspicuous home office is just one way to make good use of a formal dining room.

underfoot with their toys when you're trying to cook or clean?

Now, consider if you designed your own dream home, what room would you add to those that you have now? A study? A playroom? A sewing room? An office? Would you trade your formal dining room for one of those?

Make a conscious decision about how you want to use that room and work from there. Maybe you really want an office or a playroom that also functions as a formal dining room on the six evenings a year you entertain. That's doable. Maybe your dining-room set is a family heirloom, gosh darn it, and you never want to see anyone in there under the age of 21. That's your call.

But make the call consciously.

Keep in mind that if you use the room as a dining room, you'll need all the trappings that come with it. Then you'll need to store them. So you'll need storage for fine china, crystal, silver, linens, napkin rings, napkins, candles, matches, candleholders, chargers, runners, etc. A buffet or hutch will work just fine. With any luck, you'll still have storage space to spare. Then the dining room can do double duty quite easily, and the buffet, armoire, or hutch can also house toys, computers, or homework supplies.

Besides providing a place for fancy meals, a dining-room table provides a large, flat surface for school projects, paying bills, completing puzzles, playing games, and even cutting out sewing patterns or wrapping gifts. Be sure to protect the surface with a piece of heavy plastic like you buy for desktops.

Be adventurous here. Break some rules. Even if you use the space as a dining room, that doesn't mean you have to put dining-room furniture in there. Have a big interesting table, yes, and a few chairs. But the rest of the furnishings can be whatever you want. Like the country look? How about using antique pie safes or old ice boxes as storage? Does the room double as a home office? Put a rolltop desk in the corner or hide your computer equipment in an entertainment center or armoire.

But please. Whatever you do with this room, *use* it!

cleaning with kids: living areas

You've probably figured out that your living area is the largest area of your home. There's so much to clean! The good news is that your kids will be able to help with just about all of it.

Most living areas have pretty standard types of furniture and flooring, but each requires different types of care. We'll talk about each of these in turn: upholstered furniture, leather furniture, wood furniture, pianos, lights, window treatments, and floors.

upholstered furniture

Kids are rough on upholstered furniture. They put their shoes on the couch, jump on the chairs, pull off the loveseat pillows to make forts, and stash crumbs, pencils, quarters, etc. under the cushions to create a perpetual collection of odds and ends. We've even found tennis shoes under our cushions.

The good news is that you *can* keep furniture nice. (I highly recommend slipcovers!) Here are some key ways to protect your furniture:

- Treat fabrics with a fluorochemical solution to make them more stain-resistant. This is an invisible finish that coats the fabric so that spills and dirt don't penetrate as quickly or easily. It's safe for most fabrics.

- Protect furniture from direct sunlight.

- Rotate and reverse cushions occasionally so they will fade evenly and receive equal wear.

- Vacuum furniture monthly with a soft brush attachment.

No matter how many house rules you have about no eating in the living room, someone will eventually spill juice on your sofa. It's just one of those things a Mom can count on. Wipe up spills with a clean cloth. Blot, don't rub! (See "Cleaning Codes for Upholstery" on page 121.)

Kid-Friendly Factor: 6 to 8 on a scale of 1 to 10

leather furniture

There are two main types of leather: protected leather, which has a finish, and unprotected leather, which is natural or unfinished. Most furniture is covered with protected leathers (also called aniline plus, top grain, pigmented leather, or everyday leather) because they are more durable and stain-resistant. Aniline or unprotected leathers are less commonly used. They are colored with transparent dye so their grain shows through. There may be a light wax finish, but nothing that will really protect the leather from a child's abuse. The most porous (and easiest to stain) type of unprotected leather is suede or

LIVING AREA CHORES BY AGE

Your living areas will be spotless in a jiffy once you enlist your kids' help. Here's a guide to which chores kids can do at what ages. Once a child reaches a certain skill or age level, he can generally do the chores for his age group and those for the age groups below. Of course, some of these chores need to be done each day, others once a week, and still others once a month or even less frequently. Use your best judgment for what gets done when, and see "Mrs. Clean Jeans' Housekeeping Routine" on page 253 for guidelines.

AGES 2 AND UNDER:
- Put toys in bins or drawers
- Help pick up stray books and magazines
- Turn off the TV if the button is within reach

AGES 3 TO 5:
- Previous chores, plus:
- Put away toys and games and all their pieces in the proper boxes or bins
- Return CDs, DVDs, and videocassettes to their cases
- Return books to bookshelves
- Sponge down the play table
- Dust low furniture
- Wash or spot-clean baseboards

AGES 6 TO 9:
- Previous chores, plus:
- Shake area rugs, depending on size
- Empty and wipe wastebaskets clean, using disinfecting wipes
- Dust furniture and shelves

- Vacuum, with help depending on the machine's height and weight
- Dust lamp shades
- Wipe smudges from walls and doors
- Water plants
- Take indoor plants outside for a gentle washing

AGES 10 TO 13:
- Previous chores, plus:
- Clean telephones, computer and TV screens, video-game controllers, and remote controls
- Vacuum floors and carpets
- Disinfect light switches and doorknobs
- Vacuum furniture
- Wipe leather furniture with a soft cloth
- Clean windows
- Clean blinds
- Wash washable curtains

AGES 14 TO 17:
- Previous chores, plus:
- Organize closet
- Dust the ceiling fan
- Wash and polish wood furniture
- Clean ceiling fixtures, light fixtures, and lamps
- Dust and vacuum corners and crevices from high point to low
- Vacuum floors and carpet and move furniture to clean underneath
- Vacuum drapes
- Deep-clean carpet and upholstery. (Teens can make the call to the carpet cleaner for you.)
- Clean out the fireplace and tools

CLEANING CODES FOR UPHOLSTERY

If you look on the tags on your sofa cushions, you'll see either a W, S, WS, or X. (If your upholstered furniture doesn't have a code, test a cleaner on a hidden spot first or call a professional upholstery cleaner.) These codes tell you how to clean the upholstery. Here's what they stand for:

W = Water-based cleaning agent. Clean with a water-based product such as a little foam from mild detergent or nonsolvent upholstery shampoo. Use as little foam and water as possible to do the job; you don't want to get the upholstery too wet.

S = Solvent. Clean with a mild water-free dry-cleaning solvent. Use just a little and make sure you have plenty of ventilation. Don't put any water on it.

WS = Water-based cleaning agent or solvent. Depending on the stain, you can use a dry-cleaning solvent, the foam of a mild detergent, or upholstery shampoo.

X = Don't clean it yourself. Hire a professional. You can, however, vacuum or brush off surface grime.

By the way, zippered cushion covers do not mean you can remove the covers for cleaning separately. The zippers are there to provide a tighter fit. If you clean covers separately, they may shrink, tear, or discolor. It's deceptive, I know. I've bought couches myself on the mistaken notion that I could clean the removable covers.

In addition to the cleaning code, manufacturers use a wearability code to gauge how well a particular fabric will hold up under use. When you're shopping for furniture, ask the salesperson about the wearability of the various fabrics. Then go for the one that will take the most abuse. Here's how to break the secret code:

HD = Heavy duty. This is what you want in your family room.

MD = Medium duty. Reserve this until your kids are out of the toddler stage.

LD = Light duty. This is rather delicate fabric that is definitely not kidproof. Use it for entertaining.

DD = Delicate duty. Do we need to even discuss this one? If you have a room that's off limits to kids, pets, and husbands, buy this fabric.

---

nubuck. Avoid these leathers until your kids are grown. Or put them in your off-limits study.

Protected leathers, however, can be a good choice. You can buy leathers with very tough, durable finishes that will take

a lot of abuse. They're not as soft and supple as the aniline, but they will hold up better. Cats (usually) won't shred them. Protected leathers are fairly puncture-resistant and don't rip or tear easily. And unlike fabric upholstery, leather gets better with age. Leather is also preferable for people with allergies because you can remove all dust from its surface.

To preserve your leather furniture, keep it at least 2 feet away from heat vents or other heat sources. Don't expose leather furniture to direct sunlight or it could dry out and crack.

Each week, wipe leather with a soft cloth. Each month, clean it with a gentle cleaning agent, such as liquid Ivory soap mixed in lukewarm water. Wipe, don't rub!

Kid-Friendly Factor: 9 on a scale of 1 to 10

wood furniture

Lucky for us, the distressed look is in! If you buy painted, distressed, or farmhouse-type furniture, your worries are over. Nothing your kids can do to it will hurt it. Nicks, bumps, and scratches are all part of the "patina."

I think whoever started that trend must have had a large family.

If you choose to go against the grain and buy regular, undistressed furniture—and you want to keep it that way—I can offer you hope. Keeping furniture in good shape is completely in the realm of possibility, even with kids.

To prevent problems with wood furniture, always use coasters and trivets. Put felt under bowls and figurines on furniture to prevent them from scratching the wood. Protect wood from direct sunlight, which can dry out and bleach the wood. Keep wooden furniture away from heat vents. Protect wood tables with tablecloths.

How you take care of your wood furniture depends on the type of wood (solid or veneer) and the way it's been treated or finished. When you take care of wood furniture, you're really taking care of the finish, and there are sundry types. The wood can have a soft oil finish or a factory-applied hard finish. It can even be protected by a layer of polyurethane.

Dust wood weekly with a very soft cloth or feather duster. Gentle reminder here: *Always* use a clean cloth. My Mom had a designated "dust rag" that she used week after week. You're only reapplying last week's dirt when you reuse cloths. (Sorry, Mom!)

Wash wood once a year. Dampen a cloth with a mild soap solution and wipe the wood. Rinse, then wipe dry.

A few times a year, polish natural woods to keep them from drying out. Always use the same kind of polish. If you use oil polish one time and wax polish the next, it could cause a cloudy finish. Avoid silicone finishes because they are hard to remove and can build up over time. They also show smudges more. Laminates, varnishes, and sealed wood surfaces do not need polishing. Just wipe them off with a damp cloth.

One last note about wood: If your dining room table has leaves, don't store them in the garage or basement. The different humidity can cause the wood to swell or shrink so that the leaves may not fit when you need them. Store leaves as close to the table as possible; perhaps in a hall closet.

Kid-Friendly Factor: 8 on a scale of 1 to 10

pianos

Generally, you should treat pianos with normal wood finishes as you would any wood. Many pianos, however, have high-gloss finishes, which are sealed at furniture factories to protect the wood. This seal prevents polishes and waxes from penetrating to the wood, so using polishes only muddies the shine. All you need to do to keep a high-gloss piano gleaming is to rub the surface with a piece of damp chamois, and then buff it with a dry chamois.

Keep dust out of the piano keys by closing the cover after use. Clean the keys occasionally by rubbing them with a damp cloth. If your keys start to yellow, you can whiten them by rubbing them lightly with a little toothpaste on a cloth. Then wipe off with a damp cloth and dry.

lights

Furniture comes and goes, but lamps are (seemingly) forever. Stop neglecting your lights! They need more than just an occasional bulb change. How about a few passes with a feather duster occasionally or an occasional vacuuming?

Consider yourself enlightened. About once a month, your lamps need a good cleaning. First of all, be safe: Turn off all lights before cleaning. To clean table lamps, sconces, and ceiling lights, carefully remove the shades and clean them according to the type of material (see below). Wipe off the bulb and base with a damp cloth. Immerse ceiling-lamp covers in hot soapy water. Wash them gently, rinse, and dry.

The secret to keeping lamp shades clean is to dust them weekly. Once grime builds up, it gets more difficult to remove, especially on more delicate shades such as parchment or fabric. Here's how to clean specific types of shades:

Beaded: Vacuum regularly to prevent dust buildup. Wipe occasionally with a damp cloth.

Fabric: Dust with a soft vacuum attachment; clean professionally if necessary.

Glass: Wash in dishwashing solution; rinse and dry thoroughly.

Metal: Wipe with a soft, damp cloth.

Paper: Wipe; replace when they get too dirty.

Parchment: Dust; remove marks with an eraser.

Plastic: Wash in dishwashing solution.

Rattan: Vacuum often.

Silk: Clean professionally.

If you have a chandelier, you've got two choices: Dodge the bullet and call in the pros, or wash it yourself piece by piece, following the steps below.

Turn off the lights. You might even want to turn this one off at the breaker.

Take out all bulbs and wipe them off.

Fill two tubs with hot water. Add dish detergent to the wash tub and ammonia to the rinse tub for sparkle. Cushion the bottoms of the tubs with cloths.

Remove the crystal drops and saucers and put them in the sudsy water. (Either remove just a few crystal parts at a time or make a diagram of what goes where so you don't have a chandelier jigsaw puzzle to contend with when it's time to put it back together.)

Wipe the base of the chandelier with a cloth dampened with the wash water. Wash, rinse, and dry all parts.

Replace the parts quickly before you forget where they go, and then replace the bulbs.

window treatments

When I was a kid, part of spring cleaning was taking down every curtain, sheer, and blind in the house and washing them. A really big part of spring cleaning was hanging them all back up. (I hated spring cleaning.)

Washing the metal blinds was the only fun part. We would put them in the wading pool and scrub them. Often, we'd wash the dog while we were at it. (The dog hated spring cleaning, too!)

Nowadays most experts say that you shouldn't take window treatments down at all. Just clean them where they are. Here's your handy-dandy guide to cleaning every type of window treatment. (Dog optional.)

drapes and soft window treatments

Drapes mostly get dusty. Very dusty. The best way to keep your soft window treatments looking good is to vacuum them thoroughly, top to bottom, at least twice a year.

Another option is to take down the treatments and send them for a 10-minute spin in the dryer on the fluff cycle. Then, of course, you have to hang them up again (ugh).

Are the drapes a little soiled? Call in the pros. Most drapes must be professionally cleaned. Some cleaners use a solvent/extraction method directly on the drapes as they hang in the windows. That way you don't have naked windows while you're waiting for them to return. Heavily soiled drapes, however, will probably need to be taken down and sent to the cleaners.

sheers

Sheers are some of the most difficult window treatments to clean because they are very fragile and stretch easily. For best results, dust them weekly with a feather duster. If you use a vacuum, use low suction to keep from stretching or puckering the material. Clean only one small area at a time in short, horizontal strokes.

Experts advise using a drapery cleaning service to clean sheers. Look for one with portable injection/extraction machines that clean the sheers without solvents as they hang.

shades

Dust shades regularly. If you use a vacuum, be careful not to apply too much pressure. Or you can blow off dust with a blow-dryer set on low. Spot-clean shades with a sponge dipped in mild hand dishwashing detergent. Gently blot dry with a clean, lint-free rag.

blinds

Dust, vacuum, or blow-dry blinds regularly. To clean wooden painted louvers, tilt them almost all the way up and wipe them with a cloth moistened in a mild detergent solution; then tilt them almost all the way down and wipe again. This ensures that you clean the middle, too. Do not wet stained wood shutters because this may damage the finish. Instead, clean them with lemon oil or a wood preservative.

Probably the most efficient way to wash vinyl or metal miniblinds is ye olde traditional method of taking them down and immersing them in a bathtub full of soapy water. Rinse them, and then hang them over the shower rod to dry.

Vacuum or dust vertical blinds regularly, especially along the floor. If you have pets, use a pet brush to remove pet hair. Don't wash or dry-clean fabric vertical blinds. Clean vinyl or aluminum vertical blinds with a damp cloth. Leave a light film of detergent on the vanes to reduce static electricity.

Some valances and curtains are washable, especially if they aren't lined. Before washing, examine them for sun rotting. If they have rotted, don't bother washing them. Just replace them. If they're not washable, have them professionally cleaned.

floors

Once, there were only a couple of flooring choices for living areas: carpet or hardwood. Carpet was difficult to keep clean. And hardwood was difficult to keep unmarred. But now, we have a wealth of flooring options to choose among: carpet and hardwood, of course, but also ceramic tile, laminate, stone, and vinyl. And that's not counting the flooring trims available, such as limestone, marble, and slate.

Some types of flooring are definitely more family-friendly (i.e., durable) than others. Here is a quick rundown of the various types of flooring available, how to find the most family-friendly variation, and finally, how to take care of it once you get it home.

carpets

Carpets are one of the most popular choices for living areas. Advantages are that it's warm and soft and makes a room feel cozy. Carpeting comes in all colors and textures, so you can coordinate with other fabrics and colors in the room. Carpet also softens sound, and that, as any Mom knows, is a distinct plus. It can be installed over all kinds of surfaces on every floor in the house from basement to attic. It's also generally less expensive to install than many other types of flooring.

Drawbacks of carpet are that it's difficult to keep clean and comparatively easy to stain. People with allergies won't be happy campers with carpet because it's a giant dust sponge.

When you buy carpet for a family's needs, look for a tight yarn twist (tighter = longer-lasting), a short nap (shorter = more crush-resistant), dense stitching (denser = more crush-resistant), a good quality cushion (good cushion = longer lasting carpet), and continuous filament nylon (the carpet is woven from one long filament instead of a lot of shorter filaments = less pilling).

Here's how to care for carpets:

• Vacuum, vacuum, vacuum with a rotating brush or beater bar at least twice a week, more frequently in heavily trafficked areas. (Sorry!) Pull the vacuum back and forth to get out embedded dirt. Change vacuum bags often and keep brushes clean.

- Keep drapes closed when you're not in the room to keep the carpet from fading.

- Use coasters under furniture.

- Don't roll or pull things directly across carpet.

- Be careful using strong chemicals near carpets.

- Professionally clean carpets at least twice a year, more often if you have kids and pets or a dust-allergy sufferer in residence.

FAMILY PICKUP LINES

VACUUMING NAME GAME
Gimme an "L"! There really is more to vacuuming than just plugging in the machine and giving the carpet the once-over. To suck up all the dirt and dust hidden among the fibers requires a full 20 seconds or so of going back and forth over each area of the rug. Issue those instructions to your kid, and you'll receive a resounding, "Booooring!"

Instead, ask your son or daughter to vacuum until Mom or Dad can see the letter of his or her first name in the carpet in a neat little pattern. My daughter, Lyndsay, has learned to make a mean "L."

Out, out #&*! spot! If you've got kids, you'll get spills. And invariably those spills will be on white carpet. Most manufacturers put a stain-resistant finish on carpets, but it can only do so much. Deal with spills immediately. The longer you wait, the more the carpet absorbs them. Scrape up any solids first. Then blot up stains with a clean white cloth or paper towel. Don't rub. Put a small amount of stain remover on a clean cloth and lay it over the stain for 10 minutes. (See "Common Carpet Stains" on page 128 for appropriate remedies for common stains.) Then begin blotting from the edge of the stain to the center. Rinse the area with cold water and blot dry. Put a stack of clean white towels on the spot and weight them down with a heavy object for six hours to soak up excess moisture.

Caution: If you don't remove all of the cleaning agent, a worse stain can result. Don't skip this last step! Also, if the stain is really serious, you might want to call a professional in right away. Home remedies may worsen the problem or even set the stain permanently.

Kid-Friendly Factor: 5 on a scale of 1 to 10

ceramic tile flooring
To make glazed tile, manufacturers fuse liquid glass to ceramic tile at high temperatures. That makes a hard, non-porous surface. There are many advantages to glazed tile: It doesn't stain,

DIRTY LITTLE SECRETS

COMMON CARPET STAINS
Food and beverages are attracted to carpet like magnets. Stains happen. Here are some remedies for the most common stains. Pretest all cleaners in an inconspicuous area before you use them on a carpet.

Ballpoint pen ink: Pour a little rubbing alcohol onto a clean dry cloth and blot.

Blood: Someone get a boo-boo? After you kiss it well (and apply a happy face Band-Aid), go to work on the spot. Rub an ice cube on the stain. As it melts, so will the spot. Don't let the area get too wet, however. Blot up the stain with a clean white towel.

Burns: If a large section of carpet is burned, you will need to patch the carpet. However, small burns can be disguised by cutting away the burned tips with scissors and trimming the surrounding tufts to disguise the cut.

Fingernail polish: Some little lady's in big trouble! Remove the polish with a non-acetate nail-polish remover on a clean cloth. Work from the edges to the middle and leave the remover on for a few minutes. Then blot dry. It may take several tries.

Pet accidents: Urine is the worst. And once it soaks into the pad, you've got a big problem.

First, blot up as much as you can. Dissolve $\frac{1}{4}$ teaspoon of dishwashing detergent in 1 cup of lukewarm water, and blot it onto the stain with a clean cloth. Blot dry using a second cloth. Rinse. Blot dry. Keep repeating those steps until the spot is gone. Then mix $\frac{1}{2}$ cup of white vinegar in 1 cup of water and blot again. Finally, put a pile of paper towels on the spot and weight it down with a heavy object until all moisture is absorbed. (Hint: Don't use too much liquid, or you will inadvertently spread the urine into the pad yourself.)

Now that we've gone through all that, here's the bad news: It may not work. Pets' urine changes chemically depending on factors ranging from diet to medication to reproductive cycles. Also, urine can react chemically with some dyes and leave the affected area a different color. Here's more bad news. Odors from cat urine are difficult to remove completely. For cat stains, you might want to call in the pros. Sometimes you have to patch the carpet. Sometimes you have to patch the pad. Sometimes you even have to take up the subflooring. No kidding. If you have cats, and you're getting new carpet (brave you!), check into the type with a special backing that prevents spills from going through to the underlying pad.

scratch, or burn easily; it doesn't fade; it's not slippery; and it's easy to clean. Tiles come in all sorts of styles, shapes, and colors that will match any home's décor.

The drawbacks of tile are that it's cold, hard, and expensive. It's kid-durable, but it's not particularly kid-friendly. Here's how to care for it:

- Vacuum and/or sweep regularly.

- Avoid abrasive powders that can scratch the tile.

- Avoid ammonia-based cleaning agents. They may discolor some colored grout.

- Clean with a nylon scrub sponge using nonabrasive cleanser and water, and then rinse.

- Never use wax or sealant.

- Clean grout by scrubbing with detergent, and then apply a diluted solution of chlorine bleach and let sit for five minutes. Then wash again and rinse.

- Wipe up spills immediately.

Kid-Friendly Factor: 7 on a scale of 1 to 10

hardwood

You may think you don't want wood floors. You may have heard horror stories from friends who installed wood floors and had to move out of their homes for a few days during the installation to let the fumes and dust subside. You may have heard complaints about having to wax and scrub hardwood floors and how much care they require.

You can still have the messy hardwoods installed and stained and give them all the waxing and scrubbing you'd like. But you don't have to. Today, most hardwoods are finished in the factory with a special urethane layer that preserves their shine and also makes them much harder and more durable. And since the floors don't need sanding or staining, installation is a lot less hassle, too. If you do decide on hardwood, the prefinished wood is the way to go for families.

Also, wood floors come in a range of hardness from Douglas fir and pine (softest) to mesquite and Brazilian cherry (hardest). The harder the wood, the less work you'll have keeping it unmarred.

Here's how to protect your wood floor:

- Put welcome mats at doors to catch the dirt before you track it in. Or better yet, make the house a no-shoe zone. High heels exert up to 8,000 pounds of pressure per square inch on floors. (Not to mention what they do to the female foot.)

- Protect flooring in heavy traffic areas with area rugs.

- Put glides on chairs, and coasters or felt under all furniture that sits directly on hardwood floors. Otherwise, the furniture could scratch or dent the wood. Put rubber cups or an area rug under heavy furniture such as pianos.

- Vacuum or sweep frequently. Use a soft brush attachment on your vacuum. Grinding in dirt and grime will ruin a finish fast.

- Don't damp-mop. Even though the wood is sealed, you still don't want to put water on it. And if you spill anything, mop it up immediately with a paper towel or clean cloth.

- Choose and use products wisely. Use only the products recommended by the manufacturer. Oil or wax-based products or ammonia cleansers could damage the factory shine on urethane finishes.

- Avoid sunlight, which can change the color of the flooring. (Cherry gets darker, for instance.) Close your shades or drapes during the day when you are not using the room. Also move furniture and area rugs around occasionally to avoid uneven coloration.

Kid-Friendly Factor: Home-stained floors, 6; factory-finished (urethane-coated) floors, 9 on a scale of 1 to 10

laminate

Laminates, which are known mostly by the brand name Pergo, consist of several layers: a top "wear layer" or finish, a photograph of real wood, a layer of fiberboard, and a bottom layer. The bottom layer, also called the underside or the balance layer, is made from specially laminated kraft paper. Since the visual layer is photography, laminates can mimic any flooring material from stone to tile to wood.

The good news is that wood laminates look like regular wood, but they are more durable and easier to care for, they are more affordable, and they can be installed in places where solid or veneered wood is not appropriate. Laminates are also easy to use in remodels because they can be installed over most materials and don't require a subfloor.

You can get laminates that are finished to look like just about any kind of wood. Many people cannot tell wood and laminate floors apart. (Unless they're flooring installers, of course.)

The main complaint most people have about laminate is that it doesn't "sound" like wood when you walk across it. Laminate floors are noisier than wood.

Although laminates can be less expensive to install in an existing home, they cost as much as solid wood in new construction.

The care tips for laminate are very similar to those for wood floors:

- Use welcome mats. Grit is your floor's worst enemy.

- Use furniture casters. These floors also scratch.

- Vacuum often, using the soft brush attachment on the vacuum.

- Do not polish, wax, or use steel wool or abrasive cleansers.

- Use products recommended by the manufacturer.

- These floors cannot be polished or refinished. However, they are very easy to replace when the time comes.

Kid-Friendly Factor: 9 on a scale of 1 to 10

linoleum

Vinyl floors are often called "linoleum," but they are two different materials. Vinyl is synthetic. Linoleum, a blend of natural products such as linseed oil, limestone, resins, and wood powder, is more like a wood floor than vinyl.

Linoleum is very durable, burn-resistant, and allergen-free. It's more durable than vinyl and not as prone to indentations. It absorbs sound. And it's available in many patterns and colors, making it a good choice for family rooms or playrooms.

Here's how to care for a linoleum floor:

- Sweep or vacuum regularly.

- Damp-mop with cool water and a mild dishwashing detergent for daily cleaning. Apply a capful of baby oil to the mop to make no-wax floors shiny. (To save time, I sometimes pour the solution into a spray bottle, squirt just the areas that need cleaning, and then damp-mop.)

- If the floor is excessively dirty, use the cleaning agent the manufacturer recommends.

- Keep water away from seams and edges to prevent loosening.

- Allow the floor to air-dry before walking on it.

Kid-Friendly Factor: 8 on a scale of 1 to 10

stone flooring

There are several types of stone flooring used in living areas. Popular choices include limestone, marble, and slate. These stone floors are a very formal look that usually does not go well with children. It's also difficult to maintain, cold, slippery, and very, very hard when toddlers fall on it. Think twice before installing stone flooring in your home. If your house already has stone flooring, then you already know everything I just told you.

In general, stone floors are fairly durable because they are usually sealed to minimize staining. Here's how to care for stone floors:

- Sweep daily. Remove dirt before it gets ground in. If you have a textured stone floor, vacuuming works better than sweeping.

- Immediately after sweeping, damp-mop the floor, using a clean mop that has not been exposed to strong cleaners.

- Wash your stone floors regularly with what the manufacturer suggests. But rinse twice, so soil residues from rinse water don't dull surfaces. Squeegee away water to avoid water spots. Never use vinegar, which can strip the shine.

- If your floor has a polished surface, finish with paste wax. Skip this step if your stones are unfinished.

- Clean up spills immediately.

Kid-Friendly Factor: 6 on a scale of 1 to 10

vinyl flooring

What do you think of when you think of vinyl flooring? If ugly textured kitchen floors in browns and beiges come to mind, think again. Today's vinyl flooring can look like wood, stone, or ceramic tile. Or it can still look like vinyl. The new vinyl flooring is more durable and more tear- and burn-resistant, too. You can even buy "no-wax" flooring that has a permanent shine. It's a great choice for dens, family rooms, playrooms, or rec rooms.

Here's how to keep your vinyl floors happy:

- Ward off dirt with welcome mats at the door. (Do not use a rubber or latex-backed mat on the floor because it can stain the vinyl.)

- Vacuum regularly. (Don't use a beater bar.)

Real-Life Solutions

Here are some clever ways real moms solved their living area challenges:

Challenge: Too many horses. Connie's 10-year-old is horse crazy. She has a collection of Breyer horses, barns, fences, even a little truck that hauls the little trailer to horse shows. Needless to say, this stuff takes up a lot of room. In the summer, it's no problem; the family has devoted half the garage to make a playroom, which is defined by an 8-by-10-foot carpet. There are shelves to hold all the Breyer accessories and plenty of floor space for the barns. Plus Connie's daughter uses her Red Flyer wagon to pull it all out into the yard to set up her equestrian center. But in the winter when she can't play outside, there's a bit of a problem.

Solution: Connie has given her daughter the bottom cabinets in the entertainment center to hide the barns, truck, and trailer. The horses are still stationed in tubs in the garage, but bringing those in is not a problem because they are light and not difficult to maneuver like the heavier stuff. Now when she has a free afternoon, she can manage her play date without help from Mom. And she has no excuse for not cleaning it up, either.

Challenge: Too-visible mess. When Jessica's daughter was young, they lived in a house that had a living room/dining room combination. You walked straight into that room from the front door so whatever mess was out was visible. The kid had to play in the living room—there was nowhere else to

- Mop occasionally with a no-rinse floor-cleaning product. Sometimes, you may need to use a stripper and cleaner.

- Clean up spills immediately.

- Most stains can be removed with a floor stripper and cleaning agent.

- If the floor starts looking dull, polish it with a product recommended by the manufacturer. Inexpensive PVC vinyl floors might need a few coats of polish to help prevent scratches.

- Occasional buffing will heighten the shine.

- Never use abrasive scrubbers or abrasive cleaners, detergents, mop-and-shine products, paste wax, or solvents on the floor.

- Don't use rolling casters, but *do* use floor protectors under heavy furniture to prevent indentations.

- If a seam opens, call a professional. Do not try to mend it yourself.

---

play. But how to hide the mess? Complicating the problem was the fact that the family didn't have a lot of money to throw at it, either.

Solution: Jessica simply stationed a series of brightly colored stackable plastic cubes around the room and filled them with toys. The child could play with any one basket of toys at a time. But before she could dump another basket, she had to refill the first. That limited the clutter to a few toys and still gave the kid a lot of accessible choices at one time. Plus, this system encouraged and enabled her to be able to clean up behind herself at age 3.

Challenge: Too many toys. Another friend of mine, Sandi, has a 9-year-old daughter and 4-year-old into-everything son. Sandi has a family room and a living room back to back that are separated by a wall. Previously, the toys were everywhere, in the family room, in the living room, and in the doorway in between.

Solution: In the family room, Sandi built a floor-to-ceiling unit of shelving and cupboards. Nothing fancy. Nothing expensive. Just a whole wall of deep cubbies. The cubbies are deeper than most bookshelves, about 2 feet deep. One compartment holds the TV, and another holds the stereo. The rest of the compartments are dedicated to toys, toys, and more toys.

This way, the children can see everything they have at a glance. The only rule is they must clear the floor and have everything back on the shelves in ready-to-go mode by bedtime. The parents can either watch TV or read in the middle of the play or they can creep away into the living room next door for a little adult time. They're nearby and on the watch either way.

Chapter 7

sweet dreams are
made of this

MY SON CHRIS'S BEDROOM is a breeze to keep tidy.

Then again, Chris was born with a neat streak obvious to all from the moment he began to walk (which was way too early, by the way, at just nine months). Shortly thereafter, he began smoothing out the pleats in his fire truck–stenciled bedskirt before getting into bed each night. This was clearly not your normal organizationally challenged child.

Long before Chris learned to do most of the cleaning and organizing himself, he kept his room and the toys and books inside neat. The neatnik tendencies continue today: If there's anything out of place in his room, I just say the words "Let's organize your drawers!" (or closet) and Chris'll drop almost anything and come running. Even today at age 11.

Lyndsay arrived some 12 months after Chris. Clearly she missed the receiving line for the cleaning and organizing genes Chris got an extra set of. By nature a stuff-loving, organization-phobic pack rat, Lyndsay seemed to pop out of the womb with a penchant for disorganization. The more jumbled her crib, the happier Lyndsay was.

Long after Lyndsay grudgingly learned to clean and organize her Barbie and Beanie Babies–littered space (which has now grown to include American Girl doll and book collections and more writing journals than either of us can count), she still avoids actually doing either like the kiddie plague. And Lyndsay's somewhat proud of it. A sign on her door reads: "OFF LIMITS! My room is messy." Lyndsay is a typical 10-year-old: Honest to a fault.

Just when my husband and I thought we create but two kinds of kids—neatniks or slackers—along came Payne, a middle-of-the-organizing-road kind of kid who enjoys putting his Thomas the Tank Engine trains, Buzz Lightyear, and dinosaurs away, provided you've created neatly organized bins in which to stash them. If not, Payne is happy as a kiddie clam to play amidst a toy tsunami.

I quickly discovered that each of these personalities, not to mention age groups, poses its own cleaning and organizational challenges when it comes to keeping their respective rooms livable. Thankfully, each also has its own simple solutions.

These problems and solutions, of course, bear no resemblance whatsoever to a parental unit's bedroom challenges. That's why you'll find this chapter is really two chapters in one: kids' bedrooms and parents' bedrooms.

I've broken the kids' challenges and solutions into the following age groups:

- Preschoolers (ages 2 to 4)
- Gradeschoolers (ages 5 to 9)
- Tweens (ages 10 to 12)
- Teens (ages 13 to 17)

My bedroom advice for parents is directed toward a very different age group (which shall remain undefined) with another set of problems. But here you have to motivate only yourself and your spouse. This could be an easier or a harder task, depending on the adults involved.

a home for everything

Bedrooms are just as challenging to organize as other rooms, maybe even more so, because they're such personal spaces. Each kid will want to organize his or her own room his or her own way. Here are some of my favorite secrets to help the process along at each stage of development: preschoolers,

gradeschoolers, tweens, and teens. And
then we'll talk about parents' rooms.

preschoolers

Preschoolers have a lot of stuff.

In our house, 3-year-old Payne lays
claim to his small but cozy bedroom filled
with a Thomas the Tank Engine train
collection and the accompanying wooden
tracks, dinosaurs galore complete with
T-rex and all his extinct buddies, a
menagerie of colorful plastic animals wild
and domesticated (the latter comes
complete with a barn and chirping
chicken and horse-whinnying sounds),
cars and trucks of varying sizes, two
talking Buzz Lightyear action figures, an
airplane, and a helicopter or three. Plus,
the room needs to house a half-dozen
shoes, and pants, shorts, T-shirts, and
sweatshirts by the dozen. Oh yes. Did I
mention his jammies overload? About
nine at last count.

You get the picture. It's a big load of
stuff for a busy little guy. The problem? As
with just about every other preschooler,
it's keeping all of Payne's stuff together
and accessible in his room without
sacrificing floor visibility and some sense
of organization.

Here's what to do: It all starts on the
floor. For you, that is. That's it, squat
down. Getting down to your preschoolers'
eye level is a real eye-opener when it
comes to considering how to get her
requisite stuff organized. Grownup stuff-
holders aren't going to work here. Big
chests of drawers are hard to reach and
unsafe for little hands. Closet doors fold
closed onto little feet. Big hangers can't fit
little clothes. And those standard closet
clothing rods are nowhere near usable for
my 3-year-old (or yours, either). They'd
make a better jungle gym for him to play

on than a place to hang or retrieve his clothes.

In short: A preschooler's bedroom is usually a bonafide conundrum. Without some kind of structure and organization, kids' busy bedrooms are apt to feel like Grand Central Station (and look about as clean). But with a little forethought and a few well-crafted activity centers, you can have this busy place in order in a New York minute. Here's how:

Craft Central: Group a kid-size table and chairs, splat mat beneath, and plastic tote with washable crayons, markers, and other supplies.

Play Station: Pick a corner nook, defined by a small area rug. (Preferably a washable area rug.) Leave big toys such as trucks or LEGO sets out and ready to tackle.

Dress-Up Area: Mom, this is where you can recycle some of the excess in your closet. Just fill a plastic bin with your old clothes and fallen-from-favor shoes, bangles, and bags.

Play with Mommy Place: Inaccessible closet shelves are perfect storage spaces for games and crafts that require a grownup's supervision. I do this to keep Payne from beginning a chemistry experiment when I'm homework helper for Chris and Lyndsay.

sleeping space

As you know, sheets are tough for little ones. The top sheet always winds up at the foot of the bed. (Must be the sheet fairy at work again.) And making the bed? It's a tough skill for little hands to master. This is a good age at which to eliminate troublesome items and keep things simple. Ditch the top sheet and use only a fitted sheet topped with a comforter. You probably won't be able to bounce a quarter off it, but you won't have to make it yourself, either. If you cover the comforter with a cozy flannel or cotton duvet, you can remove and wash it weekly. The goal is to create something easy for your little one to pull up on her own.

Don't give in to the temptation to push a preschooler's bed against the wall. That makes it harder for her to make the bed. Yes, it saves space and keeps her from falling out on one side. But consider using rails instead. Pull the bed away from the wall and use it to visually divide the room into activity areas. Kids like things cozy.

Wherever you put the bed, you'll need either a bedside table or a shelf for bedtime essentials: a reading light, sippy cup for water, and books for bedtime stories. And to encourage long-winter's-night-type sleep and naps, use blackout shades on the windows. You wake up when the sun peers into your room, so why wouldn't she? Keep that sort of early-bird behavior where it belongs (outside, with the winged creatures) by ditching your pretty but impractical sheers, or at the very least installing a shade. We're thinking about everyone's quality of life here.

putting it all together

In general, as you're designing and organizing a preschooler's bedroom, simple and sturdy are the key words. All surfaces need to be easy to clean. That includes the floors. Carpets aren't the best for this messy age. If you do have carpet, cover the center or high-traffic area with a washable area rug, a splat mat, or a plastic office-chair mat.

Hardwood is easier than carpet to wipe spills off of and is a great play surface for all those dinosaurs, trucks, and Beanie Babies. Just add an area rug for softness and style.

Resist the urge to match everything in a preschooler's room. It's not necessary. As if this room is ever going to look like a designer showcase! Because you'll be changing the décor before you know it, and because your little one will make sure

that after a year the pieces are barely recognizable anyway, accept hand-me-downs. Just make sure none of the painted finishes contain lead and that the corners aren't hard and sharp.

While we're talking about paint, keep in mind that walls should be washable. Best bets for kid-friendly finishes include an eggshell or satin paint on the walls and semi-gloss for doors and moldings. These finishes are formulated to better withstand repeated cleanings. But other than that, use paint for the vertical décor zing you desire. It's easy to change and easier still to clean.

You can get creative with painting techniques. Check out removable borders,

Here's my idea of a great preschooler's room. It's open and sunny with lots of room to play, but it has plenty of kid-height storage, too.

magnetic paint (paints that are magnetized), chalkboard paint (paints that create a chalkboard that you can actually draw on), and glitter paint (paints with glitter mixed in make walls sparkle, no extra steps required). Or try corkboard walls (it doubles as a soundproofer and stuff-hanger).

Then build a theme. Avoid matching things. A room with the same print on the border, the sheets, and the curtains looks anything but relaxed and comfortable. Instead, choose a theme close to your kid's heart (or your geographic location) that you can build on. Think seashell sheers on the window, sailboat sheets, and a sand-colored area rug. Use your imagination.

Resist the urge to paper your babe's nursery in teddy bears or yellow duckies. You'll be back at the design drawing board before the kid's out of diapers. Instead, choose a more evergreen (everything's relative in childhood seasons) theme such as flowers or flag colors (the U.S.'s or even your state flag or favorite team flag) that can grow with your child with the help of a few well-chosen accessories. Until the teenage years, that is.

Now that the big things are out of the way, I think the three biggest organizational challenges in preschoolers' rooms are toys, clothes, and artwork. Here are my suggestions for each.

toys

Oh, toys. Many toys. Many big toys. There's one rule to keeping these friendly faces from taking over the room: Divide and label. Everything.

Since most preschoolers can't read, these won't be your file-folder labels. Instead, use something entirely different but equally control-inspiring: picture labels. Pictures of socks, shorts, shirts, and dinosaurs help your preschooler know where things go. Color or tape pictures on every box, bin, or bag of the items that go inside. For example, I went to the Internet and found the Thomas the Tank Engine home page, printed it out, and taped it to Payne's bin of Thomas toys. Now Payne knows exactly in which plastic tub to find and return his Thomas trains.

Here are some of my favorite ways to stash and display Payne's bulky and hard-to-stash playtime favorites:

- Buy kid-smart storage products for games and toys, such as plastic tubs that tuck under the bed, roller drawers and cubbies, small bookcases, and toy drawers.

- Create a play area in one corner where's it's okay to leave big toys out. Confine it with a small area rug.

- Put fire trucks, trains, and larger-than-life stuffed toys in big plastic dish tubs.

- Stash stuffed toys on shelves or in hammocks.

- Fill a bookcase that has deep shelves with brightly-colored storage baskets, which can in turn hold dozens of small toys.

- Save the zippered plastic bags that new comforters come in and use them to pack away whatever stuffed animals or Beanie Babies are currently out of favor.

- Recycle old kid-safe, kid-size furniture, such as discarded entertainment and computer centers—even old kitchen islands—to make great storage for a kid's room.

- Skip the clunky, expensive toy box in favor of a laundry (now toy) basket.

- Let toys double as décor. Dolls and trucks can decorate dresser tops.

- Hang space-hogging Beanie Babies and airplanes in flight from the top of canopy beds with fishing line.

- Use an over-the-door clear plastic shoe bag for Beanie Babies and airplanes in search of a hangar.

- If you're really space-crunched, create a toy library. Rotate the preschooler's faves in and out every week or so, and store the rest in another room, the basement, or attic.

clothes

As I mentioned before, Payne has a lot of clothes. Sometimes it seems like he has more clothes than I do! Here's how to keep kids' clothes neat:

- Create a dressing-for-success station. You can arrange similar items in specific drawers. One drawer for jammies, another for socks, another for sweatshirts and athletic gear. Or, arrange drawers by outfits (one-stop shopping is appealing to preschoolers, too) in a one-gallon or larger zippered plastic bag. Simply stock the essentials, from hair bow to ruffle socks, when you put clean clothes away.

  You could also have a church drawer (for Sunday-best purses and hair bows, suspenders, and tiny ties—and, of course, Bibles). A cold-weather drawer for mittens, knit caps, ski goggles, and long underwear. A beach and pool drawer for goggles, swim trunks, and pool shoes . . . You get the idea!

- Get a laundry hamper. Unquestionably, in this room and in all your kids' rooms, you'll need a laundry hamper. Big or small, round, square, corner-fit, it doesn't matter. There just needs to be a place for dirty duds to land before night-night.

  Having a hamper in each kid's room instills good habits and keeps items off the floor. Since kids like to throw their stuff, why not plan for it, even encourage it, when it works to your advantage? I'm talking basketball hoops over hampers or laundry baskets here. And in a pinch, those pre-fab hang-over-the-door (think shoe bags here) laundry catchers will do nicely.

- Remove closet doors to keep little toes and fingers safe and to keep stuff from piling up unnoticed inside.

- Organize shoes in closet shoe cubbies.

- Install a closet clothing rod extension to bring clothes down to kid level.

artwork

Another challenge of organizing kids' rooms is the seemingly endless stream of artwork that arrives home with your son or daughter after preschool. Artwork is a preschooler's (and his parents') pride and joy. Yes, we do eventually get over this syndrome of treating each and every finger painting as a Picasso. But in the meantime, if you don't have the heart to circular-file the art that comes home from preschool, here's how to display it without spending too much time or money in the process.

- Pick up a few inexpensive plastic frames about an inch thick. You can stuff a dizzying amount of colored- and finger-painted layers inside. It makes displaying the artwork *du jour* a snap.

- Hang a clothesline, a ribbon, or a jump rope across the room. Hold the daily artistry in place with clothespins.

gradeschoolers

Once your kids are out of the toddler stage and in school, their needs change. Suddenly, they are more responsible, can work and play unsupervised, like privacy, and have homework.

It's these differences we need to consider when setting up their bedrooms. Gradeschoolers need a study area, room for their collections, and a hideaway so they can just "chill." Let's talk about each of those areas in turn.

the study center

The study area in your kid's room can be a new furniture item or a cleverly arranged, well-equipped surface. It's helpful to create an attractive space where kids *want* to work and study.

This is the age where a loft bed with a desk underneath would be a great space-saving investment. After all, you don't have to worry (so much) at this age about them toppling out of the top bunk and harming themselves.

But if a new combo desk/bed isn't in your family financial plan this year, simply make sure a flat surface is accessible and pack it with the essentials: a mug filled with pens and pencils, scissors, a ruler, tape, markers, an eraser, and anything else your kid uses frequently.

the collections zone

Collected collections will make everyone look good, and gradeschoolers are no exception. This is the age when collections begin. Also at this age is when you can begin both encouraging and corralling your kid's collecting tendencies by creating space and a place in which to house the elementary treasures of life.

Start with the obvious: Drawers and shelves. They'll turn into dumping grounds unless you divide and conquer the stuff collecting inside. Group similar items, such as hair bows, in small bins or baskets to be placed inside a dresser or a desk drawer. Egg cartons and oblong pencil holders are also handy for little things.

Self-enclosed shelves with ends so books and other items won't fall off and hard-to-use bookends aren't required keep things

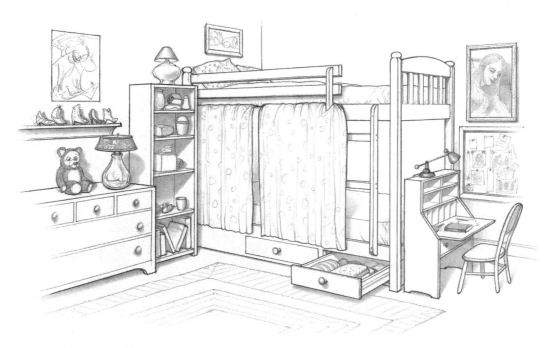

This type of room would be perfect for a gradeschooler. It has convenient storage, study space, and a feeling of privacy.

off the floor and on display. Over-the-door shoe bags work here, too, for the collection of baseball cards, Beanie Babies, yo-yos, and beyond.

From there, get creative. Install corkboard along an entire wall to display artwork, notes, and ribbons. Anything that's flat and vertical can go here. A garden trellis hung on the wall can corral cap collections. Your only rules here are that the items must be contained within the storage space, be it hooks, pegs, or push-pins, and easily reachable and expandable when used by your gradeschooler.

"secret" hideaways

The cozy hideaway areas of your kids' rooms are easy. They're 99 percent imagination and 1 percent perspiration. Usually no investment is required. This is good parenting stuff.

Chris and Lyndsay are frequent fort-makers. Their favorite campground is the one they often create directly beneath the living room stairs. Together or with friends, they drape bed sheets over the top of our open stair steps, affix blankets to the underside and sides of the stairway, and place our sofa cushion pillows on the hardwood floor. They get quite creative, actually, sometimes even bringing in lamps, decorative pillows, blankets, and drawbacks for the blanket that serves as the door. The place often resembles a house within a house.

tips for sharing bedrooms

For many families, it's just not possible to give each kid his or her own room. (I think lots of times kids are secretly glad to share a room with a sibling anyway.) When kids are very young, you may want them to share sleeping space and use the other bedroom as a playroom. That way, they can comfort each other in the dark and have more space to play in when it's light.

Here are a few ways to help them share:

• Give each kid his separate space and privacy. If possible, divide the room into halves. Try a folding screen by each bed or a curtain or bookshelves bisecting the room for really rocky sibling rivalries.

• Consider ages when doling out rooming assignments to your kids. Shared spaces work better for young children. Tweens and up want their own space.

• Set sibling rules such as who can (or can't) touch what; never borrow each other's stuff without asking, etc.

• Let each child decorate her area the way she wants.

• Give each child her own closet, even if it's a closet in another room. A rolling wardrobe works well in tight spaces.

• Finally, let each child have the room to herself for 30 minutes each day.

Since kids love hideaways so much, why not get a bit creative in their rooms? Maybe a popup tent in a far corner where he can keep favorite toys, whisper with friends, and even hide from the parents. It's gradeschool hideaway heaven.

My 10-year-old has a homespun version: a bunk tent. Because Lyndsay always sleeps on the top of her bunk bed, the lower bunk has become her secret space. It's all covered around with sheets, a girlie haven. And it's here just in time to transition her to the more-space-away-from-Mom-and-Dad-is-essential tweens.

tweens

Yes, tweens are close in age to the gradeschool stage, but developmentally, they are morphing into little teenagers. (You'll know you're there when TV is replaced by CDs and radio, and they begin knowing the names of Top 10 songs.)

Tweens have fewer traditional toys. They fall from favor and are replaced by smaller, pricier, more technological toys like CD players, MP3s, PlayStations, computers, and DVD-equipped TVs. And now the kids need places to put these things. It's time to tweak the desk setup,

This room will keep even a tween (relatively) happy. At this age, most kids are ready to "graduate" to new décor, anyway.

get rid of the tchotchkes of childhood, and clear the shelves for adolescence. Bookshelves can be double-bolted to hold a CD-player/radio combo unit with speakers. Plus, of course, the desk is home for that homework must-have: the computer.

In our house, MP3s, PlayStations and TVs aren't bedroom décor. But if you do decide to house your tween's stuff there, create a small entertainment area and set ground rules for its use. These might include no electronic games until all homework is finished and lunch made for tomorrow. Set a daily time limit (an hour or two each school day, perhaps) for these indoor energy-zappers. Yes, I know they love them. But we're the parents, remember? To avoid the socially challenged nerd syndrome, we have to kick them out of the house sometimes.

This is also the stage of sports, hobbies, and lessons. Now the stuff in his room is more focused, but you'll still need to make room to store dance stuff, volleyball gear, soccer equipment, horse stuff, etc.

Naturally, you'll also need a place to display ribbons, trophies, and certificates. It's time to reach back to the preschooler setup of (seemingly) so long ago. A canopy on a bed can make a dramatic frame for hanging your child's ribbons from riding, swimming, soccer, whatever.

Bulletin boards work wonders, but they are rarely big enough to house all the awards that come with today's sports teams. (Whether that's the right approach for kids is another book entirely!)

The tween years are the golden age of sleepovers. This is one reason why the bedroom is oh-so-very important for tweens. Don't fight it, make it less painful for both them and you.

If your tween has a single bed, now's the time to add that trundle. Or just make sure there's enough floor area for a pair of sleeping bags. Fashion and clothes have suddenly hit this group's radar screen, making a full-length mirror (hung behind a door or covering sliding closet doors) a must.

Your not-so-little-anymore darlings are at last fully capable of taking care of their own room and clothes. (A heavy sigh of relief is appropriate here.) Meaning you provide drawers, shelves, shoe rack, and a hanging clothes rod or two, and your tween can take it from there. She'll quite possibly *insist* on taking it from there. Let her, with limits. (We'll get into those limits a bit later.)

Don't be surprised if there's some rebelling against the "babyish" room your tween grew up in, no matter how it was decorated.

When both Chris and Lyndsay reached this phase, I acquiesced about some things, like paint color and linens. Chris eagerly replaced his gingham blue-and-yellow with a much more manly red-and-white motif.

Lyndsay was okay with her room's ballet-pink walls and white trim, but she objected to the pair of white duvets with pink embroidered flowers that had covered her beds for the past four years. Too Laura Ashley, Mom. More palatable are the hot pink, lime green, and sunny yellow paisley-print duo (it's a retro thing) now covering up horizontal space there.

Paint and linens are comparatively inexpensive. Which is why I gave the flag colors and '60s fabric throwbacks the nod. My philosophy is that tweens can decorate in any way they want, as long as it doesn't permanently damage the room and is not offensive.

But I put my foot down when Lyndsay

began her campaign for a new bed. The bunk bed, it seems, is suddenly so babyish. A canopy bed, queen-size, please, suddenly topped her most-wanted list. Which is where it will stay for the foreseeable future.

I just say no to expensive makeovers at this stage in the parenting game. In a couple of years, she'll again be in the market to reinvent her private chambers. Take a deep breath here. She'll be: A teenager.

teens

You'll need to take in all the considerations for the tweens here, plus

Here's a well-organized teen's room. If your teen's room doesn't quite reach this level, remember: You can always close the door if your teen's room is a total disaster area.

figure in the fact that teens *really* like loud music. Remember the money we saved putting off the big fixes during the tweens? Now it's time to sink it into cork flooring on the walls to soundproof that room. Or at least make some decibel rules.

Teens want a phone. Teens also want to be *alone*. You'll still want to supervise her (especially now), though you'll need to be discreet. But stop and think. They will be leaving your home soon. This is a way to give them freedom while still under your roof (and nose, I might add). Here you'll be taking an entirely different approach. The setup will be, for the most part, teenager-inspired.

Let them try out their organizing and setup skills with these new additions, but be waiting in the wings in case they ask for adult input. (Highly unlikely, but possible.)

Let them learn the hard lessons about cleaning, organizing, and the repercussions of a lack thereof under your parental protection. Occasionally, you'll be called on to teach them a few good lessons about responsibility and cleanliness (a relative term when used in the context of the teenage years). But resist the urge to "surprise" a gradeschooler, tween, or teen by organizing his or her room yourself. Instead, always get their input and, most importantly, their participation. A clean, organized life does, after all, start in a small place—the bedroom.

FAMILY PICKUP LINES

CRANK UP THE CLEANING   Let your kids boogie-clean their rooms to their tunes of choice. Grab your earplugs if needed. It's worth it to get them to clean their room.

A few ways to inspire a teen to get organized are to give them cool containers to put their belongings in, allow them a budget to organize and decorate their rooms, or invest in under-bed storage boxes to make cleanup easier.

parents

Well, finally. Time for us. Adult bedrooms have built-in problems. Mainly, that we do just about everything in there nowadays. We work there, chat on the phone to friends, make lists, watch TV, and work on the laptop. Some of us even exercise there. And some of us eat and drink there. (Shhh! Don't tell the kids!)

Oh, yeah, some of us sleep there, too.

Like the kids' rooms, we'll tackle this one by thinking first about what we use the room for before we set it up. Which brings us to what every bedroom needs:

• A bed. (Didn't want to start out too esoteric here!)

- A bedside table. (If you don't have one, I'll bet you have a big messy pile beside the bed. Think outside the box here. An oversize terra-cotta pot with a glass top makes a creative table.)

- Essential bedside accessories such as a reading light, an alarm clock, a container for jewelry and/or reading glasses, room for a water bottle or glass, tissues, an emery board, a notepad, a pen, and a flashlight.

- A full-length mirror.

- A dresser or bureau with drawers. (Make good use of these stuff-holders. Put the things you use daily inside. If you get up earlier than your spouse, you may actually want a dresser with undergarments, sweaters, etc. in the other room so you don't disturb him or her by turning on the bedroom light to hunt for your stuff.)

- Valet. (This could come in handy if you have a spouse who just refuses to hang things up—it's a great Father's Day gift idea.)

To make your room a reflection of the inhabitants inside, fill it with items reflecting your interests, passions, and

Ah, here's a parent's haven: clean *and* serene. Good planning pays off again.

tastes. A wall with family photographs framed in different sizes and shapes bespeaks your interest in, joy from, and love of family. A vase with a trio of roses from your garden evokes the simplicity of nature and your spouse's passion for gardening.

Reflect your passion for romance by creating candle groupings around the room. Scented candles can emit a relaxing aroma such as vanilla or rose by day, and at night, they reflect your passion for, well, your kids' dad. Or Mom.

Amidst all this beauty, you can hide some serious functionality. A bed skirt is the perfect disguise for that under-the-bed storage area. A skirted table topped with candles and freshly arranged birds of paradise is the perfect hideaway for that

oversize hat box you can't quite squeeze into any drawer or nook. Or that old collection of photographs you're meaning to cull before your child gets to college.

And since one of life's greatest pleasures is arguably a good night's sleep, make sure you set the stage for bedded bliss. Change sheets and blankets to fit the season. Use cool cotton for summer and cozy flannel for winter so you won't wake up shivering or in a sweat. Top with an all-season down comforter that you can make fresh each season by changing the duvet cover. Just make sure it's machine-washable, light, breathable, and long enough so that it extends at least a foot on each side of the mattress.

In the morning, let the sun shine in—unless you'd like to sleep past dawn, that

---

BEDROOM CHORES BY AGE— FOR PARENTS

Aha! This is the one place in the book where you'll find more parents' chores than kids' chores since we're talking about your room!

Daily Parents' Chores

- Make your bed
- Put dirty clothes in the hamper
- Declutter once a day to get rid of newspapers, magazines, etc.
- Get your spouse in on the act. You're not his maid (or his mom) either

Weekly Parents' Chores

- Vacuum the carpet and/or dust-mop the floor
- Change the linens
- Dust-bust surfaces, including your night stands, electronics, picture frames, and windowsills
- Disinfect doorknobs, telephones, and light switches. Give the ole TV remote a quick rub-down, too
- Empty the wastebasket

    Most of all, use your bedroom as a model for your kids' rooms. The best way to teach kids good housekeeping habits is to be tidy yourself—not to pick up after them.

is. In that case, drape your windows with shades, blinds, or simple fabric curtains so you're in control of the wake-up call.

cleaning with kids: the bedroom

It may feel like a constant battle to keep your kids' bedrooms clean. Why not just give up and close the door? Because the habits you're instilling now will serve them well as they go on in life. Here's how to make cleaning bedrooms with kids a bit less painful for everyone.

Especially when it comes to their rooms, kids need to know exactly what we mean by "clean." What is a clean bedroom? Not a speck of dust? Toys and clothes put away? A clear walkway? Write it down, in checklist form, so kids can easily succeed by meeting your expectations. What exactly do you expect? And how often do you expect it?

The actual cleaning of bedrooms is very similar to the types of chores I discussed in chapter 6. Your bedrooms probably have wooden furniture (See "Wood Furniture" on page 122), carpets (See "Carpets" on page 126), or hardwood floors (See "Hardwood" on page 129).

Not only do you need to spell each chore out for your kids, but you'll also have to motivate them to actually get moving on the chore. For little ones the promise of a game of Candy Land with Mommy or a bike ride around the cul-de-sac with Daddy might be all the prodding you'll need to do to get the little one to get that big-boy job done.

Where tweens are concerned, you can take stronger action. If stuff is on the floor, take control. I know one mom who got angry and packed away her kid's American Girl doll collection after

DIRTY LITTLE SECRETS

MATTRESSES   Here's how to keep your mattresses clean:

- Keep mattresses covered with a dust-barrier cover to protect them from stains, soil, and even pests.
- Turn the mattress over seasonally to keep the wear even.
- Vacuum the mattress and box springs monthly to remove surface dust.
- Treat stains quickly by cleaning with dry suds. Make suds by beating mild detergent in warm water, using an eggbeater. (Really.) Skim the suds off the top and discard the soapy water. Apply the dry suds to a small area at a time using a soft sponge. Wipe the spot clean with a damp (not wet) sponge. Avoid getting the mattress padding wet. Allow the mattress to air-dry, or use a hair dryer to speed up the process.

BEDROOM CHORES BY AGE

Here's a list of which tasks kids can generally do by which age. Once a child reaches a certain skill or age level, he can generally do the chores for his age group and those for the age groups below. Of course, some of these chores need to be done each day, others once a week, and still others once a month or even less frequently. Use your best judgment for what gets done when, and see "Mrs. Clean Jeans' Housekeeping Routine" on page 253 for guidelines.

AGES 2 AND UNDER:
- Put toys in bins or drawers
- Help pick up stray books and magazines
- Put dirty clothes in hamper if the top is low enough

AGES 3 TO 5:
- Previous chores, plus:
- Pull comforter over bed
- Return CDs, DVDs, and videocassettes to their cases
- Put toys and games and all their pieces in the proper boxes or bins
- Return books to bookshelves
- Sponge down the play table
- Take clean, folded clothes to his or her room
- Dust low furniture
- Wash or spot-clean baseboards
- Air-dry throw pillows in dryer

AGES 6 TO 9:
- Previous chores, plus:
- Make the bed
- Tidy bedroom
- Shake area rugs, depending on size
- Vacuum, with help depending on the machine's height and weight

- Empty and wipe wastebaskets clean, using disinfecting wipes
- Dust furniture and shelves
- Dust lamp shades
- Wipe smudges from walls and doors

AGES 10 TO 13:
- Previous chores, plus:
- Clean telephones, computer and TV screens, video-game controllers, and remote controls
- Change bed linens
- Clean the bedroom
- Vacuum floors and carpets
- Clean bedroom closets
- Disinfect light switches and doorknobs
- Vacuum furniture
- Clean windows
- Clean blinds
- Wash windows and wipe light fixtures
- Wash washable curtains

AGES 14 TO 17:
- Previous chores, plus:
- Organize closets
- Dust ceiling fan
- Clean lights and light fixtures
- Turn mattresses
- Vacuum drapes
- Dust and vacuum corners and crevices from high point to low
- Wash and polish wood furniture
- Vacuum floors and carpets and move furniture to clean underneath
- Remove dust ruffles from beds to wash or dry-clean
- Deep-clean carpet and upholstery (Teens can make the call to the carpet cleaner for you.)
- Turn mattresses

say adieu to allergens

The bedroom is a dust mite's home base, thanks to the proliferation of shed skin. Whether you notice it or not, your skin flakes, and that produces a mite's favorite meal. Be especially diligent here:

- Remove carpeting if asthma or dust allergies are severe.
- Dust frequently with a damp cloth or furniture-dusting product.
- Vacuum weekly using a double-bagged, HEPA-filtered vacuum cleaner.
- Launder curtains regularly; or better yet, replace curtains with shades. Avoid blinds—they're dust magnets.
- Get rid of dust collectors such as magazines, knickknacks, and stuffed animals, or store them in closed boxes or cloth bags.
- Keep the closet door closed.
- Store shoes, belts, and other small items in boxes, or keep them in cloth or canvas bags.
- Keep dressers and nightstands clear of clutter.
- Launder sheets and pillows weekly in warm water; tumble dry. Wash blankets, comforters, and mattress pads monthly.
- Vacuum both sides of the mattress for at least two minutes twice monthly to reduce the dust and allergens in the mattress.
- Keep furry or feathered pets out of the bedroom. If one takes a catnap on the bed, wash the bedding as soon as possible.

repeated infractions. Then the girl had to earn it back. For each clean-room week, she had one doll returned.

Here's an idea for teens. Make them sign a lease agreement! This could state how a room will be kept. If said teen violates the lease, no, you can't evict her, but you can yank a privilege or three. Or maybe have her pay "damages" out of her allowance.

Or try a credit-card approach. Tell your son you will give him a $30 credit card at the end of the month for his favorite store. The catch: For every day that his room is dirty (as defined in the lease) there will be a dollar deducted from the card. The beauty of this system is that you're going to spend at least $30 a month on your teen's wardrobe anyway. Why not make him work for it?

If all else fails, you can always close the bedroom door.

When it comes down to it, even though it's embedded in a mom's genes to want to simply clean a kid's room, you should try to resist the urge to do this essential chore for him or her. You're robbing your little angel of a life lesson she needs to learn.

Chapter 8

home work

LET'S FACE IT: *Everyone* really works at home. Kids do homework. Parents pay bills, manage their finances, juggle their schedules. And some people even run businesses from their homes.

Finding room for everyone to work at home (a place designed for, well, homier activities like sleeping and eating) can prove a daunting challenge indeed.

Take our home, for example. We need a cozy place for a 3-year-old to color and puzzle over puzzles that's within sight but outside the tripping hazard zone. We need a computer-equipped workstation that can be shared between tweens Chris and Lyndsay in a space-scrunched family room. And we need a safe place for Christopher and me to stash all our personal and business papers so they don't transform our bedroom into a boardroom.

So much for the computer's promise of simplifying our lives! Instead of needing less paper, it seems we are now actually downloading and printing *more* stuff to stash. While some things can arguably be stored safely on our home computers in lieu of traditional paper files, for others, we simply must have a hard copy. Like the family's birth certificates, car lease agreements, and some (but not all) monthly bills. (More on those in a bit.)

You get the picture. Paper is both a blessing and a curse, as is our ability to do just about anything, from paying bills online to researching homes for sale and everything in between, from the cozy confines of our homes. Sure, it saves time and money on fuel, but now we have the luxury of "working" around the clock. Hmmm . . . and this is really considered a good thing for our families? (We'll save that debate.)

Whether you use your home office daily for your job or just a few afternoons a week to pay bills online and send e-mails, there are four essentials for an efficient but comfy home office:

1. A private space.

2. Room for the basics (an ergonomic chair, computer, perhaps a fax machine, a printer), and room to grow.

3. A simple system for organizing paper (and e-mail) pileups.

4. Another, smaller home office for the kids so you can actually get stuff done in yours.

We'll also need to establish rules of the home office, such as: Who can use the office? Is it a no-man's land for kids? (Think so.) Of all the rooms in the house, this is one that should *not* be kid-friendly.

Finally, we'll need to know how to clean the new digs, 'cause this office doesn't come with a nightly cleaning crew. So knowing how to clean essentials like the computer and keyboard is a must.

a home for everything

In the best of all possible worlds, where should the home office go?

It's not a trick question. The answer is easy: Anyplace that meets the following needs is worthy of consideration:

- Heat and air

- Good lighting, preferably natural

- Storage options or room for storage options to be hauled in

- Phone line(s), computer hookup capability, and electrical outlets

Optimally, a home office would also be out of the way of the usual traffic patterns

CLEAN HOUSE RULES FOR HOME OFFICES

Some of these rules apply to kids, and others just to adults. Heed this advice to win the paperwork game.

For Kids:

1. Kids must be careful in the home office and respectful of the importance of the paperwork that's handled there.

2. No food or drink. (Computer keyboards are an expensive pain to replace.)

3. No roughhousing in this den of peaceful concentration.

4. No yakking on your phone.

5. No messing with stuff on the desk. Mom's stuff is private, too, Missy Tween.

6. No taking scissors, stapler, tape, or other office supplies out of the room without permission.

7. Return what you have taken—with permission—promptly.

8. No hanging out in the office unsupervised without permission.

For Adults:

1. Clean your desktop every night. Throw away what you don't need again. File what you do.

2. Label everything.

3. Clean out files at least every six months with the goal of tossing, tossing, tossing.

4. File bills by due date (at least a week before, to allow for mailing time).

5. Know your filing system, and use it.

6. Have one, or at the most two, notebooks in which you write all memos, phone calls, notes, and to-do lists.

after school, away from the kitchen (think fridge), and close to the bathroom.

a room of your own

The best-case scenario is a whole room, a spare bedroom, or an in-law unit. A separate room allows some privacy when needed, and if you're not a very tidy person, you can simply shut the door. With the addition of a Murphy bed or futon couch, the room can play double duty as a guest room, as well. If you run a business out of your home, however, the bedroom look will make meeting clients in your office less professional.

No extra rooms? What about the attic? Don't think cobwebs here; think of the attic garret that writers hang out in. Advantage: This lofty locale is definitely off the beaten path.

Attic-less? Okay, then think lower. The basement? The key here is that it be waterproof and finished. The rules of electricity, phone lines, and computer hookups still apply. As does the "let there be light" rule, unless you're going for the Dungeons & Dragons look. A basement with its own exit is an especially good choice if you get a few visitors now and then.

a corner office

Okay, so a separate room is a luxury that just isn't in the space budget right now. It's time, then, to consider getting yourself a corner office. As in a corner of the den, a bedroom, or the kitchen.

There are pros and cons to this room-within-a-room setup, of course. Let's start with the cons. It's tough to eke out adequate storage and be organized within the confines of a corner office. It's harder still to keep the kids out of your stuff when you can't close the door to keep interlopers out. Worse, you can't leave anything out on your desk to be tackled first thing in the morning. Chances are it won't be in the same place the next day. (If it's there at all.)

That said, now here are the pros! You don't tie up a whole room for home office matters. It's usually a cinch to nab a corner where you can work. All you need is a writing surface, a chair, and a light.

This illustration shows my idea of a great home office: inviting, open, and convenient.

An office that shares space in another room is a less great option. But here's one way you could organize a corner office.

Best of all, you can choose to be near the hub of the home and your family.

And if a corner just isn't sufficient? Bring in reinforcements, such as an office-in-an-armoire. This clever type of furniture keeps everything in one place, contained and safe, and it can be quickly closed so everything's out of sight when company comes.

outfitting your home office

Whether it's a palatial room all on its own or a corner of another room, here are some key items to gather for your home office.

the desk

Whether you have a separate surface or use the corner of a table, remember this: Bigger is better. So even if you are squeezing into a shared affair, define and claim as big a space as you can. Get rid of any shared items in this area, and consider setting up physical boundaries to define your home office area.

Not sharing spaces? Don't get sucked in by the home-trend hype when it comes to your work surface. Sure, all those cute little compartmentalized desks with pigeon holes look organized, but to actually *be* organized and on top of it all, you need space to spread out. Along the same lines, rolltop desks are cute, but cute doesn't cut it when you've got a family to organize and maintain. Stick to efficient. And look cute instead while you're doing it. Get a desk with a large workspace so you can spread out stacks of paper when needed. Two connecting 3-by-6-foot tables are great if you have the space. Arrange them perpendicular to each other with the printer in the middle.

the chair

Your home office chair is not to be confused with your kitchen chair. You'll be spending a good deal of time on your backside here, so you may as well be comfortable and ergonomically supported. Invest in a real office chair that you can adjust to a comfortable height. Dare the kids to mess with it.

the computer

What brand, how much memory, what chip? Your choice; I'm definitely not going there. You know your needs (if you don't, hire an expert to bring you up to speed on the latest software and hardware offerings on the market). Choose a system that works for both you and your family and has the capacity to grow with your family.

Laptop vs. desktop? If you're on the move, the kids are on the move, and you're a family that likes to be connected en route, a laptop is your best choice. We use ours constantly when traveling on family trips. We check weather and the opening time of our day's planned attractions, and we send wish-you-were-here (and the occasional be-glad-you're-not) e-mails to friends and family (especially Nana and Poppy in San Diego).

But instead, if you use your computer only at home for homework or occasional personal notes to friends and family, a traditional computer setup will work just fine for your family.

the connection

Opt for a broadband-type Internet connection if at all possible. Yes, they usually cost more. But if you can afford the few extra dollars, you'll agree that life really is too short to sit around waiting for the Abe Lincoln history page to load for your son's homework assignment or an image of your sister's kids to download. It's just good business not waste any more precious minutes than you absolutely have to in any office, including your home's.

To that end, you may want to invest in a system that networks the various computers in your home, allowing everyone to be online simultaneously. It has been a veritable godsend in our home. No more arguing about whose turn it is to be online or who gets to be next.

Each night, when my husband, Christopher, comes home, one of the first things he does (other than give kisses all around) is sink his laptop into the network hookup across the way from my computer in our home office. He immediately is online.

DIRTY LITTLE SECRETS

THE COMPUTER   The computer
gets just as dirty as anything else in the house.
Here's how to clean its various components:

THE MONITOR

Stop! I know what you're thinking. "What's the
big deal? Just spray it with window cleaner, right?"
Wrong, computer killer. Never spray anything
directly onto the monitor or screen. Some
spray will go through vents onto the circuit
boards. And circuit boards are very finicky
about being dropped in on by any liquid,
especially strong cleaners. Try this safer
method instead:

1. Turn off the computer. Don't just power
   down; turn it off at the switch.
2. Gently wipe the plastic casing with a cloth
   dampened with water and just a bit of
   dishwashing detergent.
3. Spray glass cleaner onto a lint-free cloth and
   then gently wipe the screen.
4. Never touch the back of the monitor.

THE MOUSE

Every time you roll the mouse, you are rolling
grease, dirt, and gunk into its innards. About
once a month, you need to clean it to keep it
rolling along. Here's how:

1. Unplug the mouse from the computer.
2. Open the back and remove the ball.
3. Clean the ball with a damp cloth, and let it dry.
4. Gently clean the inside with a cotton swab
   moistened with rubbing alcohol.
5. Blow in compressed air to dry.

THE KEYBOARD

Science can't explain it, but soft drinks,
crumbs, and coffee are undeniably attracted to
computer keyboards. Put them and a kid or
three in proximity, and they're bound to
interact messily sooner or later. Here's how to
clean up the inevitable mess when it happens:

1. Unplug the keyboard.
2. If liquid is spilled, turn the keyboard over
   and let it drain and dry for at least 24 hours.
   If the spill was a sticky drink—a cola or a
   latte, perhaps—try prying the small key caps
   off of the keyboard with a flat-head
   screwdriver to get better access to the mess.
3. Take a picture of the keyboard layout, or
   make a quick sketch of it before you remove
   any keys so you can put them back where
   you found them. Don't remove the spacebar,
   the Enter key, or other large key caps,
   however.
4. Gently clean the keyboard with a wet cotton
   swab. Gently pry off really grimy gunk with a
   cotton swab dipped in rubbing alcohol.
5. Rinse the key caps thoroughly, and allow
   them to air-dry.
6. Replace the key caps.
7. Let everything dry for at least 24 hours
   before plugging the keyboard back in.

Before bed, you'll often find at least three Aronsons online accomplishing a variety of things: Christopher's checking how a recent film's box office numbers are faring through the evening, Lyndsay's instant-messaging her classmates about the newest Hilary Duff song, and I'm banking online, trying to figure out if Chris's team uniform check has cleared.

acing e-mail

Save time and your sanity by setting up your e-mail to make life simpler. It's easy if you take a few moments to set up some simple systems.

Create separate addresses. You've got separate e-mail addresses for your kids, of course. So why not give yourself separate e-mail addresses for your business and pleasure? That way, when you have a minute to attend to business details, you know just where to go without having to filter through non-business communiqués.

Stop junk. Use your junk e-mail filter and block pop-ups features. You'll save precious minutes not having to delete obnoxious e-mail and close annoying pop-up windows. Not to mention what it will do to lighten your mood.

Stay healthy. Purchase antivirus software and keep it up to date to catch and quarantine the latest e-mail viruses.

the phone

If you really are running a business at home, it's essential to have separate phone lines for it and for your family. (And don't let your 5-year-old record your greeting, unless your business caters to 5-year-olds.)

You also need a separate line for a modem or dial-up computer connection if you use your computer more than an hour or so a week. (Unless you're on in the wee hours of the morning when no one would be calling anyway.) At the very least, if you are using your home phone line for the computer, set up an answering program to field incoming calls. Please.

I have one family member (who shall remain nameless) who often logs onto her (that's a clue, though) computer for hours during the day, leaving callers to wait while endless ringing continues and we finally hang up in frustration. With no way to leave a message, this system leaves plenty to be desired on both ends. For the oblivious home-computer user, an emergency call can go unreceived; for the caller, a loving sentiment or kind word goes unshared.

A second line is worth the few extra dollars a month. Really.

DIRTY LITTLE SECRETS

THE PHONE
A neighbor kid just sniffled his way to your phone to call home. Now what? Wipe the ear- and mouthpiece clean with either a disposable antibacterial wipe or a paper towel dipped in rubbing alcohol. Wipe the phone dry with a clean paper towel or allow it to air-dry. Bye-bye bugs!

Also, if you share a phone with the rest of the family, get voice mail instead of the recorder that blurts the message out for all to hear and can't record when you're on the phone. Along the same lines, call waiting is good just to alert you that there's a call on voice mail when you hang up. But please, don't be rude and switch over unless you're talking to your mother-in-law and you're expecting the school nurse to call.

Finally, if you spend that much time on the phone, a hands-free telephone headset is a must.

the copier/fax/ printer/scanner

I remember when I bought my four-in-one machine after my beloved and well-used seven-year-old printer crashed and burned a few years back. It was one of those where you had to feed in a page to be printed. That's it. I had a separate fax machine, longed for a copier, and dreamed of a scanner in my future.

These were not idle lusts, mind you. I often found myself rushing to the local grocery store late at night or early in the morning to do such mundane (and outrageously expensive) tasks as copying my driver's license for a school field trip form, a birth certificate for a passport application, photos for the kids to use in classroom collages . . . you get the picture. And so did I. But husband Christopher didn't. After chastising me for getting a bigger, more expensive unit, he needed to

photocopy a check the very next day. Wasn't he glad I'd opted for a more business-like approach to running our family? Yeah, right. This is real life. He still grumbled about the bill, all right, but he couldn't argue about the machine's essential role in taking care of our family business.

He's clearly come around. Today, Christopher has his own four-in-one machine, a lot fancier than mine, for his work-from-home stuff. 'Nuff said.

paper storage

Hang it, put it in a drawer, floor-store it, or shelve it. Those are your four options for storing all your stuff, your family's stuff, the work stuff, the home stuff, and the school stuff. No matter what you choose, or if you choose to use a combination of all of these, make sure important papers are stored together in a way that you can find what you're looking for when you simply must have it, like at tax time.

It doesn't have to be fancy. Even a shoebox for each month (filled with receipts and bills paid) that's stashed on a shelf can do the job. Group important like items such as medical information and insurance claims together in one place. (We'll talk more about paper storage on page 166.)

in 'n' out system

You'll need one to keep your sanity. In the "in" box go mail, school stuff that needs your attention or signature, and today's mail. In the "out" box go items for the kids' backpacks and outgoing mail.

The other part of the system is for pending work. On my desk are two standing file holders: one for stories I'm writing or researching and the other for personal stuff. In that one, you'll find folders for Lyndsay's dance and theatre school, summer camp, Chris's baseball league, and Payne's preschool class. Anything related to the kids' daily school or social lives resides here. These are neat tools that, when used judiciously (two or three are plenty) provide the intended goal of having everything literally at your fingertips when the phone rings and you've got a carpool to sort out.

Suffice it to say that, in today's world, we can take care of so much of today's life business at home if we set ourselves up with the basic business systems and essentials. Not to mention the time, effort, and cash we save in not having to rush out to the closest copy store at 9 P.M. to copy a book page your kid needs for his homework or send a desperate fax requesting a copy of your paid invoice.

the walls

Just look at all that untapped vertical space! Let your home office walls do double duty! I had blank wall space and a box of pictures. The solution to my less-than-homey new home office and my favorite but undisplayed pics of family and friends? Corkboard. I had pieces cut to fit the area between my desktop and the cabinet shelves above. Today, I keep my favorite friends and family within eyesight, and my home office area feels much more homey. In a pinch, bulletin boards hung end-to-end work well, too.

tips for setting up your home office

Want your home work to run like clockwork? Here's how to set yourself up right:

Keep organized. I have one notebook that I use for to-do lists and a second for everything else. These two notebooks keep me straight. The key is that I write everything in them, rather than tiny pieces of information on tiny pieces of paper. Try it! This way, no slips of paper are lost. No phone numbers are misplaced. You don't have to tear up the house looking for the napkin with the contractor's name on it. All you have to do to find a message is think, "Hmmm. I talked to them sometime last September." Then you just flip back to the pages you wrote in last September. Low-tech? You bet. Efficient? Absolutely.

When you finish a notebook, place it in the box with the dates clearly labeled on the front. Keep it for reference. You'll need it. About once a week, really try to transfer the phone numbers to your directory and the dates to the family calendar.

Give everything its own space. Think drawers, trays, file holders, and bins. Keep things nearby—but not necessarily on—

your desktop. Your goal, should you choose to accept it, is to keep 75 percent of your desktop visible at all times.

Make sure everything is at arm's length. Here's where the "near" comes in. You shouldn't have to get up to get your files, your fax, or your phone.

Store supplies that you use together, in the same place. Keep stamps, a pen that actually writes, a calculator, and envelopes together so bill time's a breeze (or at least as much of a breeze as bill time can be).

Pens, pencils, and highlighters are among the assorted essentials that need a home spot in your home office. A cute mug with your kid's baseball picture works great; a drawer will do in a pinch. Other essential stuff to stash in a supplies drawer or in a single box for easy grabbing includes staplers, tape, paper cutters, a hole punch, stamps, and thumbtacks. The bottom line: Group 'em so you can grab 'em in a pinch. (While we're talking about office supplies, choose staples over paper clips. Clips get caught on other papers and come apart more easily. Just keep a staple-remover handy.)

Save time searching through drawers by storing as many items as possible in clear containers.

Create a place for everything, and return everything to its place. If you're short on space, store supplies and less-used items in a closet or in another part of your home.

Throw out what you can. Ditch yesterday's news and last month's

magazines. Okay, so you won't read a newspaper from three days ago, why on earth are you keeping months-old magazines around? If you're saving a magazine for a reason—an article you want to clip out, say—clip it out and recycle the rest. Forget about using those old rags as a "reference." Chances are, if the time rolls around when you actually need it, you'll forget that the items are there. Instead, clip items you'd like to keep right away, and you'll have room for all the new mags that arrive daily in your mailbox.

Be prepared for a disaster. Then it won't happen, of course. But if it does, you'll be prepared. Regularly back up critical computer files on a removable, recordable compact disk (CD-R) or other safe format. Purchase—and use—a power surge protector for your computer and all your electronic items.

Get organized electronically. All those PDAs you're hearing about are popular for a reason! A handheld device can carry more information than you ever could. It can replace your date book, your address book, and even your calculator. Some even have Internet capability. I have one. I fought against them, too, but then I tried one. Today, I have a master schedule on my computer and a portable device I carry with me everywhere so I can arrange play dates and orthodontist appointments and even keep in touch with an old friend or two in Boston and Denver. Two big benefits: No more scratched-out names and addresses in a book too big to lug around in most handbags, and there's a full backup should the portable information ever get misplaced.

tips for small spaces

When space is at a premium, your organization of it needs to be, too. If you've got a cramped office, it's time to get creative and think outside the box. Maximize your floor space by not putting your desk in the traditional place, up against the wall. Instead, consider putting it in the middle of the room or perpendicular to the wall. Do have it facing the door, however, so you can greet visitors without a jump.

To make the most of your limited wall space, get one tall file holder instead of a couple of two-drawer models. Use leftover wall space for shelves. I started with just file drawers in our home office a few years ago. That idea lasted about a day. Once I began filing our myriad papers, I realized quickly that leaving the walls out of the storage and organizing routine wasn't going to cut it.

I chose cabinets with shelves, mostly so I could use the space to tuck away the more unruly stuff: odd-size books, phone books, papers and miscellany from my father's estate, a box of printed envelopes for work correspondence, etc. But to soften the office feel in our bedroom, I chose to confine some of the clunkier items in wicker baskets and even a hatbox. Whatever I have around that's big enough

to hold things inside is fair game for dual use in my house.

You may want to have a wall of deep shelving for such things as phone books and boxes of printer paper. I use my covered shelving for storing those items, too. But in a pinch, these are things you can retrieve from the basement or garage when needed. So stash the overflow in a nearby closet (or even one that's not so close). Just don't seriously attempt to get any work done when you're having to dodge file shelves and step over stationery supplies and phone books to get to your seat or sort through a mishmash of mail, bills, and letters from school and the softball team on your obscured desktop.

If you need more drawer space, however, there's at least one item that might be worth maneuvering around in your office: an inexpensive rolling cart that you can stash under your desk. Ditto for your files: If you're plumb out of options, a rolling cart for your files can be stashed out of sight in your closet when company comes, then rolled out to the home office when you're ready to conquer the world.

painless paperwork

Ah, the dreaded paper chase. Yes, the race is on at home, too. But you can win the marathon if you're armed with the latest paper-training techniques. No coach required.

You may wonder, why keep records at all? Well, there's the little consideration of being prepared for tax time, for starters. You're not given an option from Uncle Sam in this regard. If the Internal Revenue Service has a question about an item on your family's tax return, you must be prepared to answer it. This means keeping records or "proof."

In addition, you'll often need records for insurance purposes or for getting a loan. Good records will help you identify income sources if your family receives money or property from a variety of sources, such as a family trust. Organizing expenses will help you identify which expenses you might be able to claim as a deduction. Property records have important details like the original cost, and they verify any improvements you have made.

New Year? New Files! As a general rule, get a jump on the paper chase by beginning new folders each year and archiving the past year's folders.

For most families, there are four types of paperwork to be culled and considered. (Make that five, if you run a home business.) You'll need to create a separate filing system or area for each. It can be as simple as assigning each paperwork type its own unique color. You could use green for financial, for example, and red for household. Here are the major categories to be conquered, and how to organize them.

computer rules for kids

There have to be rules for computer use. So be sure to consider how much time you think is reasonable for your kid to spend playing games or sending e-mails on the computer. The amount of time will vary by family, by school workload, and by a kid's demonstrated trustworthiness. Here are some other rules you might consider adopting:

- Don't forward long joke lists.
- Don't call up attachments: none. (Kids have no reason to send attachments. In my house, this is punishable by a week of no e-mails.)
- No visiting chat rooms of any kind.
- No conversing with people you don't know.
- Never give out your phone number or address online to anyone you *do* know, either. (Who knows who's watching in cyberspace? Assume nothing's private.)
- No ordering anything. Not even "free" stuff.
- No visiting adult sites on home computers or anywhere else. (Set the computer controls so this isn't even a possibility.)

Ask kids to alert you immediately if they see anything fishy, or if something that they don't understand happens online. Pop in frequently and look over their shoulders. Nothing hulk-like, just a friendly visit. "Need any help researching that state bird?"

financial papers

Here's what you need in your financial files:

Financial cheat sheet. This is a guide to all your papers, financial advisers, documents, location of safe deposit box key, and other information. It should include copies of what's in the safe deposit box, and what to do—and who to contact first—in case of emergency. If anything happens to you (or the bill payer), this document can help the surviving spouse through the first few days.

Safe deposit box or fireproof strongbox. What goes in here? Anything extremely important that would be very difficult to replace. Usually the list includes titles; birth, death, and marriage certificates; copies of wills and deeds; inventory tapes of household goods for insurance purposes; and passports.

Bank and credit card statement folders. Easy, right?

Bill folders. Title this so that you can get what you need, fast. I name files in a way that makes sense to me and would (hopefully) to anyone else on the prowl for them. For example, although our gas bill payment goes to "Southern California Gas Company," I file the gas bills under "G" in a file tagged "Gas Company" instead of "S" for "Southern."

Credit card list. Compile a full list of the names and numbers of each credit card in the family. (This includes bank card numbers.) Include the toll-free numbers for reporting loss or theft of said cards.

Credit card receipt catcher. Reserve a folder, envelope, drawer, or other dumping ground for family credit card receipts and online order confirmations.

Estate planning folder. Even if you're just planning to plan your estate, you've got a place to file the information.

Investment folders. In these folders, store information on stocks, bonds, and mutual funds. Your records should show the purchase price, sales price, and commissions. They may also show any reinvested dividends, stock splits and dividends, load charges, and original issue discount.

Life insurance policies folder. Store life insurance papers here, or you can put these important papers in your safe deposit box or strongbox.

Loan and mortgage folder. File these papers by bank or lending institution name or simply under "Home Mortgage."

Major expenditure receipt folder. You'll want to put the purchase information for your new Sub Zero fridge and other expensive belongings here.

Pay stub folder or envelope. Each pay period, stash your stub.

Tax records folder. Anything you'll definitely be using on your income tax return should go here.

Work benefits folder. Just in case you're having trouble sleeping some night and are desperate for something to read, put all those work benefits documents here.

And a word for the tech-savvy: If you already have many of these "papers" stored on a computer program, bravo! You've saved yourself some serious file space. But you're not out of the woods when it comes to a few specific papers you'll need to keep in your possession, anyway, such as proof of payment, receipts, and deeds.

And just how long should you keep most of these papers? The Internal Revenue Service (IRS) has a three-year statute of limitations on auditing a return. Keep all records of income or deduction expense for three years. If you failed to report more than 25 percent of your gross income, the government will have six years to collect the tax or start legal proceedings. Filing a fraudulent return or failing to file a return eliminates any statute of limitations for an audit by the IRS. If you hire a tax specialist, check to see how many years you should keep your records. You may have to keep them—period.

You'll also want to keep records that show the original cost or value of your property. Also keep a record of home improvement costs to offset and/or reduce capital gains tax if your home, land, or property is ever sold for more than its original cost or value.

However, your insurance company or creditors may require you keep certain records longer. And, of course, keep records relating to property until the period of limitations expires for the year in which you sell or otherwise dispose of the property.

Of course, that's easy enough to say, but hard for some of us to do. Take my husband, for example. When we got married, he carted into our new condo box after box of phone bills, cellular phone bills, and electric bills. Some dated back more than ten years.

Thankfully, sheer space constraints, coupled with a few subtle hints from his bride that he might just be overdoing this being fiscally responsible thing a tad, led him to give those dusty papers a second life in a recycling center.

home papers

Here's what should be in your home files:

Household papers cheat sheet. This sheet can be on the computer or in a file. It's a guide to the household paperwork.

Car maintenance records. Use this to hold permits, 20,000 mile service receipts, etc.

Home maintenance records. With these records, you'll know the last time you serviced the air conditioner or had the heating vents vacuumed.

Home repairs file. This includes the names and numbers of repair people, contractors, window washers, etc.

Inventory of household goods. This is for insurance purposes. Some people even

GET REWARDED FOR YOUR GOOD DEEDS Did the April 15 tax filing bite harder than usual this year? Make sure you're being rewarded for your good deeds, and maybe next year will be gentler. Put a small notebook and an envelope in the pocket of your car door. Every time you volunteer for something at your kid's school or at any nonprofit organization, write down your expenses, and put any receipts in the envelope. Your volunteer hours aren't deductible, but your related out-of-pocket expenses are, including mileage, long-distance phone calls, office supplies, and tolls.

make a video of their home and its contents in case of an earthquake, fire, tornado, or some other act of God. A copy should go in the safe deposit box.

Owner's manuals. This file includes directions and receipts.

What's where list. This is your locator list for what's stored in the attic, the basement, the garage, the storage unit, etc.

family papers

Your family files should contain all of these categories. Organize your must-haves in a way that makes them easy for you to grab when you're trying to, say,

reconcile your daughter's orthodontic bills with the insurance coverage statements. Here's a look at what to store and how to keep all the essential papers at your fingertips:

Babysitter file. Here's the place to keep notes and numbers on your favorite sitters, who's in high school, who's in college, their driver's license numbers if they're driving your kids anywhere, and other pertinent information.

Card occasion list. Keep a list of important occasions here, and put the date on the calendar as well. As you see just the right card throughout the year, keep it here and you're be ready when the date sneaks up on you. Be sure to stash some belated greetings as well, just in case.

Clipped coupons. Limit these. Otherwise, they'll take over your home. Use your supermarket club card instead. Only save coupons for the big-ticket items, like 20 percent off kids' clothes for Labor Day at your favorite department store.

Correspondence. Your cards and letters go here.

House sitter/petsitter file. Store recent bills, brochures, recommendations by friends, etc., here.

Medical and dental records. File these by family member.

Pet records. File these by pet, naturally.

School records. File these by family member.

leisure papers

These are the papers associated with hobbies, interests, and travel:

Activity files. For kids, you need a folder for each activity they're involved in that includes the coach's name and phone number and the phone numbers of other families involved. You can also include costs, equipment lists, schedules, and volunteer duties.

Club membership papers. This includes activities and calendars.

Christmas list. I keep ours on the computer, but I also have a paper copy in our Christmas file. I try to update new addresses throughout the year, so when December rolls around, it doesn't take me days to have a workable mailing list for our cards.

Day-trip ideas. As I read about a new museum or park opening or a neat story about a funky place to Rollerblade with the kids, out of the paper it goes and into the day-trip file. It comes in handy when summer rolls around.

Decorating ideas. Nothing fancy here, just tear sheets for me. While flipping through a magazine, I'll tear out photos of rooms or fabrics that appeal. When the day comes that I can totally redecorate, I'll have a wealth of ideas to cull from.

Dining details. If your I've-got-20-minutes-for-dinner routine is limited to calling for pizza delivery, you need to expand your dining horizons file.

Hobbies. If you show your dog, there are papers for that. If you golf, have a file of courses you frequent and their fees and tips, and maybe even a few scorecards from enjoyable rounds with golf buddies. Maybe golf courses you'd like to travel to.

Maps and directions. This is where to stash directions and maps to places you frequent, just not very often.

Movie reviews. In our house, movies are king, so we keep up on these regal opening words by clipping from the newspaper or downloading the latest dish from the Internet.

Sports files. Store sports tickets themselves, as well as paperwork such as parking passes and stadium directions, here.

Summer camps and activities. I create files by year and begin filing them in January. It seems that just about every club, organization, or school has some special offering over the summer. I keep them all together until it's time to send in confirmations. Then, with the kids, Christopher and I review all the offerings (and our budget) and get the applications in for our favorites, on time.

Travel file. This would include places you'd like to go as well as your latest frequent flier miles statement, hotel cards, and rental car coupons. Stash here anything you need or may need to refer to when you're ready to plan—or take—a trip.

Upcoming events. Keep postcards and brochures on concerts, plays, and festivals you'd like to talk over with the family (and possibly attend) here.

Wish lists. This can be for kids as well as the grownups in the house. For example, it could include a wish list of golf equipment that you can hand out to the family at birthdays and Christmas, perhaps, or something to give grandma when a birthday is coming up. Have the kids write down what they can't live without the next time they're begging you to buy them something. Then file it away for someone's future reference.

Party ideas. After noticing that I was reading great party tips and techniques, but always at times when a birthday party or barbecue wasn't in our near future, I began cutting the great ideas out and filing them in a party file. That way, when birthdays roll around, I'm not searching alien Internet sites looking for some novel ideas for a Buzz Lightyear birthday bash.

As you can see, that's a lot of paper. Some of it is stored in the computer. To make sure that you can find stuff once you enter it into the computer, set up your computer files like you do your paper files. Start with the main folder labeled "My Documents." Then break down the information into four folders for different categories (five if your kid shares your computer). Then make any sub-folders as needed. If you don't do it in an orderly fashion, your computer will be unnavigable. Trust me.

homework central

Yes, it may be your home office, but you'll likely be sharing it with your kids. Kids have paperwork, too. Tons of it. And they need their own desks, computers, and files so they can keep track of their own stuff, too (with your setup help, of course).

Yes, I did say to keep the kids out of your office. But that's not always possible, is it? Sometimes kids share the computer. Sometime I have to watch little Payne while I (try to) work. Sometimes the kids just want to ask a question or visit for a few minutes when they get home from school. My door is always open, deadlines be damned! If it weren't for my distractions (I mean kids), I wouldn't be writing this anyway.

Remember you're a mom first, a worker second. Stay up late to finish up what needs finishing. Whatever it takes to keep your priorities straight and make time for the kids. Consider it a homework pass. Speaking of homework, that's very likely what your kids will need to share your office for.

Best-case scenario: Your kid has her own desk complete with computer and chair in her own room. That computer is networked to mom's computer and printer downstairs. The family has broadband so more than one computer can be online at a time. This is the picture of 21st century homework bliss.

If you're not living best-case scenario, there are a few easy ways to make do. You could place a kid-size desk in the office or kitchen. Or share your desk with the kids but give them their own rolling carts, drawers, or bookcases. Or you could designate one spot in the house for each kid's study hall. It should be in a quiet corner far from distractions. A friend's daughter likes to study at the kitchen counter while Mom cooks. Another child works at the dining room table. Wherever a child studies, she will need a large, flat surface and good lighting. Make sure she also has the tools of the trade. Keep a drawer or basket of school supplies nearby so she doesn't have to jump up and down every time she needs to erase or staple something. She will also need a file drawer or bucket to file papers or ongoing projects. Older kids will need access to a computer, too.

Whichever location you choose, here's how to transform it into a kids' homework station.

Start by setting up a file system for various subjects. Per child. You'll need to set aside a file cabinet or box for each child's use. If you're sharing homework spaces with your kids, this is the perfect time to bring home those cute home-office portables you see in

Here's an example of a homework station. Make sure the furniture is kid-height and the storage and accessories are kid-friendly.

mom's magic homework project basket

Here's the answer to the "But Mom, it's due tomorrow!" demand. This is a cleaning caddy chock-full of all those items I used to have to dash to the store for: posterboard, glue, sequins, fabric swatches, permanent markers in several colors, pipe cleaners, and a zippered plastic bag filled with aquarium leftovers and other glueable figurines.

the home décor mags. The rattan-lidded file box. The everything basket.

Next, outfit the desk with necessary homework tools. This will vary by your child's age, grade, and the subjects he's studying this school year. But the basics include pens, pencils, highlighters, erasers, tape, stapler, and probably a hole punch.

Create a bookshelf reference library with resource books and current texts. To cut down on back strain, consider buying a duplicate set of texts at the beginning of each year. I'm doing it for Chris and Lyndsay for the first time this year. Seeing them lugging bulging backpacks that they can barely pick up, let alone carry, has convinced me that it's a cost-effective

alternative to corrective surgery. I'm going to try to keep the kids from writing in the books I buy, and perhaps sell them to the next grade. We'll see how that goes.

I've gotten out of the silly habit of tossing shoeboxes. They're now beneath our bed awaiting new life as a class project or diorama. As for the odd-size posterboard: I stash the blue, white, and red paper behind our tall bookshelves in the living room.

cleaning with kids: home offices

Your home office probably is 75 percent for you and only 25 percent for your kids. But still, they should pitch in to help clean—after all, you help them with their rooms, I'll bet.

Not surprisingly, the actual cleaning of home offices is very similar to the chores you'd do for your living and family rooms. I discussed these in chapter 6. Your office may have wooden furniture (see "Wood Furniture" on page 122), carpets (see "Carpets" on page 126), and maybe hardwood floors (see "Hardwood" on page 129).

Next, we'll move on to a particularly challenging area of the house to keep clean: the garage.

OFFICE CHORES BY AGE

Here's a guide to which chores kids can do at what ages in the home office. Once a child reaches a certain skill or age level, he can generally do the chores for his age group and those for the age groups below. Of course, some of these chores need to be done each day, others once a week, and still others once a month or even less frequently. Use your best judgment for what gets done when, and see "Mrs. Clean Jeans' Housekeeping Routine" on page 253 for guidelines.

AGES 2 AND UNDER:
- Put toys in bins or drawers
- Help pick up stray books and magazines

AGES 3 TO 5:
- Previous chores, plus:
- Return books to bookshelves
- Put toys and games (and all their pieces) in the proper boxes or bins
- Dust low furniture
- Help prepare papers for recycling
- Wash or spot-clean baseboards

AGES 6 TO 9:
- Previous chores, plus:
- Take out trash and recycling
- Vacuum, with help depending on the machine's height and weight
- Empty and wipe wastebaskets clean, using disinfecting wipes

- Dust furniture and shelves
- Dust lamp shades
- Wipe smudges from walls and doors

AGES 10 TO 13:
- Previous chores, plus:
- Clean telephones, computer and TV screens, video game controllers, and remote controls
- Vacuum floors and carpets
- Disinfect light switches and doorknobs
- Vacuum furniture
- Wipe leather furniture with a soft cloth
- Clean windows
- Clean blinds
- Wash screens and miniblinds
- Wash windows and wipe light fixtures
- Wash washable curtains

AGES 14 TO 17:
- Previous chores, plus:
- Organize closets
- Dust ceiling fan
- Clean lights and light fixtures
- Deep-clean carpet and upholstery (Teens can make the call to the carpet cleaner for you.)
- Wash and polish wood furniture
- Dust and vacuum corners and crevices from high point to low
- Vacuum floors and carpet and move furniture to clean underneath
- Vacuum drapes

Chapter 9

grungy garages no more

FAMILY HOUSEWORK, of course, does not stop at the house. You have to get *in* the house, right? Many families have garages, a common entry point that is frequently known (it was around our house, anyway) as the "big black dump hole."

At least that's what I dubbed it soon after Christopher laid claim to the concrete collector space—otherwise known as the garage—early on in our marriage.

I was pretty okay with that at first. A guy's gotta have someplace to house the family tools to his liking, right? Fair enough. So I refrained from contributing my organizing two cents—as long as I didn't trip over Rollerblades while bringing in the groceries, and the paint, cleaners, and other dangerous stuff was stashed well out of reach of curious little Aronson hands.

The result of this divide-and-conquer approach to garage management? It went something like this: Christopher would clean the garage. He'd dutifully take everything out, trash what he could, and then neatly pack up everything else. And I do mean neatly. No dish ever broke; no vinyl record ever got scratched.

Christopher would find a nook for every little thing and a corner nesting place for the bigger stuff that we stashed in the garage. He ran these weekend-long organizing marathons every month or so. After them, our garage looked perfect—until Monday morning rolled around, that is. (Sometimes until Tuesday, even.) That's when a "new arrival" would be taken out to the garage for storage—with no storage space in sight.

Today, our garage isn't perfect, but there's room to grow. Here's a look at how we won the wasteland-no-more war by creating a system that makes room for the castoffs and castaways of daily life together.

a home for everything

By its very nature, a garage is a no man's (or in my case, woman's) land. Garages aren't exactly part of the house, but they're not outdoors, either.

As a result, this transitional area can become junky in a heartbeat. Even when someone does take responsibility for the garage, it is out of sight, out of mind. We see it only as we cruise through on the way from the car, usually shedding backpacks, shoes, and umbrellas in our wake. Oh, no problem, we think, we'll pick them up later.

But we rarely make time to do that. We don't really put things away in the garage. And kids are the worst offenders. They toss the soccer balls in the general direction of the corner. Oops! They throw their bikes on top of the pile of clothes we're going to take to Goodwill . . . sometime. (That's the same pile that's been there six months.) Hey, clothing keeps.

But because it's usually the family entry to the home, we'd like to keep the garage

---

CLEAN HOUSE RULES FOR THE GARAGE

1. Put things in their proper place the first time.

2. No dumping stuff in the garage. If it goes inside the house, bring it inside.

3. Store dangerous chemicals and tools high up, far out of reach of kids.

somewhat clean. Otherwise, we're continually tracking dirt into the house. Yet it's difficult to keep the garage floor clean because half the time the outer door is open and dirt and leaves blow in. Mud rides in on car tires. And then to complicate matters, there are often oil leaks (not many, we hope) under the car on the concrete floor.

There are several things going on here. First, because no one really hangs out in the garage, it's last on our list of priorities for keeping it tidy and clean. Even Christopher, in his it's-mine-all-mine days, only gave it cleaning attention every month or three.

Second, all sorts of disparate activities go on here. The garage is used for an entry to our house, for storage for everything from kids' large toys to sports equipment to gardening tools, for working out, for workshops, for recycling, and the list just goes on. How much can one room do? (Oh, yeah, and we'd like to park the car there, too—if there's any room left over. There's nothing like leaving your second-biggest investment out to rust in the driveway!)

The good news is that the garage can meet most of your needs. But that's if— and only if—you and the family organize it correctly. And once it's organized, everyone who sets foot in no-woman's-land should maintain that system.

Here's how to tackle the dirty job:

First, divide the garage into areas of use, just like rooms. Consider these options:

- Automotive supplies

- Car park (if you can squeeze it in)

- Entry

- Gardening tools and supplies

- Home and car maintenance supplies (paint, duct tape, caustic cleansers, and poisons up very very high, or better yet, locked up)

- Outdoor toys and equipment (bikes, trikes, skateboards, scooters, hula hoops, pogo sticks)

- Pantry (Costco extras)

- Short-term storage (sports equipment, pet carriers, and pet food)

- Mid-term storage (luggage, camping equipment, seasonal items, and decorations)

- Long-term storage (mementos, old financial records, and hated heirlooms)

- Trash and recycling area

- Workshop (tools and projects in process)

- Workout area (treadmill and weights)

Wow! It's a wonder we can walk through there, let alone park. Of course, not everyone will have all these areas. And some will have all these—and more.

the garage as entryway

Most of us enter our homes through the garage. That's one reason why it's so junky. At the back door, we kick off our muddy shoes, throw down the umbrella, and toss in the ball we found outside the garage door.

Wherever your entry area is, it is essential to make it functional. Create a user-friendly entry area in your garage for the family. Again, consider what you do and what you're carrying (and dropping) as you enter the home, and then design a place for it. Here's how:

Accessories: Whatever the season, we always need something. In the winter, it's gloves, hats, and scarves. In the summer, it's sunglasses, raincoats, and hats. Give each member of the family a small basket or bin to store the items that they always seem to need as they go out the door. No more running back inside to track it down at the last minute.

Backpacks: Those poor kids lug home monstrous backpacks and, of course, they cannot possibly take them all the way to their bedrooms, now can they? If the answer is no, find a temporary holding place for the backpacks in the garage. They're in the way inside, anyway. Options include:

- *Bins:* Put big plastic bins of different colors near the door to capture backpacks. Assign one color for each kid.

- *Hooks:* Sturdy—very sturdy—hooks on the wall are another good alternative.

- *Shelves:* Keep 'em low and make sure they're deep enough to fit the whole massive backpack.

Coats: We all have one favorite coat that we wear day in and day out each season. This garment never sees the inside of the closet because it's always at the ready. Hang favorite coats and rain gear on hooks near the kitchen door, or wherever your usual departure spot is.

Gear: Busy families need lots of stuff: saxophones, tennis rackets, swim goggles, etc. And they need a place to stash it till they need it again. You do not want this stuff sitting by the back door for Grandma Ellie or little Payne to trip over.

Ideally, the kids would walk over to the pegboard wall that's there just for this purpose and hang the tennis rackets on the appropriate peg; then they would walk over to the bin that's there just for balls and insert the soccer ball. And yes, that is something to strive for. But when they are going to be using the tennis racket again the next day, that might not happen. They're human.

Avoid conflict and crashes and give them each a bin or a space on the shelf that's just for their stuff. Consider making the space big enough for their backpacks, too. Tell your kids that they have to empty the bin or shelf once a week. But they *do* have that week's grace period. And Mom won't even look to see what's there.

Bikes: Bikes are so big and they tip over so easily they require extra thought. I have a rule that bikes always go in their prescribed "parking places."

A friend of mine actually marked parking lines on the floor of her garage so her kids know exactly where to put their bikes. My friend never has to get out of her car just to move a bike an inch. Another friend had her husband install one of those nifty racks that suspend cycles from the ceiling. This is the perfect solution for occasional riders.

Shoes: Many families have a no-shoes-inside policy. Most families have a no-muddy-shoes-inside policy. That means a lot of shoes piled beside the door. Here are some alternative places to put them. The good news is they won't be piling up in your closet or sullying your carpet or rug.

- *Basket:* If you have a small family and need a place for only a few shoes, just have a basket by the door.

- *Shelving:* If you have a lot of different kinds of shoes (especially athletic shoes with cleats or riding boots) of awkward sizes or a bigger family, just designate certain shelves for shoes. Add a bench or chair so Grandma can

DIRTY LITTLE SECRETS

GARAGES   The secret to a clean, well-organized garage is giving the kids just a *bit* of space. Do not give them the run of the garage. You will never find anything, and everything will be a mess. This is not a family room. If anything, you will need stricter rules for this area because they will be unsupervised more here.

sit down while she takes off her shoes, or so you can have a seat while you take off your little one's shoes.

- *Shoe cubby:* If you have a *lot* of shoes, invest in a closet shoe cubby to organize and store them all. Or try a shoe rack.

the garage as storage zone

If you have space, the garage is a very good storage place. Not all storage is created equal. Some things need to be accessible at all times; other things we see only every 10 years when we move, but we want to keep them anyway. Think of your storage in three distinct categories.

Short-term storage: This is for things you'll need in the next three months or things that you need intermittently, such as items you buy in bulk. Short-term storage also includes items that you don't use often but need to keep handy, such as boots, flashlights, and umbrellas.

Mid-term storage: These are things you use seasonally, such as Christmas trees, grills, hammocks, and skis. Put them in lofts or stack them in boxes, but don't push them all the way to the back of the garage.

Long-term storage: These are things you don't really need but can't really part with, either, such as old tax records, your daughter's first dress, your children's artwork, mementos, and family treasures that you can't stand but will pass down anyway. Put these at the dark back inaccessible corners of the garage.

setting up your space

The first challenge of using the garage for storage is that unlike most rooms, the garage is not exactly furnished. You will need a lot of storage "furniture" to make the garage work for your family. We did. Thankfully, our home came with floor-to-ceiling cabinets and shelves that made transitioning our systems a cinch.

But that's pretty rare, I think. So if you're furnishing your garage from scratch, the good news is that these catchall furnishings don't need to be attractive, just functional. And they don't have to be expensive, either. Here are some systems that you might consider for

Pre-empt muddy footprints and piles of soggy coats and backpacks with a convenient unloading zone. Here's one way you could organize the entry from your garage to your house.

your garage, depending on what you use it for. None of them are ideal for storing everything. You will probably need a combination to meet all your needs. These furnishing options are roughly arranged from most to least expensive:

Floor-to-ceiling cabinets: This is one of the most attractive options, and it's also one of the most expensive. I'm glad ours came with the house. However, we could have bought (or custom-built) wood cabinets with shelves, hooks, whatever we needed. You can, too.

The advantages of this system is that all your unsightly items are out of sight. You can organize them well. And you can keep them relatively dust-free and clean. For neatniks, this might be the right choice.

The bad news is that floor-to-ceiling cabinets are not deep or large enough to store big boxes or bulky items such as luggage. And small items can get lost within big cabinets unless you put boxes on the shelves to contain them.

Friends of mine, a retired couple, Pat and Sam, use their garage as a workspace for their hobbies. Ken likes to mount and frame artwork and prints. Pat likes to refinish old furniture. Neither hobby is an indoor activity. So Pat and Sam keep their equipment and supplies along opposite walls of the garage. When they're ready to work, they just back the car out of the garage into the driveway, pull their tools up front and center, and get down to business.

Counters and cabinets: Some people install counters and cabinets in their garage, just like you'd have in a kitchen. Some even have a sink in the garage. This is helpful to wash up after gardening or working on the car without messing up the sinks inside.

Of course, this, too, is an expensive solution. You do have the convenience of drawers for small items. And you can keep things relatively clean. But it's obviously not for everyone.

Lofts: For the long-term storage items that you use only once in a blue moon, you might want to invest in lofts. These are platforms suspended about 4 or 5 feet from the ceiling. They are great for storing mementos, old financial records, and other stuff you don't need but can't part with. It keeps them dry and out of harm's way. You can put things that you might need more often, such as luggage and pet carriers up on the loft, but store them at the front where they're pretty accessible.

Instead of building them from wood, you can buy wire lofts that are about 4-by-4-feet that hang from the ceiling.

If you don't want to actually create a loft, you may be able to store large items such as rafts or tents in the rafters. You can even devise a pulley system to pull them up and down. The sky—or the roof anyway—is the limit.

Specialized racks: For just about anything that you want to hang or store, there is a specialized rack designed specifically for it. There are racks to store balls, bikes, tennis supplies, you name it. Most people would not need such costly solutions. However, if you have a passion—biking, tennis, fishing, golf—and have expensive equipment, you might want to invest in proper storage for it.

Industrial shelving: These are the aluminum shelves you can get at hardware stores. They are inexpensive and light. They can hold everything from pantry items to sodas to boxes.

Capacity on these shelves range from 50 pounds to more than 200—so make sure you know how much weight yours can hold. This will be helpful when you're considering what to store where, but it's essential that you know if the kids try to climb them. For safety and a lot of other practical reasons, make all your garage's storage units no-play zones. And if the kids don't comply, make the garage and all its contents off-limits for a day or two. You shouldn't have to tell the kids twice.

Pegboards: These are boards filled with holes on which you hang things on special hooks. Pegboards are very handy garage storage because everything is accessible and in plain view yet not on the floor. Pegboards are great for storing bikes, gardening tools, work tools, and sports equipment.

Specialized racks like these are great storage solutions for bulky items such as garden equipment and sports gear.

A friend of mine, Kathy, has a family that's really into sports. An entire wall of their garage is covered by a sturdy pegboard with even sturdier hooks. Everything from bikes to skis to swim goggles is hung on the pegboard. All balls are stashed in a series of bins at the bottom. Water bottles and energy bars are stored alongside the bins. Gym bags are on the counter, ready to go with fresh, clean towels. Running shoes and hiking boots are in shoe cubbies at the bottom. A canoe and a rubber raft hang side by side from the ceiling. This is a family that's ready to play anytime. Tennis, anyone?

Plastic containers. Remember that the garage is a really dirty place. Protect anything that's not sealed by storing it in plastic containers. Wheeled containers are great for toy pickup at the end of the day.

what you shouldn't store in the garage

The garage is very enticing for storage. But there are certain things that don't belong there.

- No clothing or bedding. Rats would just love to nest in your expensive duvet. Let them find a B&B farther down the block. Also, garages are usually too damp for storing clothing; it will mildew.

- No fresh foods. In theory, a nice cool garage would be a great place to keep extra potatoes, carrots, onions, etc. Ants, mice, and rats think so, too.

- No wine. Since garages are uninsulated, the temperature fluctuates too much to make it a good spot to keep the fruits of the vine.

cleaning with kids: the garage

At least once a year, set aside a Saturday for cleaning the garage. Actually, you should do it twice a year: when you get out the summer stuff, and again when you get out the winter stuff.

Garage-cleaning day is the ideal time to ooh and ahh over all your old treasures and reevaluate whether to keep them. Is the patio umbrella dirty? Clean it. Is the artificial Christmas tree bent? Repair it or toss it. (You rarely need a backup Christmas tree.)

Try to send the little ones away for this occasion. Ages 8 and up will be of help. Anyone younger will be of hindrance.

Have big plastic bags everywhere: for charity, for trash, for sale, and for resituating.

At the end of the day, cart away the bags for trash and charity. (Do it today or you'll leave them cluttering the garage for another five months.) Set aside stuff for a superduper garage sale. Let the children benefit from their hard work.

Be sure to clean the garage while it's empty. Sweep it out, get rid of oil stains, brush away cobwebs—you get the picture.

If you have oil stains on the floor, here's how to get rid of them. Scrape up any accumulation. Absorb oil with a noncombustible material such as automatic dishwasher detergent or cat litter. Grind it into the oil a bit. Leave it on for several minutes, and then pour boiling water on the stained areas. Scrub the floor with a stiff brush or push broom, and then rinse it with water. Sprinkle baking soda over the cleaned area to neutralize the solution that you've used. Never clean with gasoline. And get that leaky car fixed!

Treat other garage-floor stains with Spray 'n Wash, let them rest, and then scrub them away with automatic dishwasher detergent.

If you see any evidence of rodent droppings, send the kids away. Put on a mask. Wet the area first. Then wipe the droppings up. You do not want to accidentally inhale any of the rodent droppings because they harbor viruses and/or bacteria.

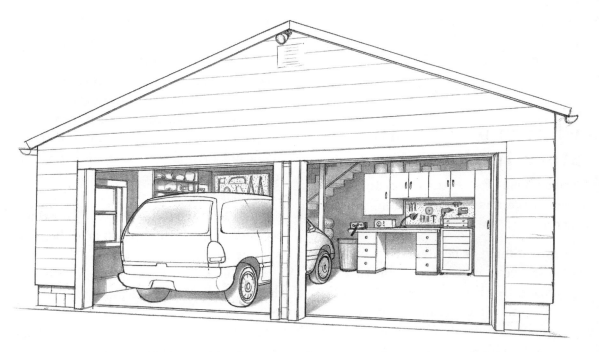

A well-organized garage like this would make coming and going so much more pleasant. There's even room for the cars!

It's a good idea to wet all dusty areas before sweeping or wiping. This keeps the dust from swirling around and giving you an allergy or asthma attack. Or use a sweeping compound. This mixture of oil, sand, and sawdust catches and holds dirt instead of throwing it up in the air when you sweep. You can purchase it at hardware stores.

Once the garage floor is clean, apply a cement sealer to seal the concrete floor and protect it from spills. Cement sealers are a great primer if you want to really get fancy and paint the floor.

To limit the amount of dust and dirt that your family tracks into the house, place a small indoor/outdoor carpet or large doormat in front of the entry door.

GARAGE CHORES BY AGE

Here's a guide to which chores kids can do to care for and clean up the garage. Once a child reaches a certain skill or age level, he can generally do the chores for his age group and those for the age groups below. Of course, some of these chores need to be done each day, others once a week, and still others once a month or even less frequently. Use your best judgment for what gets done when, and see "Mrs. Clean Jeans' Housekeeping Routine" on page 253 for guidelines.

AGES 2 AND UNDER:
- Put toys in bins or drawers
- Pick up wrappers and small trash

AGES 3 TO 5:
- Previous chores, plus:
- Put toys and games (and all their pieces) in the proper boxes or bins
- Help prepare papers for recycling
- Sweep the garage floor with a push broom

AGES 6 TO 9:
- Previous chores, plus:
- Wipe up spills
- Sweep floor
- Empty and wipe wastebaskets clean, using disinfecting wipes
- Prepare recyclables for pickup
- Vacuum out car
- Help wash car
- Clean all doormats

AGES 10 TO 13:
- Previous chores, plus:
- Disinfect light switches and doorknobs
- Take trash and recycling containers to curb
- Wipe clean the car's dashboard and upholstery
- Help clean the garage
- Wash screens and miniblinds
- Wash windows and wipe light fixtures

AGES 14 TO 17:
- Previous chores, plus:
- Wash the car
- Wash the car's undercarriage (each spring)
- Spring-clean the garage

Chapter 10

taking it outside

I LOVE THE LAZY DAYS OF SUMMER. The kids are blissfully free after nine months of indoor imprisonment (a.k.a. school), meaning outdoor anything is preferable to a day inside. It's a time for playing in the sun, entertaining outside, and enjoying friends and family. After all, less indoor kid and family time means less mess. Right?

Well, sort of. Housework, of course, does not stop at the house. While the indoor traffic may have slowed to a near stop (at least by day), once spring arrives, it's rush hour on patios, flower beds, and lawns. Yet tidying up around the outside of the house is not a top priority. At least not among my three free spirits.

After all, planning gardens and pool parties is a lot more fun than preparing the yard and garden before them and cleaning the pool and hot tub after them. But since a summer-fresh outdoor area is a necessary part of making the fun stuff really fun, why not get the kids to pitch in outside as well as in? And maybe teach them a thing or three about how things grow?

Let's take it area by area, with a little help from my friend and alter-ego, Mrs. Dirty Jeans. In real life, Mrs. Dirty Jeans is Connie Ballard, a freelance writer with more than 20 years of newspaper experience under her bib overalls. (Full disclosure: Contrary to her pseudonym, Mrs. Dirty Jeans actually keeps her bib overalls and other gardening attire sparkling clean following Mrs. Clean Jeans' laundry tips.)

While cleaning and perfecting the patio is a subject near and dear to my heart, when it's time to tackle the green stuff I consult Mrs. Dirty Jeans. She's been gardening since she was knee-high to, well, you know.

It all started with Connie's grandmother, who lived with her, loved houseplants, and filled every window with pots of begonias and philodendrons. (This sparked an ongoing war with Connie's mother, who hated the associated mess and "accidentally" knocked pots off windowsills whenever she had the opportunity.) When Connie was 8, her grandmother gave her a small philodendron. This was Connie's first houseplant. She promptly killed it by trying to pry open the unfurled leaves to

rush Mother Nature along. Now she waits for Mother Nature.

Mrs. Dirty Jeans has lived all over the country and gardened in climates ranging from snowy Philadelphia to tropical Houston to drought-stricken California. Connie has been in Marin County for 13 years, and she says she's had her tropicals wiped out by freezes only twice.

Since her daughter, Marisa, was born in 1992, Connie has become increasingly interested in gardening with children. Marisa was born with a green thumb. She has her own succulent garden plus her own annual garden beside the mailbox that she tends year-round. (You can do that in California.) Marisa can discuss propagation methods and composting techniques with any adult. I've heard her.

As a certified master gardener, Connie does volunteer work for community gardening projects. She also volunteers at Marisa's school garden, a one-acre, totally organic enterprise that uses composted food from the school cafeteria seasoned with manure from the school's stable.

Today, Connie has a postage-size garden she designed and landscaped herself. It's totally organic, of course. And she does worm composting at home. It's icky stuff, but the plants love it.

For all these reasons and many more, Connie is my source for the gardening lessons I've used with great success to teach my kids how to help make things grow—and have a great time doing it.

Let's get growing!

party-perfect patios and decks

Since most families practically live outside during the warmer months, the patio or deck becomes an outdoor room where the kids play from dawn to dusk and the parents hang out and relax. (What a wonderful concept!)

CLEAN HOUSE RULES FOR THE GREAT OUTDOORS

1. No running or roughhousing in the hot tub, pool, or yard.

2. No glass outdoors for the kiddies.

3. The hot tub stays covered and locked when not in use.

4. Kids can be in the hot tub only with adult supervision.

5. No infants or toddlers in the hot tub.

6. The hot tub temperature stays below 104°F.

7. No swimming without adult supervision.

8. Slide down pool slides feet first.

9. No diving! Backyard pools aren't deep enough.

10. No rolling toys are allowed near the pool.

Since we're out there so much, we'll need to organize our seasonal "room" to make it as livable as possible. Think about what you do on your patio or deck. Then arrange the furniture so that you can do it more easily and efficiently. Our deck is filled with activities: Kids play, parents read or talk, and we entertain. Essentially, you need one area for eating and entertaining and a separate area for the kids.

the adult entertainment area

This part's a breeze. All you need are a table and some comfy chairs. This is not the place to scrimp. Sink-in-and-stay-a-spell kind of comfortable chairs will make your moderate investment pay off big time.

Top it all off with an umbrella for shade, and your parlor is open for business. Optional furniture includes a storage chest for adult toys and stuff you always need outside—such as sunscreen, hats, and bug spray—and folding tables by the grill for serving and cooking. An ice chest would be nice, too. Steaks, anyone?

the kids' deck zone

For safety's sake, set up the play area away from the grill and the table. You might even want to make the kids their own little outdoor room delineated by container plants. I have a sturdy blue kid-size table with six multicolor chairs in our family room that's easy to take outdoors for just such occasions.

Keep favorite toys in a wheeled container or a wagon so kids can roll them outside to play. Or consider a deck storage chest for them to use as a toy box. Another way to keep your yard tidy is to provide ample, accessible toy storage in the kids' corner of the garage (see "A Home for Everything" on page 178).

Consider what you would put in a conventional room. For little ones, provide protection from the sun with a "ceiling" (umbrella or awning), a "floor" (a quilt, splat-mat, or old blanket), and "walls" (some sort of barrier such as container plants, toy chests, or fences) that will keep them from wandering off. (Or at least slow them down.) The older kids might want more privacy, but keep the little ones in view.

If you have a yard and small kids, you're probably running out of room. Outdoor toys, for some reason, tend to be big— *very* big. It takes only a few gifts from the grandparents to seriously junk up the yard. Let's see, there's the swing set, the plastic playhouse, the sandbox, the wading pool, and the bikes and trikes. Arrgggh! Just moving the stuff to mow the lawn can take an hour.

Here's an example of a patio set up for entertaining and relaxing.

You'll be hard-pressed to get the kids to come inside from a great outdoor kids' room like this.

Unless you're running a day care, set some limits on how much plastic you want in your yard. You wouldn't fill up your lawn with junked cars, why is a trashy swing set any different? Try setting some boundaries. Give the kids one area of the patio and yard as their play area. Confine toys to that space. Then you and the hubby can have some unobstructed areas to garden, entertain, and just plain relax. You deserve a corner of paradise, too.

Help the kids keep their area tidy by limiting the number of toys that can be out at any given time, just as you do indoors. Just because your kids have more room outside doesn't mean they can play with ten toys at one time. And the sheer quantity of toys strewn about also reduces the odds that they will actually pick them all up at the end of the day.

cleaning with kids: the patio and yard

I use the term "cleaning" loosely here when we're talking about yards. But you get the drift, we're talking about keeping your patio and yard well kept in all of its splendor, with help from the kids.

spiffy patios

Keeping patios and decks, and all of their assorted decorations, clean can be a challenge. Have you ever tried to clean a glass patio tabletop? It's an exercise in futility. You wipe it, it dries, and streaks appear. Dirty streaks. You wipe it again, it dries, and the dirty streaks multiply. The same types of challenges arise with other outdoor pieces—you're battling Mother Nature here, after all!

Here are the dirty little secrets to mastering the art of cleaning outdoor furniture:

Cushions: Most cushions today have synthetic covers and polyester fill and are designed to withstand the elements. Still, they could use some help if you'd like them to last for the long term (or at least a few seasons). Here's how to take care of polyester-coated cushions with polyester fill (cotton, foam-filled, and floral acrylic covers require different care).

Hose down cushions occasionally. Turn them often for even wear and sun exposure, just like you do your couch cushions. Avoid getting sunscreen on the cushions. Hose off spills or sunscreen smears immediately. To deep-clean, use a spray enzyme cleaner on stubborn spots. Set the cushions on their ends in the sun until they are completely dry. If you detect mildew, put the cushions on the driveway and saturate them with a solution of 1 cup of bleach, 3 gallons of warm water, and ¼ cup of laundry detergent. Let the wet cushions sit in the sun for several hours. Rinse. Let them dry in the sun for several days if necessary.

Be sure to clean away any remnants from the outdoor season before storing cushions for the winter because set stains are nearly impossible to remove. Store clean cushions in plastic bags (I use trash bags) for the winter.

A word of caution here: There's a very popular fabric that looks like cotton but is really acrylic fabric, usually in a floral design. Never put these cushions in the dryer or clean them with bleach. Always check the tags to be sure.

Furniture: The problem with "outdoor living rooms" is that they get dirtier a heck of a lot faster than the indoor ones. Fortunately (or maybe wisely), outdoor furniture is constructed to take abuse—and soil. Generally speaking, if your furniture is near a pool or spa, hose it down once a week because chlorine will damage most finishes.

Here's a guide to caring for the most common outdoor furniture materials.

Aluminum: Wash aluminum with mild liquid detergent; rinse and dry. Coat with an automotive wax every six months. Warning: Sunscreens that contain PABA can stain aluminum and many other kinds of outdoor furniture. If you're wearing sunscreen, protect the chair you're sitting in with a towel.

OUTDOOR CHORES BY AGE

Here's a guide to which chores kids can do around the yard, organized by age group. Once a child reaches a certain skill or age level, he can generally do the chores for his age group and those for the age groups below. Of course, some of these chores need to be done each day, others once a week, and still others once a month or even less frequently. Use your best judgment for what gets done when, and see "Mrs. Clean Jeans' Housekeeping Routine" on page 253 for guidelines.

AGES 2 AND UNDER:
- Pick up outside toys
- Collect snails in a pail

AGES 3 TO 5:
- Previous chores, plus:
- Put away outside toys and games (and all their pieces) in the proper boxes or bins
- Help with planting
- Water outside plants
- Debug plants
- Sponge down the outdoor play table

AGES 6 TO 9:
- Previous chores, plus:
- Hang up (pool) towel
- Rake leaves
- Sweep the patio and porches
- Wipe patio table and chairs
- Do easy yard work such as weeding

- Help test the pool or hot tub water
- Help balance the pool or hot tub pH
- Help clean the pool strainer baskets
- Prepare recyclables for pickup
- Clean all doormats

AGES 10 TO 13:
- Previous chores, plus:
- Take trash and recycling containers to curb
- Clean the patio and patio furniture
- Plant plants and bulbs
- Harvest vegetables
- Mulch plants
- Take compostable material to the compost pile
- Cut flowers for the house
- Vacuum the pool once a week
- Scrub the pool sides occasionally
- Fish surface litter out of pool (with a grownup's supervision, of course)
- Shovel snow

AGES 14 TO 17:
- Previous chores, plus:
- Mow the lawn
- Wash exterior windows
- Do yard work such as pruning
- Spring-clean the garage
- Check the pool or hot-tub filter
- Maintain the compost pile
- Clean out the fireplace and tools
- Change furnace filters

Resin: This substance doesn't require much care. Wash it with a mild soapy solution, hose it off, and towel dry. Avoid products with ammonia, but use a diluted bleach solution for stains. Polish resin furniture with car wax if desired.

Teak: Teak is a popular choice for outdoor furniture because it weathers well. Do not use teak oil on outdoor furniture because it will act as a dust magnet. Clean teak with a mild soap solution and a soft brush. Rinse well. Keep teak furniture in the sun because dampness will cause mildew.

Vinyl: Clean vinyl with warm soapy water. Never use bleach because it can damage the finish, allowing the porous material to stain, fade, and weaken faster.

Wicker (natural): Clean wicker only once a year unless you have spills (ha!). For natural wicker, first tip the chair to one side and vacuum it well. Then wash it with a solution of mild detergent and water, using a toothbrush to get at those hard-to-reach spots. Rinse it with a garden hose. Towel the wicker dry, and let it sit for 24 hours before using.

Polish wicker furniture with furniture polish occasionally. Natural wicker will rot in the sun, so place it in a shady spot or beneath your umbrella. Never cover wicker with plastic because it will trap moisture and encourage mildew.

Wicker (resin or vinyl): Wash synthetic wicker in soapy water, and then rinse and dry it. You can polish it with a spray-on polish.

Wood: Clean outdoor wooden furniture at least once a year. Wash it with a mild detergent and scrub brush. Store it indoors over winter if possible.

Wrought Iron: Wash wrought iron with soapy water; rinse and towel dry. Wax or polish it twice a year. Touch up any rust spots immediately. During the winter, either bring wrought iron indoors or cover it.

Floors: Most patio flooring is designed for easy care. Simply sweep and/or hose it down frequently. Some flooring (such as finished concrete) must be sealed. Many patios could benefit from pressure washing every couple of years. Decks are best cleaned professionally. Consult an expert if your flooring needs cleaning beyond sweeping and hosing down.

Hammocks: Cotton hammocks soak up water like a sponge. When you first bring them out in the spring, spray them with a water repellant to minimize water retention. To clean hammocks, lay them flat and scrub them with solution of hand dishwashing detergent in warm water using a nylon scrubber. Rinse and clean the other side. Rinse again and hang to dry. Never use bleach on these natural relaxers—it will rot the fibers.

Tabletops: These are really hard to clean flat. The trick to cleaning a patio table is to turn it on its side (very carefully, if you're dealing with glass), and hose it down first. Then wipe it off with a sponge dipped in soapy water. Hose again. Then wipe dry. If you can't turn it sideways, move the chairs back and hose from the traditional angle (but it might take a couple of tries!).

Umbrellas: To really clean an umbrella, take it apart and put the top part back into the stand so that it's within reach. Then crank the umbrella open and wash it with a liquid cleaner and a sponge. If your umbrella is vinyl, use the detergent made for convertible car tops. It works wonders on these sun-beaten skin-savers. Dry the umbrella open in full sun for a day or two. Never put an umbrella away even slightly damp. That's a recipe for mildew.

playing safe

Keeping up the yard is a full-time job, and most of us cannot afford gardeners. Instead, we enlist our children in the process. Lucky them. And lucky us! Getting kids to help with yard work is usually easier than getting them to help with indoor chores. Kids love to be outside. They love to play in the dirt. They love anything to do with squirting water. Kids and yard work go together like peanut butter and jelly!

Some yard jobs, such as mowing, require no motivation. Kids love to handle anything that has a motor and the power to maim or kill them. Kids, especially boys, are born with a love of lawn mowers. They're big, they're noisy, they're dangerous—what more could a growing boy ask for?

Therein lies the problem. Adults, especially moms, don't like lawn mowers for precisely the same reasons. Therefore, it suits both parties if older kids do the mowing, as long as a few safety precautions are observed.

No one under the age of 14 should handle a lawn mower, a weed wacker, a chipper-shredder, or other potentially dangerous, sharp-edged, debris-spewing machines. Or, for that matter, pruners and other sharp-edged tools. And parents should never take kids for joy rides on a riding mower. It gives them precisely the wrong message. Mowers are not toys. Kids are apt to slip and fall under the blades. In fact, don't even let kids near when you're mowing because the mower could spit rocks out, or you could even accidentally back over them. Send the kids (and pets) inside while mowing.

While you're mowing, set a safe example and always wear long pants, sturdy shoes (not sandals), gloves, and goggles. Do not try to free objects that are stuck in the mower blade with your hand, even if the mower is turned off. There could be residual tension that will spin the blade once the object is removed.

(continued on page 200)

THE DRILL FOR GRILLS

Come Memorial Day, Americans light up—
their grills, that is.

Before you light that match or turn on the
gas in the spring, stop and think. That grill has
been sitting out in the yard for six or seven
months accumulating dirt, insects, and rust.
Just as you wouldn't fry an egg in a dirty frying
pan, you wouldn't throw a juicy steak on a
dirty grate. Would you?

CHARCOAL GRILLS

Here's how to get your charcoal grill ready to
glow:

Clean the cooking grate with a brass grill
brush and warm soapy water. If you meet
resistance, try rubbing it lightly with steel wool.
Rinse and dry. (Lightly coat cast-iron grates
with cooking oil.) Never use oven cleaner on
your grill. It can damage the finish, plus it's a
bad idea to put a caustic substance on the
grates where food's going to go.

Remove last year's ashes. Then clean the
inside and outside of the grill with a grill
brush. Wash the inside and outside of the grill
with warm soapy water. Rinse and wipe dry.

Now to keep that grill clean, treat it just like
you would any other cooking surface. If you
wipe up spills immediately—before they get
cooked on—cleanup will be much easier. (The
grill will look nicer, too.)

After each use, while the grates are still
warm, clean them with a wire grill brush. If you
have cast-iron grates, oil them lightly after
cleaning. Then remove the ashes.

GAS GRILLS

If you're like most people, you've got a trusty,
much-used gas grill sitting on your patio or
deck. And if you're like most people, you haven't
cleaned that thing since you bought it. Are you
crazy? You're really going to light up a tank of
propane without checking things out first?

I didn't think so. Here are some tips for
cleaning and inspecting your gas grill before
you fire up this summer. (Warning: Always
check your manufacturer's directions before
doing anything to your grill. There may be a
specific way to clean your particular model.)

Before you fire up, read your owner's
manual. Bring it outside with you for reference.

Spread newspapers under your work area to
protect your patio or deck. Shut off the gas at
the tank and remove the tank. (Follow
directions in your owner's manual for
removing the burner and pulling the gas or
venturi tubes off the gas lines.)

Clean off any external dirt or grease with a
cloth dipped in soapy water. Wipe the grill dry.
Spider nests and grease can clog ports (or gas

connections). Remove clogs with a toothpick, wire, or paper clip. Clear the venturi tubes with a non-wire bottlebrush.

Remove grill grates (or grids) and briquettes, and set them aside. Wash the burner grates and drip pans with soapy water and a plastic scouring pad, and then set them aside.

Cover the gas openings at the control panel with plastic bags and/or aluminum foil to keep them dry. Then clean the inside and outside of the grill with a brass bristle brush and warm, soapy water. Rinse it with a garden hose, and then wipe it dry. Remove the plastic/foil covering on the gas openings.

Check the hoses for leaks or cracks. Make sure that there are no severe bends in the hoses.

Hook up the propane tank. (If it's dented or very rusty, do not use it. There could be a leak. Replace it immediately.)

Check for connection leaks by painting the connections with a solution of half water and half soap. Turn on the gas. If any connections bubble, you've got a leak. Tighten the connections.

To clean the briquettes and grate, put them in the grill, flipped over so that the greasy side faces the burner. Close the lid and "cook" on high for 15 minutes. When cool, remove them and scrub with a brass bristle brush and warm soapy water. Dry and replace. Oil grates to ward off corrosion. Replace any briquettes that are disintegrating. (They usually need replacing once a year.) Then replace the burner grates and drip pans.

To keep your gas grill in top-grilling shape, after each use close the lid and turn heat on high for 15 minutes. Scrape the grates with a wire grill brush. If the grates are cast iron, season them with oil.

Clean the grill every six months, or at least at the beginning and end of the grilling season.

Before storing a gas grill for winter, it's important to winterize it. Clean the briquettes and grates by flipping them greasy side down, closing the lid, and firing up the grill on high for 15 minutes. Cool and wash with warm soapy water.

Turn off the gas at the tank and remove the propane unit. Clean the tank with warm, soapy water and wipe it dry. Clean the gas connections with a paper clip.

Clean the outside of the grill and check for chips. Sand and touch up chips with a paint designed for high temperatures.

If you store your grill outside, replace the propane unit and cover the grill. If you store your grill inside, keep the tank off of it. Store the tank outside (away from kids and dryer vents) in an upright position. Cover gas line openings with plastic bags to prevent bugs and spiders from nesting there.

Still more safety advice: Parents usually like having a lush green carpet for their kids to play on. But just make sure that that carpet isn't poisoning your kids (and pets). Some of the ways people grow such lush green carpets is with lots of fertilizers (to make it grow), herbicides (to keep out weeds), and pesticides (to kill bugs). Do you really want your toddler (who puts everything he touches into his mouth) playing on that bed of chemicals? And even if your lawn is just for show and the kids never go near it, those chemicals wash off your lawn, down the gutter, and eventually into our water supplies. In this chapter, we will show you how to garden organically, so chemical fertilizers, herbicides, and pesticides are not needed.

For example, if you buy the right kind of grass for your climate and soil, you'll have denser, healthier grass that will choke out most of the weeds. You can also weed by hand. Or you could plant a groundcover such as chamomile or creeping thyme instead of grass. Your call.

One natural alternative to commercial herbicides is applying a layer of corn gluten, which keeps weed seeds from germinating. An organic alternative to fertilizer is simply leaving the grass clippings on the lawn after you mow. When the clippings decompose, they will return nitrogen to the soil.

If you insist on chemicals, be as safe as possible. Know everything you can about the chemicals that you are using. Always store them out of the reach of children.

And never let kids help you fertilize or spread herbicides or pesticides. Apply commercial fertilizers in late October after the kids have come indoors for the winter. This timing will also help the grass develop a strong root system for the winter ahead. Sermon over.

As I mentioned before, mowing is not a safe chore for small kids. Instead of mowing, there are other, safer, ways kids can help with yard work. Our job as parents is to figure out how to get them to help out with the kid-friendly aspects of yard work such as weeding, watering, or just picking up their bicycles.

For example, after an adult or older kid has finished mowing, younger kids can help gather up the grass clippings and take

mowing tips

Follow these tips for the best mowing results. (And share them with your older kid who's saving up for basketball camp by running a mowing service this summer.)

- **Don't mow wet grass.**
- **Mow when grass is 2 to 3 inches high.**
- **Alternate directions when you mow** (vertically, horizontally, diagonally).
- **Keep mower blades sharp.**
- **Don't crop grass too short.** It needs some length for photosynthesis, plus higher grass blocks out weeds and is less susceptible to browning from drought.

them to the compost pile. Kids are also great at edging—using a spade or special edging tool to outline a garden bed, drive, or path. One of the hardest parts of lawn care is keeping it from taking over the driveway and sidewalks. This is a great chore for kids because they're low to the ground, anyway. Another task kids can usually do is operate leaf blowers—and they usually love to do so! These are safe to use, but tell kids not to aim them at anyone—including the poor dog or cat!—and to wear a mask and ear plugs when using them.

let's get growing!

Working outside with younger children is a bit of a challenge. You need to childproof your yard so that you don't have to keep an eagle eye on them every second. And you need an enclosed area so you don't have to worry about them running out in front of cars.

But just getting your family outside to help shouldn't be a problem. In the spring, we're all itching to be outdoors. It's the beginning of the growing year. And it's a great time to introduce kids to the joys of gardening. They seem to be born with a love of growing things. Even toddlers watch sprouts poke their little green heads out of the backyard soil with a sense of awe.

Kids start off in the right frame of mind. They want to be in the garden, and they like the work. Our job as parents is to keep them in that frame of mind and not wreck a good thing. That's tougher than it sounds because gardening can be hard and tedious. We have to devise ways to keep that sense of wonder alive throughout their childhood.

making the (garden) beds

Garden beds need to be prepared. You don't just march out one day, dig a hole, and stick a plant in. Well, maybe *you* do. That might explain that brown thumb of yours! Let's do it right. You want your child's introduction to gardening to be successful.

First, tidy up. Rake up all the debris and dead plant material left over from winter and put it on the compost pile. Now dig prepared compost into the flowerbeds to reinvigorate the soil for the growing season. This can be compost from the store, from your compost pile (remove the finished compost before adding new material), or even aged manure that you can probably get for free from area stables. (You haul, though.)

the planting plan

Now it's time to decide which plants go where. Get a big sheet of paper and help the kids draw the garden designs. If you

worm composting

A fun year-round family project is worm composting. You simply put some worms in a worm box and feed them with table scraps (no dairy, fat, or meat). In a couple of weeks, you can drain off the excess liquid for a powerful fertilizer. In a couple of months, you can use the new soil in your garden. Worms are good for composting, and also in the garden, because their excrement is high in nitrogen, plus they aerate soil by tunneling. That improves tilth and allows water and air to get to plants' roots.

Here's how to make a worm compost bin and put your worms to work:

1. Get a big plastic tub (not see-through) with a lid. Shoot for a tub 30 gallons or larger.

2. Drill holes along the sides about $\frac{1}{2}$ inch from the bottom for drainage. Poke some air holes near the top.

3. Put in about a 4-inch layer of shredded newspapers. Spray the papers with water until they are damp but *not* soggy.

4. Add about three or four handfuls of garden soil.

5. Mix in about 1 cup of chopped food scraps. (Chopped foods decompose faster than bigger pieces.)

6. Now add the worms. Red wigglers are the best. You can usually buy them at garden centers. (Don't use nightcrawlers, the worms sold for bait.)

7. Add more table scraps every week and keep the soil moist but not wet. (If it starts to smell, it's too wet.) To keep flies from laying eggs on them, be sure to cover scraps with soil. Also add more paper or yard scraps each week.

8. Store your worm compost bin in a shady place, such as a basement or garage.

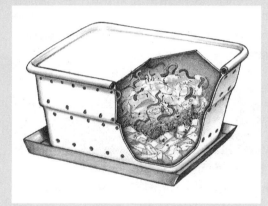

This is a convenient indoor compost bin.

When you're ready to put your compost in the garden, separate the worms out first so they can continue to compost for you. The easiest way is to spread the contents of the box on a plastic garbage bag on the driveway on a sunny day. Cover half the soil with a box to shade it. The worms will crawl to the shady part. (Because your box is sitting on lumpy soil there are small raised areas for the worms to, well, worm their way out.)

making compost happen

If you'd prefer to compost without worms, that's fine. Here's what to do. This process takes a couple of months because you have to wait for stuff to decay. Start in an out-of-the-way place in your yard. Make a heap of table scraps (not dairy, fat, or meat, which will attract rodents and other critters). Add garden wastes such as grass clippings, leaves, or plant prunings. Avoid anything big or woody because it won't decompose quickly.

When your heap is about 3 feet tall, cover it with 2 inches of aged manure, which is available at garden centers. Water the pile, cover it with black plastic, and let it cook. It will get very hot inside. Turn it with a pitchfork about once a week so that everything "cooks" consistently. The more often you turn it, the faster it cooks. If it doesn't cook, add more manure.

If you don't have a good spot on the ground for a compost pile, consider getting a plastic composting bin. You can even get rounded composting bins that you roll instead of turning. Kids love this type.

You can buy a bin or make your own.

Over the season, continue to feed your compost pile with garden waste, sawdust, manure, table scraps, coffee grounds, eggshells, and shredded paper.

don't want your yard designed by a 4-year-old, consider giving him an area that's just his. A little patch under the tree in the backyard, perhaps, or some pots for container gardening. Just let him be master of some part of the gardening universe.

I gave a gardening friend signs for her garden with her name and her daughter's name on them. Her daughter promptly claimed one area of the front yard with her sign and has tended it ever since. Ownership is important.

As you're planning your garden, make it a learning experience. Talk to the kids about how different plants have different needs. Show them how to read plant labels to see how much sun and water particular plants require. Walk around the yard and discuss which part looks sunny, which part looks shady, and which plants might be happier where.

Talk to the kids about using contrasting textures and complementary colors in their designs for more interest. Explain how putting short plants up front and tall plants in the back makes it easier to see them all.

Next, make it fun by having your child choose a theme for her garden. Some of our favorites include: a pizza garden with tomatoes, oregano, and peppers; a salad garden with lettuce, tomatoes, and carrots; a scented garden filled with sweet-smelling plants; a snacking garden of carrots, cherry tomatoes, and celery; a tactile garden bursting with plants with interesting foliage to touch; a butterfly garden of plants that attract butterflies and provide food for butterfly larvae; an exotic garden of fruits and vegetables in unusual colors, such as yellow tomatoes, orange peppers, and blue potatoes; and an edible flower garden. Choosing a theme makes gardening much more special.

Garden planning is a fun activity for the whole family. Kids love going to nurseries and poking around. Let them help you pick out plants. Give them a budget and let them choose the plants for their own plots. They will be honing artistic and mathematical skills while they shop. The more that kids are involved in the conceptual part of gardening, the more they will be interested in the maintenance. You need to make them feel responsible.

planting time

Once your kids have their own little plots, help them be successful gardeners. Show them how to dig a bigger, better hole for a happier plant. Teach them how to handle the roots carefully to prevent injury. Help them gently water the plant and then return to water it some more after the initial watering has settled. Explain how just-planted plants will need more water until they get established.

If you haven't prepared the soil already, this is your last opportunity to work some finished compost and/or aged (not fresh) manure into the top few inches of soil.

versatile vegetable gardening

While any gardening help is good, it's especially great to have kids help with veggie gardens. Nothing encourages children to eat their vegetables more than growing the vegetables themselves. Plus, when you grow your own vegetables, you can be sure that they have not been sprayed with pesticides.

Birds and bugs will be your problems if you grow seeds. You will have these cute little seedlings poking up through the soil one day and zilch the next. Protect your seedlings by covering them with a special cloth called a sponbonded row cover until they are a couple of inches tall.

Here's an important safety tip: Never let your kids taste the seeds they are planting. Many have been treated with fungicide to help them grow. These are poisonous to kids.

Some plants, such as root vegetables like carrots and radishes, have to be started from seeds. But you can get a head start on tomatoes, peppers, and other plants by buying growing seedlings, called transplants.

With seedlings, be sure not to rush the season, especially with tomatoes. If you plant before the nights are warm, tomatoes are susceptible to fungus. Be patient!

creative container gardening

Another type of garden that's especially good for kids is a container garden. Kids love having things in pots. And to make it even more fun for them, let them create their own pots. Containers don't have to be boring old terra-cotta pots. (Plastic pots are safer around kids, and they don't need to be watered as often.) Let the kids pick out a collection of pots of various sizes and shapes. Maybe they could plant a strawberry pot with different little plants in each of the holes. Or they could even make their own containers. Old sneakers and boots make great whimsical pots. You could even have a shoe-in with all different types of shoes. Just remember that these pots dry out faster than clay or plastic and will need frequent watering.

Watering is the prime drawback of container gardening because container plants dry out much faster than the in-ground variety. You might want to consider hooking up a little irrigation line running from pot to pot so you can go on vacation without suffering any casualties.

the marvels of mulch

After you've planted, it's helpful to mulch. And mulch again. And mulch some more. You can use wood chips, straw, or even compost for mulch. I prefer using organic material because it will eventually release nutrients to the soil after it breaks down. Mulch accomplishes three things: It helps hold water in the ground so you don't have to water as often, it helps hold warmth in the ground so plants grow faster, and it helps keep weeds from sprouting. Mulch is a serious weed deterrent only if you mulch 4 inches deep. But any mulch at all helps because weeds in mulched soil are easier to pull.

After planting, encourage kids to make little markers for their plants saying things such as, "Hi, I'm Marigold."

harvesting

You don't need to motivate your kids for this one! Kids love to pick veggies and fruits. In fact, this could be one of the gardening chore motivators. Tell kids that they can't pick the produce until they've picked off the pests. (Or weeded. Or watered.)

GETTING YOUR GARDENERS IN GEAR

With gardening come routine jobs that are fun at first, but they might get a bit boring with time. Your challenge as head gardener is to keep that interest level high with a combination of education, games, and contests. Here are my favorites:

Flower rangers: Gardeners define a weed as any plant in the wrong place. Roses can be weeds if they are invading your watermelon patch. Weeds are bad because they steal nutrients that our flowers and veggies need. Show the children how to distinguish the good guys from the bad guys. Set up an adversarial relationship with weeds. They are "invaders" and must be eradicated. As the Flower Rangers, your kids must eliminate these evil enemy forces. (Oh, heck, let them wear costumes if they like.)

Weed whackers: Start a contest: Who can pull the most weeds each week. The winner gets to pick a movie to see. And the reward for a morning of weeding? A rain dance in the sprinkler!

Rain, rain come and play: Kids like to water. Buy a watering wand or a nozzle with several settings. Show the kids how to set it on a shower setting so that you don't wash the plants away with a powerful jet of water. You can also buy hose heads of different shapes to spray the lawn or flowerbed.

This is also a good opportunity for lessons about runoff. Let the kids water for five minutes. Dig down a couple of inches and show them how the soil is still dry underneath. Explain that if you don't water often, the topsoil creates an impermeable barrier and sheds the water.

Snail races: Set a timer and see who can collect the most snails (or slugs) in 10 minutes. This is a good game for dusk when the little slimy creatures come out for a snack. Or you could make it even more fun and do it by flashlight.

The grateful deadheads: To keep annuals blooming, you have to cut or snap off spent blossoms. This is a very fun task for kids.

Aphids away! Aphids are those little black, green, or white bugs that swarm on your prize roses and leave nothing in their wake. The best way to get rid of these little pests is just to wash them away! Turn the nozzle of your hose on "jet" and take aim! The first kid with an aphid-free rosebush wins!

Be sure to supervise at harvest time, however, or you may be dining on those trendy "baby" veggies. Kids usually can't wait to pick veggies until they're fully grown! Show them which colors mean "ripe" for which veggie. (A yellow tomato is usually only half-ripe, for example, unless it happens to be a yellow-fruited variety like "Yellow Pear.")

Now for the best part: Enjoy!

Earwig booby trap: Leave a damp newspaper rolled up in the garden. Earwigs crawl in. You throw it away.

Snail stomp: Nuff said. This one is not for the squeamish.

Snail trap: Put a board about an inch off the ground. Snails will crawl under it for shelter. See who can trap the most.

Tulip garden: Plant bulbs in a pattern that spells out your kid's name or initials. For best results, plant on a hillside or in an area that can be viewed from above, such as from a second-story window.

Teepee garden: Arrange three poles in a teepee shape and plant fast-growing vines such as climbing nasturtiums or morning glories at the bottom. In a couple of months, she'll have a leafy tent.

Sunflower clubhouse: In a sunny spot, plant an outline of rows of sunflower seeds in a shape about 5-by-5-feet square. (Leave an open space on one side for the "door.") You can even plant baby's tears inside to form a "carpet."

Frozen flowers: Harvest edible flowers and freeze them in ice cubes for conversation "ice breakers" at your next party.

Goofy gourds: Growing gourds can be a lot of fun if you have a long growing season (at least 120 days of sun). After the gourds dry out, you can carve them, make birdhouses out of them, or even paint faces on them.

Personalized pumpkins: Plant pumpkins and when they are about the size of a baseball, help your child write his name on one. Then take a paper clip and punch shallow holes along the name. When the pumpkin is ready to harvest, you'll know whose is whose. The name will be visible in a hue lighter than the pumpkin skin.

Cucumber bottles: This is a little wacky but fun. Plant cucumber seeds. When the cucumbers are about an inch long, slide one at the bottom into a plastic bottle. (Keep it shaded or else it will cook.) When the little cucumber grows up, take it off the vine, bottle and all. You'll have the horticultural equivalent of the ship in the bottle.

Seed savers: At the end of the summer, let the kids go around collecting seeds from spent flowers and vegetables. Help them put labels with the seeds and dry them. Then put them in paper (not plastic) bags and label the bags. Next summer, they have their own stash of seeds to plant. You could also talk to them about the different kinds of seeds and discuss why some are shaped differently.

the 10 most wanted

In this case these really are wanted! These bugs are good bugs; they're bugs you *want* to have in your garden. What's that you say? No such thing as a good bug? The only good bug is a dead bug? Shame on you! Good bugs eat bad bugs. So if you kill off the good bugs, you're going to have twice as many bad bugs on your hands. And twice as much spraying. Here are the top 10 good bugs:

1. Earthworms: They aerate the soil by tunneling, and their excrement fertilizes it. I call them "poopers."

2. Pillbugs: poopers

3. Dung beetles: poopers (The name says it all!)

4. Bumble bees: pollinate plants

5. Lacewings: eat aphids

6. Ladybugs: eat aphids and other pests

7. Praying mantises: eat bad bugs

8. Braconid wasps: eat hornworms

9. Butterflies: pollinate plants

10. Wasps: pollinate plants

the dirty dozen

These bugs are wanted in the Wild, Wild West way—dead or alive. These guys eat or suck the juices out of your plants. And since they go from plant to plant, they also spread diseases. Teach your kids how to recognize these bugs and get rid of them. If you're handpicking, you have two options: pick and crush (not for the faint of heart), or pick and toss into a jar half full of water and a dash of liquid soap.

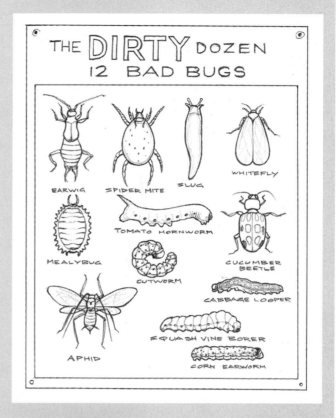

1. Aphids (spray off with water)

2. Corn earworms (handpick)

3. Tomato hornworms (handpick)

4. Squash vine borers (insert wire in hole in stem and skewer)

5. Cucumber beetles (handpick)

6. Cutworms (use cutworm collars— 2-inch sections of toilet-paper or paper-towel rolls pushed into the ground around stems of transplants)

7. Cabbage loopers (handpick)

8. Mealybugs (spray off with water or swab off with alcohol)

9. Spider mites (spray off with water)

10. Snails and slugs (handpick, crush, o r set out beer traps)

11. Earwigs (trap and crush)

12. Whiteflies (spray off with water or set out yellow sticky traps)

Part III
Guests and Getting Around

Chapter 11

mastering the minivan

WE MOMS SPEND much of our lives in the car. We run errands. We take kids to school, to soccer, to piano, to swim lessons, to the beach, to play dates, to baseball, to birthday parties, to orthodontist appointments, and on. And on. I know the world's supposedly a smaller place these days. But I'm still driving 20 minutes to get anywhere.

What all this time on the road *really* means is that the minivan has to function like a home on wheels. What do you do when you're speeding down the highway and your toddler throws up in his car seat? Or your son spills his grape juice down his shirt on the way to his piano recital?

When you're a freewheeling single and the car breaks down on the thoroughfare, you're about to embark on an adventure (that's another book). When you've got a minivan-load of 4-year-olds, you're about to encounter deep doo-doo. There's nothing the least bit adventurous about it. Instead, it's time to shift into crisis-management mode. If you're prepared for all these situations, you and the carload of kids will be moving again in no time.

a home for everything

I know: This looks like a lot of stuff to stuff into your home on wheels. But it's really not—if you package it right. Also, depending on your kids' ages and hobbies, you probably won't need all of it. I've divided the stuff into categories. Just consider each category a survival kit, and package that stuff together in zip-close plastic bags or clear plastic bins. You'll be glad you did. Make room in your vehicle for these survival kits: accident survival kit, bad-hair day survival kit, boredom survival kid, chaos survival kit, injury survival kit, mess survival kit, pet survival kit, safety survival kit, and sanity survival kit.

accident survival kit

This is the stuff everyone needs in case you have a car problem or accident, whether kids are on board or not. Keep these in the glove compartment.

CLEAN HOUSE RULES FOR THE CAR

1. No screaming or shouting in the car.

2. No arguing. (Yes, arguing *can* be legislated. Try this: Once you say "stop!" the next kid to continue to argue in any way, shape, or form loses one day of TV or other coveted privileges. Each additional offense loses another day. Hey, you could give away the TV one day.)

3. Big fights will result in the car being pulled over. (Don't try to resolve disputes while driving.)

4. Seat belts must be fastened at all times.

5. No one under 12 rides in the front seat (if you have a passenger-side air bag).

6. No touching window, radio, or any other controls unless expressly directed to do so by the driver.

7. All leftovers and wrappers must be put in the car trash can or in a bag.

8. No one can go into the house until everything is unloaded from the car. Each child is responsible for getting his or her stuff—all of it—to and from the car. Yes, kids, this does mean you'll sometimes have to make two or even three trips after arriving home. Just like Mom.

- Auto manual

- Auto membership club information and phone numbers

- Gas cards

- Insurance cards and information

- Registration

bad-hair day survival kit

Not really just for bad-hair days, this survival kit is there for those days your makeup needs a touchup or your hair

needs help. Stash these items in a small bin in your car:

- Brush

- Contact lens solution and case

- Hair ties

- Lint brush

- Makeup kit

Along the same lines, keep a change of clothes for you and each of your kids at the ready in the car, too. Spills happen, so be prepared. My friend Marisa's daughter wears a uniform to school. And at least once a month, she will get ink, milk, or

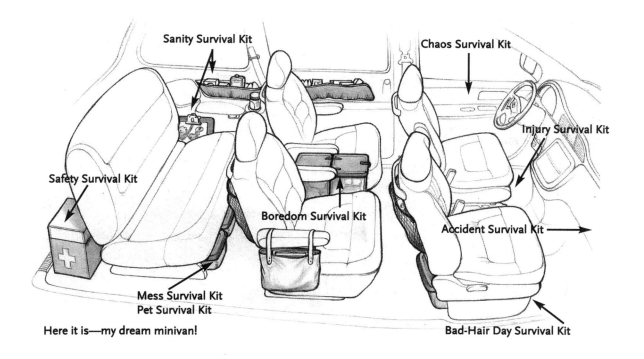

Sanity Survival Kit

Chaos Survival Kit

Injury Survival Kit

Safety Survival Kit

Boredom Survival Kit

Accident Survival Kit

Mess Survival Kit
Pet Survival Kit

Here it is—my dream minivan!

Bad-Hair Day Survival Kit

some other goodie on her uniform between home and the bus stop. No kidding! My friend packs an extra uniform for just that reason.

Don't forget the just-in-case clothes and accessories: umbrellas, rain ponchos, gloves and mufflers in the winter, walking shoes, sun hats and visors, sunglasses, jackets, and sweaters.

boredom survival kit

I get so cranky with parents who do not bring toys or games to amuse their small children in restaurants and other public places. If you *must* bring toddlers to a nice restaurant or doctor's office, at least keep them amused and quiet. I pack activity kits for each kid. The kids can take the activity kits into restaurants, meetings, or even boring visits with relatives and stay occupied. That way, I can enjoy myself, too. The kits also keep kids happy on both short errands and long drives. Good kid kits for little kids include:

- Aluminum foil (Do you know how much art kids can make from this stuff? Think rings, crowns, and necklaces.)

- Action figures, small dolls, or plastic animals. (Bonus buy: A lot of them come in little kits designed to be portable. Choose these whenever possible. I picked up a clear vinyl-like backpack filled with toy soldiers for

Payne recently. He takes them just about everywhere, including the grocery store.)

- Coloring books

- Crayons

- Magnetic board games and wipe-clean games (these are really great choices because pieces can't get lost or bumped)

Good kits for big kids include:

- Books

- CDs and portable players

- Deck of cards

- Game Boy–like games (with the sound off please!)

On the road again? If it's a long trip, consider buying each kid a new book, craft, or toy that will occupy him or her for a while. Let each kid bring one plastic box or backpack filled with personal stuff.

My favorite part of my new minivan is that it came with a DVD player and three sets of headphones. Now, during our regular 100-mile jaunts to San Diego to visit Nana and Poppy, the kids spend 2 hours each way watching movies instead of annoying each other. And Dad and I can catch up uninterrupted. If your car isn't equipped, consider renting or buying a VCR or DVD player for the back seat. With headphones, of course; they're a must.

It's also a good idea to bring a pillow for each kid to encourage naps. And pack water bottles and healthy snacks that are minimal mess-makers such as frozen grapes, cereal o's, fruit roll-ups, and juice boxes.

chaos survival kit

Life is so hectic. As you probably do, we Aronsons live at the speed of kids. It's hard to keep up. The cardinal rule of chaos control is: If you have something, you won't need it. How many times have you been on the road and suddenly remembered that you neglected to call Aunt Shawna to tell her that dinner has been canceled tonight? And then you realize you haven't memorized her number? How many times have you needed to call another parent in your kid's class, but you didn't have the number? I

FAMILY PICKUP LINES

CAR GAMES Here are some easy games to play in the car to make the drive fly by:

Talking: Each person gets to choose a topic every 15 minutes. (My choice is usually silence.) Or you could all listen to someone else talk. Bring along books on tape or a CD the whole family will enjoy.

The Silly Sentence Add-On Game: This game starts with a single person uttering a single sentence and generally ends in a free-for-all laugh fest among the tongue-tied passengers. It's great for getting everyone's mind off the clock and the odometer, and on listening to each other. My 10-year-old daughter, her friend Stephanie, and I made a 40-mile trip to Disneyland recently. Here's what I can remember of our silly game:

"The car in front of us is taupe. It's a Yukon. Stephanie is wearing a bandana. There's a really big plane flying into LAX. The call box is blue. There are surfboards on the car in front of us. Lyndsay (she had choked while laughing and drinking from her water bottle so this too became a sentence), are you okay? Yes, I'm fine. Happy birthday, Lyndsay. The Disneyland castle needs to be repainted. The sky needs to be taller. I really want that limo in front of us. Put a sock in it, Stephanie. Lyndsay is loony. . . . "

Navigation: Let older kids help navigate. Give 'em a copy of the road map on a clipboard and a highlighter to chart your progress.

The License Plate Game: Print a U.S. map from the Internet and have the kids color in the states as they see a license plate from each.

Counting Cows: Things get crazy when you pass a field full of 'em. If you pass a cemetery on your side of the car, you lose all your cows, but only if the other side calls it: "Cows buried." You can pretty much make a game out of counting anything. Try billboards, red signs . . . you get the picture.

always carry an old school directory in my car, just in case. (I keep the current one at home inside beside my phone.)

You'll need your personal phone list, too. I have all my essential numbers (and non-essential numbers, actually) in my personal electronic organizer. If you aren't using one, carry a printout of numbers you frequently need. My friend Connie keeps her list in the pocket behind the driver's seat along with all the other directories.

And, of course, a pen or pencil is essential. You always need one, and there's never one in your handbag when you do.

Here are some other handy business basics for the road warrior:

- Coupons (If you don't have them with you ready to use, what good are they? Stash them in an envelope in the door pocket.)

- Maps (There are some places I go every couple of months and when the time rolls around to return, I draw a map-blank. Guess I'm occasionally geographically impaired. To remedy this missing map gene, I print out maps or directions from my favorite Internet map site and keep them— along with state, city, and county road maps—behind the passenger seat of my car. Sometimes there's no place to ask directions—even if your spouse will let you.)

- Mileage book (No, you *cannot* deduct all those hours you volunteer at the school or the local food bank. You can, however, deduct the miles that you drive to do the volunteer work. So keep a record each time you venture out on a mission of mercy. Jot it in the notebook, and store it in your second door pocket envelope.)

- Receipts (Keep a third envelope in the door pocket to stash credit card, gas, and minor purchases receipts.)

Another handy thing to keep in your car is a master errand list. If you don't tame this seemingly benign monster of a time-taker, you'll never have time for the fun stuff. Write down all the errands you need to run for the week, and then group them geographically. Check your schedule for the week, and plan which days you'll complete which runs.

injury survival kit

We all know we need a first-aid kit at home when we have kids. But do you carry one in the car? Since we spend so much time on the road with rambunctious kids, being prepared for minor overzealousness and medical mishaps is essential. (Not to mention the need for aspirin to treat the occasional headache caused by a long drive with loud, active kids.)

So, what goes inside your portable first-aid kit? Use whatever you have handy, such as an art supply box or a simple tackle box, to stash and store:

- Adhesive tape

- Antiseptic wipes or ointment, burn ointment, and hydrocortisone cream

- Bug spray

- Emergency contact list (Just in case your babysitter or your mom is driving when an accident occurs. Include mobile numbers for you and your spouse, as well as names and numbers for the doctor, the orthodontist, and even the veterinarian if you bring the dog along for most outings.)

- First-aid manual with CPR instructions

- Instant cold packs

- Over-the-counter medications such as kids' Tylenol or Motrin and aspirin (not for anyone under 12, however)

- Prescription drugs (Store what you or your kids might need if you get stuck unexpectedly, including inhalers for your little athletic asthmatic, in childproof containers.)

- Sterile gauze

- Stretch bandages

- Sunscreen

- Tweezers for bee stings or splinters

Finally, complete your emergency kit by storing a "Send Help" sign nearby. You can buy these almost anywhere. Just pray that you or your designated driver never needs it. If you remember to charge your cell phone, you probably won't.

mess survival kit

Here's what you need to keep the car, and the little passengers inside, moderately clean. Store these items in a small clear bin in the back of your car, but make sure it's easily accessible:

- Bottled water (You can drink it or you can use it to clean up spills.)

- Napkins (Leftover fast-food napkins are perfect.)

- Plastic bags for wet clothing or other items

- Roll of paper towels

- Tissues

- Trash receptacle or bag (I have one of those sturdy vinyl-like pop-open-and-close bags that hangs over the seat. It's easy to unfasten and dump daily. I've even been known to send it for a spin in the washer with a dash of bleach when food grows mold inside of it.)

- Wet wipes or a tub of baby wipes (Payne has been out of diapers for more than a year, but I still carry wipes in my handbag and in the minivan.)

pet survival kit

For many people, the dog is a member of the family. Our schnauzer, Heidi (gone to doggy heaven last summer), was like that to us. When soccer Saturday rolled around, she was bundled into the minivan along with the rest of the family and the duffle bags of sports stuff. At the time, I didn't go for the doggy car seat, but today I've warmed to them. They're a good idea if your dog has a tendency to roam or jump around visiting the rest of its family members, seat by seat.

carpool survival

Carpools are very useful arrangements for busy moms. But there's a bit more to them than just alternating driving days. Being part of a carpool implies a commitment both on your end and on the other moms'.

Before you firm up an arrangement with other parents, consider the following: Do you have enough liability insurance? The minimum usually won't go very far if you are involved in a serious accident. Yes, I know. You're a safe driver. But what about the uninsured motorist who plows into you at the stop sign, injuring several kids in your car? Who do you think the other parents (and their insurance companies) will sue to make sure their children get the best medical care? Many schools require a minimum of $300,000 liability for field-trip drivers. So there's a ballpark number for you. At least check with your insurance agent to see whether you have enough coverage to feel safe.

Here are my other carpool rules:

• Set up carpools with parents at your kids' school or parents whose kids are involved in the same weekly activities as yours.

• Try to find other moms in your neighborhood. If you have to drive 10 miles out of your way every fourth day for one far-flung kid, the carpool may not be worth it.

• Make sure the other parents have a valid driver's license and sufficient insurance, too. Unsure? Ask. Arrange to swap or buy car seats for younger kids if necessary.

• Make sure the other moms are somewhat reliable and are safe drivers. Want to know for sure? Ask your kids the first week. They'll tell you whether they drive like you or not. (You can interpret the results.) These are your babies we're talking about here.

• Arrange a schedule that's actually going to work for your family's commitments. Establish how to change the schedule, and how to notify other moms if your kid is out that day. If there are more than two of you, you'll probably want

Yes, I know cats travel, too. But dogs are the more frequent travelers. I've yet to see a family let Fluffy the cat bound out of the hatchback at a soccer practice or baseball game. If you do take a cat in the car, I would advise putting her in a carrier. Cats will slink under the brake pedal without your realizing it—until you can't press the brake pedal. If you want to confine your cat or dog on a somewhat regular basis, invest in a gate for the back of the van or car.

Essentials when pets ride along include:

- Bags for scooped poop
- Leash
- Pooper scooper
- Water dish

to arrange a phone tree for this as well as for emergencies.

- Establish that unruly children will be dropped from the carpool after three incidents. If you work this rule in ahead of time, it's easier to address when an incident actually occurs.

- Make it clear that no one else may pick up your child without your permission. Do you really want your neighbor sending her teenage drag racer son to fetch the kids one day while she's getting a manicure?

- Insist that all drivers have cell phones, and that they keep them on. Keep a carpool directory and schedule in the car for last-minute changes or questions.

- Insist that the other moms don't run errands with kids in the car. The kids need to get home. They've had a long day. Older kids may have other activities to rush off to. And parents will worry.

- Wait until a child has entered her front door before driving off. Make sure the other parent drivers do, too.

- Consider signing a medical release consent form for your kids.

- Establish how long you will wait for stragglers.

- Do not use a cell phone while driving a carpool.

Set carpool rules for the kids, too, such as:

- Everyone wears a seat belt. The car cannot run unless seatbelts are fastened. (I actually had my daughter convinced this was true until she was about 7.)

- No one under 12 rides in the front seat (if you have a passenger-side airbag).

- No eating in the car without permission.

- All body parts must be in the car at all times.

- No loud voices or yelling inside the car.

- Keep your hands to yourself. No touching anyone else.

- Mom gets to pick the radio stations or music, if any.

- Politeness is mandatory.

safety survival kit

Think like a Girl Scout before you head down the road. Here's my list of staples you simply must have for safe journeys:

- Antifreeze

- Blanket

- Corkscrew (trust me)

- Flares or reflective triangle (these are critical to let other drivers know that you've had a problem on the road)

- Flashlight and batteries

- Ice scraper

- Identification, registration, and insurance cards

- Jumper cables

- Rubber squeegee

- Small set of tools

- Tools for changing tires and spare tire (properly inflated)

- Unopened cans of motor oil

sanity survival kit

Each morning before leaving the house, I make sure the kids have stocked the van with all the equipment they will need for their afternoon activities. These include a baseball bag with Chris's glove, bat, hat, balls, and shoes, and Lyndsay's theatre bag filled with her script book and jazz and tap shoes.

Whatever your kids are into or doing that day, prepare for it first thing in the morning. That way if something is missing or dirty, you'll have hours to locate or clean it. And always keep a ball or scooter in the minivan or trunk. That way your little one can amuse himself on the sidewalk while he's waiting for Sis to finish soccer practice or big brother to come out of the orthodontist's office. This has saved my sanity on more than one occasion, I'll admit it.

cleaning with kids: the car

Prevention is a large part of the cure here. You don't let junk and dirt pile up in your house, do you? Well, your car is much more on public display than your house will ever be. Here are a few things to consider:

Consider leather seats. If you're lucky enough to be car-shopping, choose leather seats over upholstery. They wipe up more easily. Clean leather upholstery with a special cleaner/conditioner to keep it looking good and to help it last longer. Always wipe up the excess.

If your seats are upholstered, cover them with waterproof seat covers, especially the seat that's home to your toddler or the dog.

can you hear me now?

The number-one survival tool is a cell phone. This is your most vital piece of safety equipment. Yes, a cell phone can be dangerous in the car if misused. But if you break down on the road or if you're stuck in traffic and your 4-year-old is playing the lead in the preschool play in five minutes, you've gotta make that call. I've seen distraught parents caught in a traffic jam on the Golden Gate Bridge frantically running from car to car trying to borrow a cell phone. In this commuter age, cells are not a luxury, they're a safety necessity. And always keep yours turned on so that your children can reach you in an emergency.

I've experienced the results of not following this cardinal rule. Recently my friend and neighbor, Diana, asked me to bring her 3-year-old son home with mine after preschool while she went to a doctor's appointment and to lunch with a church friend. The two boys are friends, so we planned a lunch at our house.

Well, we weren't home 10 minutes when I heard the scream. You know the one I'm talking about, it's a bloody murder wail all moms know instantaneously. I turned to see little Drew holding the back of his head, crying. As I took him into my arms and removed his hand, I felt a warm rush of blood. Seems while I had my back turned making the boys peanut butter and jelly sandwiches, a push led to a head bonk on a corner cabinet. I placed a frantic call to Diana's cell phone. No answer. I called little Drew's home and got the babysitter, who provided Drew's dad's work and cell numbers.

Alas, Drew Sr. was unreachable, too. Out of the office for lunch; his cell phone turned off. (He was lunching with an old college chum from Philadelphia and had turned off his cellular.)

Two long hours later, having rushed Drew Jr. to the nearby office of my friend, neighbor, and doctor for a quick look-see, we came home and waited. (Lori was willing but unable to provide the needed stitches without a signed medical release form from Diana and Drew.) The little guy was a trooper, happy and untroubled by his head wound or my pushy son, who was really living up to the phonetic part of his name that day. When Diana called on her way home, she said she knew something was up immediately upon powering up her phone. She'd received more than a dozen calls.

Husband Drew (who got at least as many calls, trust me) got home first. They took Drew to a local emergency room. Three staples and some six hours later, the ordeal was one for the memory books. At least from my end.

"I didn't want to be one of those affected women who sits her cell phone on the table at lunch," Diana recalled, shaking her head. She's since come around. And not only because she lives in West Los Angeles.

When it comes to being there for our kids, vanity rules don't apply.

If you don't have floor mats, get them.

To keep the car tidy, empty it of shoes, backpacks, papers—everything—after each outing! This includes emptying the trash. During the summer months, a single missed dumping can lead to some pretty rancid smells. Trust me on this.

to eat, or not to eat?

Now here's a topic of great parental debate: Do you allow your family to eat in the car? Different parents have different tolerance levels and different-size families to be considered. If you have only one child, you can probably be a little more lenient about car activities than if you're chauffeuring a mob. But think before you set the rules. I don't know of a single parent of a toddler who has a no-food rule for the car. I'm talking the main car here, the one the kids ride in regularly. My husband instituted a no-food rule with his new car last year. Suffice it to say we rarely use it to take the kids anywhere.

CAR CHORES BY AGE

Here's a list of which tasks kids can generally do by which age to care for and clean up the family car. Once a child reaches a certain skill or age level, he can generally do the chores for his age group and those for the age groups below. Of course, some of these chores need to be done each day, others once a week, and still others once a month or even less frequently. Use your best judgment for what gets done when, and see "Mrs. Clean Jeans' Housekeeping Routine" on page 253 for guidelines.

AGES 2 AND UNDER:

- Take the toys they brought into the car out of the car

AGES 3 TO 5:

- Previous chores, plus:
- Take their backpacks from the car into the house

AGES 6 TO 9:

- Previous chores, plus:
- Pick up trash in car and empty the bag
- Wipe up spills
- Vacuum out the car, with help depending on the machine's height and weight
- Help wash the car

AGES 10 TO 13:

- Previous chores, plus:
- Return to cases and organize the car's CDs, DVDs, and cassettes
- Wipe off the car's dashboard and upholstery
- Detail/dress the car's tires

AGES 14 TO 17:

- Previous chores, plus:
- Wash the car
- Wash the car's undercarriage each spring

I, however, like my moderately new minivan quite a bit. But I have to chauffeur kids from school to sundry lessons with nary a second to spare, so I have to let the kids eat a snack in the car, or they don't eat. Yes, it's best if kids don't eat in the car—for the car, their clothes, and our nerves. But real-life schedules aren't always conducive to obeying that rule.

That said, you know that if you have a 500-mile road trip, you'll give the little one anything that will keep him quiet part of the way. But as kids get older and easier to shush, some parents start getting strict about eating in the car. It doesn't matter which way you go, just stick with it. And consider these rules of the road if food is allowed in the car: It has to be of the nonsticky, nonstaining food group. No chocolate, no grape juice, nothing difficult to clean up. One father has banned fish crackers and popcorn from his car because they're difficult to remove once they're (inevitably) ground into the carpet.

If your kids eat in the car, vacuum the inside of it weekly. If you don't let the kids eat at the dashboard diner, you can probably get away with vacuuming monthly.

Clean up spills immediately, using upholstery or carpet cleaner for carpets and fabric seats. My baby wipes come in handy when those spills are on the plastic console between seats. I've wiped up more tea spills from my own travel mug than any spills from the kids. But the baby wipes work so well you'd never know it.

Each week or at least once a month, clean the dashboard and doors with a damp cloth or the old standby, baby wipes. Use a damp brush for vents and hard-to-reach spots. Then apply a vinyl cleaner and restorer.

the weekly car cleaning

Here are all the tools you'll need for that weekly car cleaning with the kids:

- Car vacuum or handheld vacuum that plugs into your car's cigarette lighter

- Hose with power nozzle

- Bucket filled with warm water and a few squirts of hand-dishwashing liquid

- Soft, natural fiber scrub mitt or sponge (Old rags will do in a pinch.)

- Clean, dry towels or a chamois cloth for drying

Start by rinsing the loose dirt from the car with your hose. Lift the windshield wipers and spray beneath. Don't forget the undersides of the wheel wells and the hubcaps.

Starting with the roof, wash 3-foot (or so) sections using your mitt or a rag dipped in soapy water. Rinse immediately. Continue this routine as you wash the hood, the sides, and the trunk. Don't suds the windows. You'll wash them separately. Here's how:

Use either a mild, home-made cleaner and as little soap as possible to minimize streaks (such as a squirt of dishwashing liquid in a bucket of warm water or one part white vinegar to two parts warm water) or your favorite commercial glass cleaner. Don't use ammonia-containing cleaners: They can damage the tint on the inside of your windows. Use either a sponge or a clean cotton cloth to do the washing and another clean cotton cloth to dry. Just make sure there aren't any traces of fabric softener or dryer sheet residue on the towel(s) as these can cause streaks on your windows, too. Why make your job any more difficult than it already is? Finally, grab a section or two of yesterday's news, and we're ready to roll (up your sleeves and down the windows, that is).

Let's begin by removing that annoying dirt line around the top of your car door window. Lower the window an inch or so. Clean the outside first, dipping your sponge in the bucket or spraying your cleaner of choice on the towel. Wring any excess from your sponge then gently rub the window using a side-to-side motion, removing road grunge as you go. Roll up the window, finish cleaning the bottom portion; wipe dry with the clean cotton towel. Move in a clockwise motion around the car cleaning the outside glass in a similar fashion.

Next, move inside the car, where we'll use the same tools but an up-and-down cleaning motion instead. (That way, when you're finished, you'll know on which side lingering streaks lie.) Be sure to get way down there in the crevices of the windshield. That's where the scary stuff settles. When clean, use the second towel to dry your surfaces. The pièce de résistance? Crumble yesterday's news and polish the windows and windshield to a sparkling clean perfection—inside and out. Mirrors, too!

To loosen gross gunk such as flicked-on tar, dip a scrub sponge in ¼ cup of vinegar mixed with ½ teaspoon of linseed oil and rub it onto the stubborn spot.

Rinse the car thoroughly to remove any suds hidden under the door handles and inside the rear-view mirrors. Dry the car immediately with chamois or rags.

Really think about it before you wax your car. If you do it once, you'll get to do it over and over. That's because once you start waxing your car, you'll need to keep it up or your finish will begin to look dull. Wax only if you're really into watching water bead up or tormenting your argumentative teen. Otherwise, you're just adding more time to your weekly car-cleaning routine.

Use a silicone-based polish for plastic bumpers. Spray the tires with a silicone product for a sleek, finished look.

Don't wait till wash day to attack the dreaded tree sap. Wipe it off immediately

mastering motion sickness

Bleah!

We've all been there, done that. Here are some ways to keep your kids' tummy contents where they belong:

• Position motion-sickness-prone kids in the middle of the back seat so their eyes are directed straight out to the road. Kids often get sick when what they're looking at (a book or the scenery whizzing by) doesn't match the motion that their bodies feel. If they still feel motion-sick, suggest that they focus on something motionless and far away, like the horizon.

• Don't let kids read in the car, especially on windy roads.

• Open a window and let a little fresh air in.

• Avoid heavy meals right before departure.

• Provide cold ginger ale for sipping and crackers for nibbling. (Here's a great reason to keep a small cooler in the car.)

• Put a wet, cold cloth over the child's face.

• Pack an ice scraper (great for scooping up chunks, ick), motion-sickness bags (a.k.a. plastic trash bags), and wet wipes for quick cleanups.

• Have a change of clothes for the motion-sickness-prone child handy.

• Finally, if your kid is likely to get car sick, ask your doctor about giving him or her a safe medication for kids that contains Hyoscine before the trip begins. Remember that it doesn't start working immediately, so medicate before the motion starts.

with a damp sponge or rag before it has a chance to stain your car's exterior.

It's important to spring clean your car just as you do your house. Give your winter-weary car an undercarriage wash each spring to remove road salt, sand, and anything else that might have hitched a ride there during the stormy winter months.

Here's the best hint of all! Do what I do when time is short and errands are piled up: Leave the car at the car wash while you go grocery shopping. Just make sure it's a soft-cloth wash and that a rinse comes first. Consider a "touchless" car wash if you're concerned about scratches. Those with handy husbands or teenagers have yet another option—a homemade car wash. Use it!

Chapter 12

be our guest

DEATH, TAXES, GUESTS, AND PARTIES are all unavoidable. The first two are out of my area of expertise! But I know a thing or two about the latter. Let's start with guests.

hosting overnight guests

Wonderful! Your parents are finally coming! You want everything to be perfect so they will come again. After all, they hate to travel. What can you do to make sure Grandma and Grandpa feel at home in *your* home?

Plenty. But by far the most precious thing you can give a guest is privacy. It's so awkward to be a guest; you feel on display, like you have no control over your situation. Provide a little sanctuary for your guests. Offer them a retreat where they can go and regroup.

Of course, the flip side of making your guests cozy in their rooms is that you and your family get an occasional breather as well. (You keep remembering why you moved so far away. . . .)

readying a room

If you don't have a spare bedroom, kick one of the kids out of his or her room for the visit. (You can make it up to him later.) Guests need a quiet refuge, especially older people who aren't used to being around rambunctious youngsters. (At least, not anymore.) Here are the basics to equip a comfy, cozy guest room:

Freshly made bed. Consider using only a fitted sheet topped by a comforter, especially if your guest has limited use of his hands (such as arthritis causes). The comforter or duvet (a removable, washable comforter cover) replaces the bedspread and top sheet. As an added guest bonus it's a cinch to make—just fluff and go.

Pillows. Foam or down? Ask their preference.

Extra blankets. On my father's occasional overnight visits, I got into the habit of equipping the designated guest room with at least two extra throw blankets. He never again asked me whether I had the heat hooked up or if I felt cold.

Dresser. Clear out a couple of drawers so your guests can unpack and get rid of their suitcases.

Bedside table and light. Make sure the table is close to the bed so your guest can read before drifting off. A good rule of thumb: The base of the shade should be at shoulder level while sitting up in bed.

No bedside table handy? A spare chair will do in a pinch. Just set a light on it, and your guest can hang her necklaces or robe on the back.

Tissues. Allergies, colds, whatever the cause, make sure you have a solution.

Water carafe. This can be one of those fancy carafes with a glass that fits on top or simply an individual-size bottled water.

Closet. Make room to hang stuff. Filled to the brim? Relocate some stuff for the weekend or week so that your guests can have things the way they like them. Stock the closet with hangers—the plastic ones you see at home stores are a great option. Thin wire hangers from the dry cleaners crease pants and dresses and simply aren't adequate.

Room to spread out. Clear floors and shelves of your stuff to make room for theirs.

Trash can. This is basic, sure, but it's too often overlooked. No one likes others to see their personal trash. (And while you're at it, make sure there's a trash can in the bathroom your guests will use.)

Chairs. A comfy place to sit invites relaxing. And that's what the visit is all about, right?

Window coverings. Install window treatments that provide privacy and light control for quality (and quantity!) sleep. I have one relative at whose home I seldom stay nights because I can never sleep much past dawn. The sheer floral curtains allow the sunrise into the room long before I would if I had my druthers.

An extra set of house keys. Have a few extra sets made in advance, and code them by having each set printed in a different color. Add car keys to the sets of those who might be driving while visiting. Keep a computer or written record of who has what color key set, and mark off when the sets are returned.

Security instructions. Have an alarm? Tell them about when it is on and when it is off and how they can tell on their own. Provide written instructions if your guest will be turning the security system on and off, and if there is a gate code or other security measures they'll need to know about in your home or neighborhood.

Nightlight. A small light is essential for guests because they're not accustomed to the layout of the room or your home. It's helpful to put in a few plug-in nightlights, such as en route to the bathroom, but you could also give your guests flashlights.

Finally, clear a corner spot to plop luggage down in case your guest is the type who actually likes living out of a suitcase instead of enjoying all your cozy preparations. At least you tried, right?

When guests are coming is a great time to nurture the kids' natural tendency to please. Have them help ready your home for guests, too. You son can choose flowers from the garden for you to place in a bedside vase. Your daughter can create "welcome to our home" cards to leave on the dresser. And a few days before visitors arrive, go grocery shopping with the kids for the feeding frenzy ahead. And let them choose the chocolates you'll place on the guest's pillow.

sharing sleeping spaces

If a room of one's own simply isn't in the (house) plan for guests, you can make the most of a cot or inflatable bed placed in the living room. Here's how:

Provide privacy. Or at least the feeling that there is some. A decorative screen or room divider placed between the sleeping area and the main area can make a world of privacy difference. You can use it as a decorative accent when guests aren't around. Position the sofa so that it faces a wall or corner instead of directly into the room.

Remind the kids that this room is not to be used until your guest rouses herself. (Emphasis on the last part.)

These aren't essential appliances to offer, but providing them might get you back in the will.

- Alarm clock/radio

- Coffee maker and cups (for really early risers)

- Hair dryer

- Phone

- Reading lamp

- Small refrigerator (You know, the kind you used in the dorms. Stock it with a few bottles of water and juice and a snack or two.)

- Travel-size steamer or iron

- TV

More Extras: These lovely amenities are simply icing on the cake. You could, of course, provide these for a guest with a room of her own, but I have them here out of guilt for the guest sharing space!

the guest briefing

Sharing some information with your guests will go a long way to making them comfortable in your home. Now, I don't mean a three-star-general operational briefing here, just a little useful information.

Before your guests arrive, tell them about any activities you've planned. Also send them brochures on activities in your area and a list of restaurants. Ask them to look the information over and let you know what they'd like to do during their stay.

And while you're at it, jot down your family's daily routine. What time do you usually get up for breakfast? Is it a serve-yourself affair? When is lunch and dinner? When do the kids usually take a nap? Do you go on afternoon walks? What time do you usually go to bed? Make it clear that your guests can adopt any routine they like, but at least they'll know what the rest of the family is up to. There's nothing worse for a guest than sitting in your room wondering what the day holds in store for you. You want them to feel like guests, not prisoners.

Once your guests arrive, give them The Royal Tour. If you don't want to be waiting on them hand and foot, you'd better show them where everything is. Show them:

- How to use the coffeemaker.
- Where the coffee and breakfast foods are kept.
- Where bowls, cups, glasses, and plates are stored.
- Where you hide the napkins and silverware.
- How to use the microwave.
- How to use the remote for the TV.

Finally, give guests their freedom! If you have a second car, let them poke around by themselves if they feel up to it. Give them a key to the house so they can go for a walk and get back inside.

If all of this seems like too much trouble, consider reserving a room for them at a nearby hotel. You want their visit to be fun, not work. It might be worth your money.

But really, if you're prepared, you can have as much fun as your guests. Happy entertaining!

- Basket of food (fruit, cookies, crackers, tea bags and instant coffee)

- Basket, bowl, or other empty decorative container so your guest has a visible place for keys, jewelry, and other essentials.

- Books and magazines

- Full-length mirror

- Laundry bag

- Lint brush

- Pen and paper

- Warming rug next to the bed (if the floor is hard and cold)

- Vase of flowers

making a luxurious bath

If there is any way to give your guests their own bathroom, do it. No one likes sharing bathrooms with folks outside the immediate family. Yeah, you love Uncle Joe, but do you really want to negotiate around his shaving supplies? Finally, make sure the door locks. If it doesn't, add a hook-and-eye closure so that your guest will know your 3-year-old won't be walking in on her.

Stock the guest bath with:

- Bath gels, salts, and bubble bath

- Bath mat

- Cups (an individual cup for each guest or the disposable variety)

- Disposable razor

- Hair spray

- Hand and body lotion

- Soaps (one fresh soap for each guest)

- Shampoo and conditioner

- Tissues

- Toilet paper (plenty of it)

- Toothbrush(es) and toothpaste

- Towels (two thick, fluffy towels per person)

- That all-important trash can

- Wash cloths (one each)

Finally, always stash a tub of disposable disinfecting wipes in the guest bath so you can sneak in and clean up when guests arrive unexpectedly or for a quick touchup during the weekend visit.

Consider these luxuries, too, if you can:

- Aromatherapy candles

- Basket or rack of magazines

- Bath pillow

- Fresh flowers or houseplant (Nothing says "welcome" quite as elegantly.)

- Loofahs or sponges

- Pretty (and unbreakable) tray with trial-size bubbles, lotions, shampoos, and soaps

No-nos in the guest bath include adding anything scented. What smells fresh and clean to you may gag your guests. And some people are allergic to certain fragrances. (Really.) The best scent is no scent, and that includes air freshener sprays, scented drawer liners, and scented candles.

sleepover survival

It's a whole other story if your overnight guests are the youthful variety! It's a fact of life—kids love sleepovers. Sleepovers are quite different than slumber parties (which are to be avoided at all costs if you value peace, quiet, and a bit of sleep at night). Sleepovers, at least with nice kids (and you don't let the not-nice ones come) can be quite pleasant, actually. So long as you follow the rules. Here are my Top 10 Rules for a successful sleepover:

1. If your kid shares a room, don't make (or even allow) the sibling share the sleepover. Put the sleepover kids in sleeping bags in the family room. The sleepover contingent won't want to include the sibling. And there's no reason to force the issue (sibling). It's not his or her sleepover.

2. Plan an alternate activity for the left-out sibling. If you can arrange a play date or sleepover for him, too, great! If not, plan an evening's activity, such as a family movie, that will keep him with you—and out of the way of the sleepover kids.

3. Plan ahead. Give your child some good-host guidelines before the guests arrive: if TV's okay, how long they can watch, and an appropriate lights-out time. (You'll notice I didn't say bed-time. We have lots of sleepovers at my house.) Remind her that solitary pursuits, such as computer games, prevent interaction instead of encouraging it. Suggest board games or outdoor play instead.

4. Give first-time guests a lay-of-the-land home tour. You don't want a 3 A.M. visitor roaming the house in search of the bathroom.

5. Make sure guests know your house rules, and follow them. This should include notice as to where in the home (such as Mom and Dad's room) is off limits to visitors.

6. Make contact with the parents. You'll need to know where to reach them (cell phones, restaurant number) that evening, overnight, and in the morning. Ask whether the child has any food or pet allergies you should be aware of. If you're planning a movie night, find out what rating of film the child is permitted to view. Set a pickup time now. Clear any plans you have to go out and leave the kids with a

babysitter with the guests' parents be-fore they drop her off. Keep the par-ents' phone numbers handy.

7. Stay within earshot of the kids at all times.

8. Prepare some comforts for each guest. Keep out a clean glass. Provide guest towels on a guest-towel rack. If there's no room for another rack, put a hook on the back of the bathroom door just for guest towels. Keep one drawer empty for guest toiletries. If space is a problem, a caddy or basket will work nicely. Make a manicure/pedicure sta-tion for teens. (It might keep them off the phone for a while.)

9. Let the kids know when you're going to bed and that you expect them to dial down the activity volume accord-ingly. This is the time to reconfirm your previously chosen bedtime.

10. Prepare a really cool—or hot—treat. Bake gooey chocolate-chunk cookies, order an extra-cheesy pizza. Do what-ever it takes to make your home the place kids want to go for serious fun.

surviving parties with kids

Maybe your plans for guests are on a slightly less grand scale—guests for a few hours instead of a few days. Sounds simpler, but don't be too sure.

Every neighborhood has a perpetual hostess. You can drop by any time, day or night, and the house is clean and inviting. A pot of coffee or tea is always "just made," and the welcome mat is always out.

That couple throws the best parties, too. There's always good food, an interesting mix of guests, and lots of places to have intimate conversations. And the house is immaculate! It's obviously a lot of work, but the host and hostess never seem to be frantic or frazzled. You would hate them—if you didn't want to keep getting invited back.

How do they do it?

Ah, the genteel art of entertaining takes practice and lots of preparation. It is not for the faint of heart nor the pinched of purse. But it can still be done fairly easily and without blowing your budget. And you can even have fun doing it. Sure, adding kids to the mix makes it more challenging, but honestly, it can make it more fun, too. (Really, no kidding! Just keep repeating that to yourself over and over.)

After 13 years of marriage, I'd like to think Christopher and I have come a long way from our newlywed style of entertaining, inviting friends over spur-of-the-moment for takeout Chinese. Today when we're planning a get-together, there's a bit more preparation involved. And almost without fail, it pays off.

CLEAN HOUSE RULES FOR YOUNG GUESTS

Okay, I admit, you can't exactly post these rules for your guests like you might post rules for your kids. But still, they are guests in your home, and it's good to have some guidelines in mind, should you need to enforce them. Especially for the pint-size guests!

Also, kids need to be able to have friends over. But they also need limits they understand ahead of time. This is partially for their benefit. If a friend wants them to do something they don't feel comfortable about, they can always fall back on, "Sorry, I can't. My mom's got a weird rule about that." Let them use you as their excuse. It's what we're here for.

Whatever your house rules are, they should address neatness, politeness, and safety. Your child needs to go by all your standard house rules as well as rules for company. Mine include:

1. Hosts, and this includes kid hosts, plan ahead for guests. Have some activities in mind and perhaps even set up for when the guest arrives.

2. No eating anywhere but outside and the kitchen (for kids anyway!).

3. No shoes on in the house.

4. No loud music.

5. No running, shrieking, or roughhousing inside.

6. Put away toys, CDs, etc. after use and before moving on to the next activity.

7. No movies or TV without permission. (It's a good idea to check up on the kids for this one!)

8. When siblings have guests, they are the sibling's guest, and other brothers and sisters are not allowed to horn in on the fun unless invited.

9. Phones are for business. Conversations must be five minutes or less. No making crank calls.

10. Did I mention no running, shrieking, or roughhousing inside?

11. Guests must abide by all house rules.

Take our recent Saturday evening Philly feast, for example. It was the wildly successful culmination of two goals: to give a proper sendoff for one set of friends and neighbors before they moved to their new home a few miles away, and to get to know a second set of friends and neighbors better.

When Christopher and I talked about entertaining at home, both families came up. Initially it didn't seem like a match made in entertaining heaven. The husbands hadn't met. And while the wives had, that was the extent of their association.

Then we realized they did have a connection. It came via Philadelphia. The new-friends couple both hailed from the city of Brotherly Love, and the dad of the departing family had grown up there as well. The Aronson solution? Philly Family Night.

Since the weather was unseasonably cool and not cooperating for an outdoor grill fest (our preferred method of entertaining), we took the Philly connection in a totally different direction and ordered out for authentic Philly food. (I really liked this part. I didn't have to cook for once.)

With gooey Philly cheese steaks and spicy fries warming in the oven for the adults alongside the kids' cheese pizza, we had plenty of time to get those first awkward moments after the introduction off to a chatty start.

We had one family bring their favorite Philly CDs (Frank Sinatra is clearly still a Philly favorite), and the other brought an antipasto platter. With these serving as an icebreaker, within minutes the couples had found a connection of their own, a high school friend both families had in common.

An hour later, the laughter level had reached fever pitch. Round two on the sandwiches was underway. And a mischievous rogue diner had ditched Frank's crooning in favor of a more danceable '70s disco CD. Moms bounded up from the table. Little boys dropped their trucks and suddenly appeared on the kitchen dance floor. Dads were toasting the festive scene with a potent Italian lemon-ice beverage that supplanted coffee as the after-dinner drink of choice.

The night ended before midnight only because little dancing boys were falling asleep in our arms.

That night was one of those wonderful times when you realize it's less about what you're eating or where you're eating it and more about who you bring to the table and how you choose to celebrate your friends' unique traits.

Of course, not all of our entertaining is so wildly spontaneous or laid back. We have business dinners. Kids have sleepovers. Neighbors drop in for a drink. Relatives visit from out of town. We have birthday parties, Thanksgiving dinners, and Christmas open houses. All of this entertaining is fun, and it makes our home a gathering place. It's also a plus to have your kids' friends at your home, instead of vice versa, so you can keep an eye on things.

But constant visitors can take a toll unless you're set up for entertaining. How

sense-ible preparations

To make your home feel cozy and warm, try appealing to the five senses.

Sight: Try to always have fresh flowers near the entry. Pick some roses or daisies from your own garden or just buy whatever is on sale at the grocery store. Flowers make a home feel fresh and inviting.

Smell: Every realtor knows the old trick of baking cookies on open house days to fill the house with a homey aroma. You don't have to have an eternal batch of cookies in the oven (think of the weight gain!), but keep aromatherapy, seasonal-scent candles, and potpourri on hand. If unexpected guests arrive, just give a quick spray or light a candle to freshen the air.

Sound: When company drops by, put on a favorite CD or turn on a tabletop fountain. The gurgle of flowing water soothes the soul and sends people rushing for the bathroom (so make sure it's clean and fresh-smelling).

Taste: Preparedness is key here. In the winter, always have teas and coffee on hand that you can easily brew or perk at a moment's notice. In the summer, keep fresh iced tea or lemonade in the fridge. Keep one little area of your pantry stocked just for these occasions. You might have biscotti, scones, muffins, little tea cookies, or specialty crackers or chips with condiments or dips. In the fridge, always keep at least one interesting cheese and some raspberries, pears, or other fruit. Other ideas are wine, veggies, nuts, miniature frozen quiches or pizzas, soft drinks, and sparkling waters. Keep a nice serving dish at the ready, too. Even the simplest feast looks elegant if you arrange it attractively on a nice platter.

Touch: Ever wonder why modern décor is so cold and uninviting? It's all those hard surfaces. Warm up your home with soft fabrics. Put woven place mats on that wood counter, drape a tablecloth across the kitchen table, and arrange a chenille afghan on the leather recliner. Outfit your home in a variety of textures for visual interest.

Now when that doorbell rings, you're ready!

can you maintain a job, a family, and a home, and still be able to entertain a drop-in guest?

Here are my tried-and-true tips to keep your home visitor-ready with minimal effort, to plan for parties and overnight guests, and to get your kids to participate in the entertaining effort.

a party-friendly home

Being a good hostess is not just about having people over (though it is about that, too). Being a good hostess is *really* about making everyone—from drop-in guests to your kids' sleepover friends to your big New Year's Eve party people—feel both special and at home.

This doesn't require fancy interior design (in fact, it precludes that look-but-don't-touch décor). Good hostessing does, however, require keeping the home somewhat tidy most of the time so that you can let people in without visibly cringing.

If you can't keep your entire home visitor-ready, at least resolve to keep one or two rooms clutter-free, just in case. In my house, I keep the kitchen and the living room company-ready. The living room is presentable in case business associates or more formal acquaintances drop by. The kitchen is where I herd my friends. We can chat while I brew tea or make coffee.

And if my guests drop in while I'm busy . . . well, I'm usually busy in the kitchen, so that works, too. They can sip their tea while I clear the breakfast dishes or prepare dinner.

I have to admit that in real life, it seems that whenever you have ten loads of laundry spread across the kitchen floor and the cat has just barfed in the entry hall, the doorbell rings. And the one time that you pray that it's a solicitor, it's your fastidious empty-nest neighbor dropping by. This must go in the "Life Is Not Fair" category. In the past, people solved this by having a parlor. Guests would go directly from the front door to the parlor, without the chance to steal a peek at the messy kitchen and work areas. Today we're more casual. (And we've repurposed the parlor/formal living room into a more frequently used space!) But we still need to keep up appearances. Here are a few tips to get that accomplished and still have a life:

Kitchen klatch: With all the granite counters, stainless steel appliances, and fluorescent lighting nowadays, kitchens can feel cold. The trick here is to make the kitchen seem inviting. To warm kitchens up, always have the kitchen table or counter set with place mats and flowers. Put a basket filled with different types of tea bags there along with a tin of cookies. Think of the little cafés where you just want to sit and linger. Go for that look.

This means, of course, that kitchens can't be dumping grounds. Make kids put away their backpacks. Keep the heart of your home uncluttered at all times. It will make cooking more enjoyable, too.

Linger in the living room: If you decide to use the living room for drop-ins, make sure that it's cozy. On a cold day, that's easy enough to do simply by lighting a fire and gathering two easy chairs around it. If a fire is not in the cards, group two cozy chairs with a small table in between. Then you can enjoy an intimate conversation with tea or coffee even in the most formal living area.

Patio pizzazz: If the weather cooperates, outdoors is always best for spontaneous entertaining. You don't have to worry about cobwebs. Hey, it's all part of nature, right? Just have a nice tray handy, throw on some iced tea or lemonade and cookies, and zip outside. All you need are two comfy chairs, a table, and some shade. A view would be nice, but it's hardly required.

Kids' rooms: Remember that kids have drop-in guests, too. Usually, they will be off to the resident child's bedroom, but it's a good idea to have designated places where kids can offer their guests a snack. Let your kids know in advance which snacks are allowed and where they are to be consumed. (And be sure to remind the kids that they have to clean up behind themselves and their guests.)

A friend of mine has a rarely used front porch secluded from the street view by big leafy plants. There are two wicker rockers and a table, so this is where her 10-year-old takes visitors to chat out of earshot of the grownups. The kids can enjoy messy, drippy Popsicles while discussing the trials and tribulations of the fifth grade.

let the kids help

There are lots of ways to get kids involved in party planning and help make them feel part of the fun. Here are just a few:

Prepare place cards: It's really handy to have place cards for any kind of a sit-down dinner, even an informal one. Place cards eliminate the uncomfortable where-do-you-want-everyone-to-sit dance. This is a definite enlist-the-kids project. Have them paint the little cards gold or apply sticker decorations. You can write the names on yourself, unless your tween or teen has terrific penpersonship. Use first and last names (John Smith), titles and names (Dr. Musto), or simply nicknames (Nana and Poppy) for more intimate affairs. Place the cards on top of or in the napkin's center. Better yet, place them on the tablecloth at the exact center of each place setting.

Make place mats: Have kids create leafy place mats. They're perfect for fall gatherings.

Start by gathering a variety of leaves of different sizes, shapes, and textures. Position white paper place mats over the leaves. With a peeled crayon, lightly rub the top of each place mat until the outline of the underlying leaf appears. Repeat with other leaves and different colors of crayons until you have a festive pattern. Cover the place mats with plastic and enjoy. You might want to make some for the grandparents, too.

Choose a centerpiece: Even if you're not eating a sit-down meal at the dining room table, a centerpiece is a lovely decoration. You can tie it into your theme! Get your kids to help brainstorm ideas. Whether you choose flowers or fruit, your centerpiece is one of the most important pieces of your table setting. Create or order yours well in advance, and, if you ordered it, pick it up the morning of your dinner.

As the name implies, place your centerpiece in the exact center of the table. Place your brand-new white candles at each end of the table, halfway between the places of the host and the hostess and the centerpiece. (You already knew that the host and hostess sit on opposite ends of the table.)

Ready the patio: Casual parties are often outside, or else they eventually spill outside, so make sure your patio and all the patio furniture is clean. Wash off glass tables. Make sure the umbrella is operational. Put out enough chairs so that people can rest somewhere. Arrange potted plants in nice groupings.

If you're barbecuing, make sure the grill is clean and that you have plenty of charcoal or propane. Position the grill in a corner where kids won't be running by. (But choose a spot where there's enough room for the Dads to hold court over the flames.)

kid-friendly family parties

Have you noticed that many parties today are family affairs? This means the hosts have to worry about entertaining not only other adults, but their offspring (and maybe their parents) as well. While it's great to be able to spend even more time with our kids and our friends' kids, more bodies (regardless of size) mean more work. And when you have to cater to different interest levels and food preferences, a "simple" gathering just keeps getting less simple.

Laying out a buffet this way makes it easy for people to get their utensils and food.

DIRTY LITTLE SECRETS

SPOTLESS SILVERWARE

Your party ware—brass, copper, pewter, silver, and stainless steel—each require special care to look their best on your festive table. First, however, you'll need to know a few basics.

Rinse your pieces under warm running water and use a mild soap such as dishwashing liquid to remove surface dirt. Resist the urge to submerge. Less is more with these precious metals! Wear gloves to protect your hands from the metal polish and the metal from fingerprints. Cotton is best, but rubber works as long as you wash a new pair first. (Any sulfur that remains on the gloves could tarnish the silver.) Always test a small area first to make sure the polish is compatible with your piece before tackling the entirety. Follow directions carefully! Finally, polish the utensils dry with a clean, lint-free rag such as an old T-shirt or well-worn towel.

Here's how to restore the lovely finish of special pieces:

Brass. Place the tarnished brass item in a pot, pan, or plastic container. Cover it with ketchup, Tabasco sauce, or Worcestershire sauce. (Seriously!) If you don't have these ingredients, try vinegar or lemon juice, both of which have the acidity to remove oxidation or tarnish. Allow the brass to sit for two hours. Then scrub it with mild dishwashing liquid and a soft fingernail brush or toothbrush under cool running water. Dry the brass with a smooth, lint-free cloth. To retard future tarnish, rub the brass with a cloth moistened with olive oil.

Copper. Wash copper with soap and warm water, and polish it with a commercial copper polish following the label's directions. Or make your own polish by moistening salt with vinegar or lemon juice to make a paste for a bright finish, or a paste of rotten-stone (a soft,

You could make your affair "adults only." But sometimes it's fun to include the whole family. Plus, sitters can be difficult to find, especially during the holidays. So your job is to plan a soiree where people of all ages will be comfortable, entertained, and safe. It's easier than you might think. Here are a few ideas.

Most adult parties are boring for kids. No clowns. No balloons. They just don't get what we enjoy about talking to each other over a glass of wine or a martini and nibbling smelly shrimp and cheese. To keep kids from running wild at your soiree, take the following precautions:

Behavior warning: Remind your children that parties are grownup events and we must use prim and proper behavior. No running. No loud voices. No roughhousing. Pretend that you are a prince or princess for the evening.

Damage control: Put breakables on higher shelves. Anything than be bumped decomposed limestone that is used in powder form as a polishing material) and olive oil for a dull finish.

Here's an important tip: Never use your copper utensils or pans with copper interiors to store acidic foods such as fruits, salad dressings, tomatoes, or anything containing vinegar. Toxic compounds can form if acidic food is cooked, stored, or served in copper containers.

Pewter. Rubbing alcohol will get rid of most of this metal's grime. And it's a cinch to care for: It's *supposed* to look aged! The only major caveat for this very thin metal: Avoid serving acidic foods on your pewter, because they eat away the metal.

Silver. Place a clean cotton tube sock on your polishing hand. Dampen the sock slightly under cool running water. Squeeze a pearl-size drop of toothpaste on your "gloved" fingertip. Apply the toothpaste to the silver using up-and-down rather than circular strokes until the tarnish is gone. Use a twisted bit of rag or a toothbrush to get between silverware tines and other tight spaces. Rinse the silver well and polish it dry with the clean, dry side of the sock.

Store silverware in an airtight plastic bag or in a chest lined with tarnish-resistant flannel. Avoid serving sulfur-containing foods such as mayonnaise and eggs from your silver platters—they'll cause tarnishing.

Stainless steel. This material is aptly named, thankfully. It resists stains, but it can retain oily fingerprints. You can throw these items (or even gently place them) into your dishwasher. If marks persist, wash stainless steel silverware by hand with phosphate-free dishwashing liquid to remove stains, or use club soda to remove streaks or heat stains.

off or into and broken will be. Move delicate possessions to higher ground until the pint-size stampede is over.

Fire safety: Do not leave lighted candles unattended in bathrooms or anywhere little hands might reach. Fireplace candles or lighters go atop the mantel, not alongside the firewood in easy reach.

Pet protection: Put all pets away for the evening. Yeah, they're cute, but dogs and cats can get nippy when mauled by 2-year-olds. More fragile animals like hamsters or birds could be injured. You also lessen the risk of someone accidentally letting the pets escape if you put them in a safe place during the party.

Kid zone creation: Set aside a study or den as a play area. Equip it with a few toys, videos, computer games, coloring books, and crayons. The kids don't have to stay there—that would be unsociable. But at least you've provided a kid-friendly environment where they can amuse themselves. Be sure to provide a

she planned with pizzazz

Here's a sample plan that a friend did for an end-of-the-school-year recital party. The theme was music, of course. And all the kids either performed or functioned as the audience.

_____ Themed elements: Musical invitations (scan sheet music for front). Black-and-white color scheme. Cake in the shape of an upright piano with a vase of flowers on top. Program for guests. Piano and musical note confetti on the tablecloths. Individual bouquets in vases as floral arrangements. (Each participant got to take one home for her performance.)

_____ Two weeks ahead: Create and send invitations. Include an ending time so guests don't arrive while you and the troops are cleaning up the patio.

_____ One week ahead: Order piano-shaped cake. Plan menu. Begin tallying RSVPs. Make recital program.

_____ Three days ahead: Clean living room, kitchen, dining room, and patio. Make a list and go grocery shopping.

_____ Two days ahead: Arrange furniture for recital. Figure out seating arrangements. Decide on serving dishes and tableware. Decorate the party rooms. Set up the buffet table with flatware, plates, platters, and serving utensils. (They don't all have to match, mind you; sometimes mismatched sets add a down-home warmth.)

_____ One day ahead: Marinate meat. Prepare crudités.

_____ That morning: Cut yellow and white cheeses into musical notes with cookie cutter. Prepare salads, dips, appetizers, and side dishes.

_____ Early afternoon: Bring cheese snacks out of the fridge and onto the table so they're room temperature by party time.

_____ Afternoon: Doorbell starts ringing at 3:30 P.M. Recital begins at 4:00 P.M., followed by hors d'oeuvres and drinks.

_____ Evening: Dad begins barbecuing. Dinner is served on the patio at 6:00 P.M. By 8:00 P.M., the last guest leaves and the cleanup begins.

All the girls in the class got a chance to dress up and show off their talents. Parents got a chance to chat. It was a fun start to the summer.

separate teens-only space away from the little kids to make grumpy teens smile.

If you can possibly find a babysitter for the event, hire one. Your neighborhood high schooler could probably entertain the mini-masses nicely for a few hours—at a bargain rate. It's well worth your investment. It might even save your carpet.

If you really want an adult affair, but want to make it easy on parents who might not have regular sitters to call on, arrange for your sitter to watch the kids at one of your guest's homes (preferably nearby). If you're having a late party (such as a New Year's Eve gathering), it could even be a sleepover affair where guests pick up the kids the next morning. Just make sure your sitter/kid ratio stays at about one sitter for every five children. If you have more than five kids, hire two (or even more) sitters.

Menu planning: Make a few kid-friendly foods. Kids like carrots, cheese, Goldfish, peppers, popcorn, and pretzels. If you're having a dinner party, a good bet for the kids would be grilled chicken or burgers, stovetop mac and cheese, or cheese pizza. Make or buy some special drinks for the kids, like lemonade or juice boxes, or buy some "kid champagne" (a.k.a. sparkling cider). Make sure they have a kids' table where they can reach their special snacks. This way, they won't be dripping dip all over the adult fare.

Give gifts: One way of keeping the kiddies happy is to give them each a little gift. It amuses them for a while, and their parents will love you. Hint: Beanie Babies are inexpensive and adored by kids of all ages.

Cave in to videos: If you absolutely cannot find a sitter (try very, *very* hard), suggest that the parents take turns supervising the kiddie table. Most kids

she learned a lesson

When a friend's child was 4 years old, she had a buddy over for a sleepover. The next day, Mom opened her bureau drawer to find that her household stash of cash was missing. She called her daughter and asked whether the girl had taken the money. The child immediately ran to her room and returned with a fistful of $5s and $1s. "Did Bridget take any of these?" Mom asked. "Oh no," replied the child. "All hers had 2s on them."

The lesson? If your children have visitors, you probably don't want them roaming all over your house. Establish parameters with the kids ahead of time and let them know which rooms they are allowed to take friends into and which rooms (such as Mom and Dad's bedroom) are strictly off limits. You might want to lock the door to these rooms, just in case.

Also, you probably have some heirlooms or keepsakes—the untouchables—that your children know not to play with. Sometimes, however, they may be tempted to show these things off for company. Tell the children firmly what things are untouchables, even for company. And lock up your jewelry.

pet precautions

How could anyone not love Fluffy? And Bruiser wouldn't hurt a fly, would he?

Tell that to Grandpa who sneezes when you say "cat." Or to Aunt Alice who's terrified of anything that barks. Or to Great-grandma Susan who broke a hip when a friendly pup jumped on her.

Yes, this is your pets' home. But they have to make compromises, too. Warn guests if you have a boa constrictor, like my friend Rada in San Francisco does. Ever since she let Michael, her teenager, bring "Rosy" home, I've been inclined to be a bit more attentive when our little guy, Payne, is with us there. Your guests may decide to sidestep the overnight route altogether and decide the nearest Embassy Suites would work better. If not, well, they were warned.

Keep all animals and reptiles safely confined during a guest's visit as much as possible. Dogs can get territorial when strangers are wandering around the house in the dark. And you don't want Cousin Flora to be afraid to go to the bathroom at night. Think of where she might wander. . . .

will actually prefer to have their own table in another room, especially if you let them watch a video, and on this special occasion, I certainly would. You're in survival mode here.

creating great grandparent affairs

Okay, you know how to entertain folks your age, but what about their Mom who travels with a walker? People will sometimes ask if they can bring their extended family along for a visit. This is a good opportunity to find out their guests' ages and whether their guests have special needs.

Here are some good strategies for elderly guests, but also for a safe party for all:

Assure a safe entry. Make sure your house number is clearly visible. Clear sidewalks and porches of kids' toys or anything someone might trip over. Make sure the entry is well lighted.

Clear walkways. Inside, make sure there is a clear, well-lit walkway that someone in a wheelchair or with a walker could navigate safely. Take up slippery area rugs. Mark any changes in floor level with plants or furniture.

Arrange seating. Even if you're planning a stand-up cocktail party, you should always have a few seats arranged in small cozy groups. This makes conversation easy and audible. And it provides a restful place for those who can't stand for long periods of time.

Position tables. Position small tables near some of the seating so guests can put their drinks or food down. Make sure the lighting is pleasant but strong enough so that the tables can be seen en route to finding another cheese ball.

Prepare food for all. Prepare some plain low-fat foods that have little or no salt. Regardless of your theme, make it easy for people with allergies, on diets, or simply finicky to find something to munch on. What could be worse than having a guest leave hungry?

Put up pets. See "Pet Precautions" on the opposite page.

Now you can relax and enjoy your party, knowing you've done all you can do for all of your guests.

party cleanup with kids

The party's over. It's time to call it a night.

But not quite yet. The guests are gone, but the mess remains. It's late, and all you want to do is get horizontal. But leaving the stuff as is can make foods become one with your cookware—never a good thing unless you're trying to get your cookware to multiply. Or offer an invitation for a second party with your resident insects. Ick.

Instead, let's just give in and decide to do the dirty job before we retire. Here's how to speed through cleanup so you don't have to wake up to a headache-inducing morning mess.

Start by delegating the following jobs among your still-awake family members. Hint: If you've got any under 10, they're better off in bed and out of the way. Older kids, however, are fair free-labor game. Take advantage of it while you can.

Trash patrol: Give your youngest non-sleeper a trash bag and instruct him to collect all disposable products. Remind him that your best silver is not disposable.

Scrap scrapers: Have one kid collect dishes, plates, and silverware, and another scrape the leftovers into a garbage bag or into the disposal.

Leftovers inspector: Mom or Dad can decide what is salvageable. But be careful here. If perishable food has been sitting out too long, you're better off tossing it. Two hours is the rule for most meats and prepared foods with cheese or eggs. You don't want food poisoning along with a hangover, do you?

Glass collector: This worker carefully gathers all glasses and deposits them very carefully by the sink.

FAMILY PICKUP LINES

CASTING CALL Don't hire help for your party, cast it! One child can be the greeter. A younger child can serve nicely as the napkin dispenser. Another can be the designated coat-taker. Yet another might get KP duty. The family that serves together, stays together, right?!

Laundry tosser: Now that the table is clear, assign a child to hunt and gather tablecloths, napkins, and washable place mats for the laundry. Treat any stains tonight, not tomorrow. Toss 'em in the washer. Don't forget to turn it on before you retire.

Dish washers: On the counter by the sink, organize the dishes by type. Glasses together, plates, serving dishes, and pots and pans. Now you have a logical order in which to rinse the dishes and load the dishwasher.

This is a two-person job, by the way. Once the dishwasher is full, run it while you hand-wash the pots and serving dishes and anything else that didn't fit in the dishwasher.

PARTY PREP AND CLEANUP CHORES BY AGE

Here's a guide to which chores kids can do to prepare for and clean up after a party. This list is really focused on party-specific tasks. It doesn't include the general cleaning you might also wish to do. (Check out "Mrs. Clean Jeans' Housekeeping Routine" on page 253 for lots of advice on that!) Once a child reaches a certain skill or age level, he can generally do the chores for his age group and those for the age groups below, too.

AGES 2 AND UNDER:
- Put toys in bins or drawers
- Help pick up stray books and magazines
- Help set the table
- Turn on the dishwasher

AGES 3 TO 5:
- Previous chores, plus:
- Put away toys in the proper boxes or bins
- Return books to bookshelves
- Return CDs, DVDs, and videocassettes to their cases

- Place dirty dishes on the kitchen counter
- Help unload the dishwasher

AGES 6 TO 9:
- Previous chores, plus:
- Sweep the patio and porches
- Wipe the patio table and chairs
- Set and clear the table
- Do simple cooking tasks such as rinsing vegetables
- Put the dishes in the dishwasher
- Prepare place cards
- Wipe up spills

AGES 10 TO 13:
- Previous chores, plus:
- Pour beverages for meals
- Help hand-wash dishes
- Put out fresh towels and soap
- Polish silver

AGES 14 TO 17:
- Previous chores, plus:
- Clean out the fireplace and tools
- Clean the powder-room sink and toilet

DIRTY LITTLE SECRETS

PARTY STAINS

It's pretty inevitable that someone will spill something somewhere at your party. Here's how to clean up the mess as gracefully as possible.

Cleaning wine stains from tablecloths: On a fresh, wet stain, sprinkle coarse salt to absorb liquid from the fabric. Shake or brush off the salt (outside, if possible). Then blot the fabric with cold water, or rinse it under cold water to remove excess sugar and prevent oxidation.

For older stains, rub a bit of diluted liquid laundry detergent onto the stained area. Launder the fabric in the hottest water that is safe for it, using laundry detergent and color-safe or chlorine bleach (whichever is safer; check the label). Repeat as needed until the stain is gone.

Removing wax from carpeting: Place ice cubes in a plastic bag and place the bag over the wax until it hardens. Gently scrape off the excess wax using a spatula or a spoon. Then set your iron on low heat. Place a brown paper bag without any writing or design on it over the stain. Press the iron on the bag for no longer than a couple of seconds. Keep the iron heat low so that the carpet fibers don't get scorched. Repeat and replace the bag as necessary until the wax no longer transfers to the paper when heated.

Blot the spot with dry-cleaning fluid until color is no longer being removed. (Use cleaning solvents like these sparingly to prevent damage to carpet backing.) Then blot the area with a cleaning solution of ¼ teaspoon dishwashing liquid and 1 cup warm water to remove all traces of cleaning fluid. Rinse and blot dry.

Next time, buy dripless candles.

Floor sweeper: Your little helpers can now be wiping counters and sweeping floors. Save vacuuming for later. As in tomorrow.

Safety checker: Someone—preferably a grownup someone—needs to make a whole-home sweep to make sure that all candles have been extinguished and the fire is out. I usually count how many candles I light so that I don't accidentally leave one smoldering somewhere.

Now, finally, turn off the music and the lights. Say Goodnight, Mrs. Clean Jeans.

After all of the guests have gone, things have been cleaned up, and life is returning to normal, hold a Monday Morning Quarterback session. Gather the family for a post-party or visit mortem. Discuss what worked. The kiddie and teen tables? Serve-yourself bar? Did the cheese blintzes flop miserably? Keep a notebook to record your party hits and misses. It's the best way to help you plan your next shindig!

Part IV
Cleaning Around the Year

Chapter 13

mrs. clean jeans' housekeeping routine

AS YOU'VE READ THE CHAPTERS in this book about rooms to be cleaned and activities to be done, I've talked a lot about which chores kids can do and how old they need to be to do them. I've been less specific, though, about which chores need to be done *when*. This is because it's a very individual choice. Your family's chore list is sure to be very different from my family's list. Your list will differ depending on so many factors, such as how many kids you have and how old they are, the layout of your home, whether or not you have pets, where you live, how much (or how little) your family is home, and how meticulous you and the family intend to be with your housekeeping routine.

But to give you a guide to create your own chore list, I'd like to offer you mine! This list includes all of the chores listed in the "Chores by Age" sections of each chapter. But here I've organized the chores by frequency of chores: daily, weekly, monthly, seasonally, and yearly (or spring cleaning).

Within each category, I've listed appropriate chores for each age group. (Remember, the age recommendations are just that, recommendations. Your tidy 11-year-old who has been cleaning his room since age 2 can probably tackle some of the chores listed for teenagers if safety isn't an issue. Conversely, if you've been the maid for your 13-year-old since she was born, you might have to start her off with some of the simpler chores recommended for younger children.) Once a child reaches a certain skill or age level, he can generally do the chores for his age group and those for the age groups below.

daily chores

Let's come clean here. The daily grind is challenging enough—and I'm just talking about the kids, carpools, and errands here—so don't let this daily cleaning list ruffle your feathers. After all, now that you've rallied the troops, you'll have plenty of help getting the essentials done daily. And exactly what those essentials are in your home is entirely your call! However, for the record, here's what we do at my house:

Daily chores for kids ages 2 and under:

- Get diaper

- Put toys in bins or drawers

- Put dirty clothes in hamper if the top is low enough

- Help pick up stray books and magazines

- Help set the table

- Turn on the dishwasher

- Turn off the TV if the button is within reach

- Wipe feet before coming inside

- Close cabinet doors and drawers

- Help rinse out the tub

- Hang up towel (on hook)

- Pick up wrappers and small trash

Daily chores for kids ages 3 to 5:

- Previous chores (except for the diaper!), plus:

- Pull comforter up over bed

- Put toys and games (and all their pieces) in the proper boxes or bins

- Return CDs, DVDs, and videocassettes to their cases

- Return books to bookshelves

- Place dirty dishes on the kitchen counter

- Help unload the dishwasher

- Sponge down the play table

- Damp-mop any spills

- Rinse out the sink after use

- Fill the pet's water dish

- Take backpacks from the car into the house

Daily chores for kids ages 6 to 9:

- Previous chores, plus:

- Make the bed

- Hang up towels

- Decide which clothes are dirty and which can be reworn

- Squeegee the shower

- Rinse out the tub

- Feed pets

- Exercise pets

- Clean pets' bowls and cages

- Help make breakfast

- Set and clear the table

- Do simple cooking tasks such as rinsing vegetables

- Put dishes in the dishwasher

- Wipe up spills

- Wipe kitchen table, chairs, highchair, counters, and cooktop or range

- Wipe down interior of the microwave

- Sweep or vacuum kitchen and bathroom floors and damp-mop any spills

- Take out trash and recycling and remove compostable material

- Pick up trash in car and empty car trash bag

Daily chores for kids ages 10 to 13:

- Previous chores, plus:

- Pour beverages for meals

- Help hand-wash dishes

- Make lunch for school

- Unload the dishwasher

- Disinfect kitchen and bathroom countertops

- Return to cases and organize the car's CDs, DVDs, and cassettes

Daily chores for kids ages 14 to 17:

- Previous chores, plus:

- Prepare meals

- Clean coffeemaker thoroughly

weekly chores

Here are the chores that I feel should be done once each week. (Because these are a bit harder, I've exempted the 2-and-under crowd here.)

Weekly chores for kids ages 3 to 5:

- Remove clothes from the dryer

- Take clean, folded clothes to his or her room

- Dust low furniture

- Help fold laundry

- Help prepare papers for recycling

Weekly chores for kids ages 6 to 9:

- Previous chores, plus:

- Bring groceries in from the car

- Put away groceries

- Tidy bedroom

- Sweep floors

- Shake area rugs, depending on size

- Water plants

- Empty and wipe wastebaskets clean, using disinfecting wipes

- Prepare recyclables for pickup

- Take hampers to the laundry room

- Fold simple laundry items

- Match socks from dryer

- Dust furniture and shelves

- Dust lamp shades

- Vacuum out the car, with help, depending on the machine height and weight

- Scoop and clean out the litter box

- Scoop up the dog's poop

Weekly chores for kids ages 10 to 13:

- Previous chores, plus:

- Disinfect kitchen and bathroom countertops

- Do a surface cleaning of fridge

- Clean telephones, computer and TV screens, video-game controllers, and remote controls

- Sort, wash, and fold laundry

- Change bed linens

- Put out fresh towels and soap

- Clean the bedroom

- Clean the shower

- Wipe chrome fixtures and mirrors clean and polish them

- Vacuum floors and carpets

- Mop floors and dry- or damp-mop wood floors

- Disinfect light switches and doorknobs

- Take trash and recycling containers to curb

- Clean fish/reptile aquarium

- Give pets medication

Weekly chores for kids ages 14 to 17:

- Previous chores, plus:

- Clean toilets, sinks, and tubs

- Wash the dog and/or cat

monthly chores

Here are chores that should be done once a month:

Monthly chore for kids ages 3 to 5:

- Sweep the garage floor with a push broom

Monthly chores for kids ages 6 to 9:

- Previous chore, plus:

- Wipe smudges from walls and doors

Monthly chores for kids ages 10 to 13:

- Previous chores, plus:

- Clean bedroom closets

- Wash out kitchen trash container and surrounding area

- Vacuum furniture

- Wipe leather furniture with a soft cloth

- Clean windows

- Clean blinds

- Wipe off the car's dashboard and upholstery

- Help clean the garage

Monthly chores for kids ages 14 to 17:

- Previous chores, plus:

- Organize closets

- Dust the ceiling fans

- Clean lights and light fixtures

- Clean the shower curtain

- Wipe down walls

- Disinfect the sink and drain

- Sew on buttons and mend torn clothes

seasonal chores

Some chores need to be done only in certain seasons. Here are a few examples.

Seasonal chores for kids ages 2 and under:

- Pick up outside toys

- Collect snails in a pail

Seasonal chores for kids ages 3 to 5:

- Previous chores, plus:

- Put away outside toys and games (and all their pieces) in the proper boxes or bins

- Help with planting

- Water outside plants

- Debug plants
- Sponge down the outdoor play table

Seasonal chores for kids ages 6 to 9:

- Previous chores, plus:
- Take indoor plants outside for a gentle washing
- Rake leaves
- Sweep the patio and porches
- Wipe patio table and chairs
- Do easy yard work such as weeding
- Help wash the car
- Hang up the (pool) towel
- Help test the pool or hot tub water
- Help balance the pool or hot tub pH
- Help clean the pool strainer baskets

Seasonal chores for kids ages 10 to 13:

- Previous chores, plus:
- Clean the patio and patio furniture
- Plant vegetables, annuals, and bulbs
- Harvest vegetables
- Mulch plants

- Take compostable material to the compost pile
- Cut flowers for the house
- Vacuum the pool once a week
- Fish surface litter out of the pool (with a grownup's supervision, of course)
- Scrub the pool sides occasionally
- Detail/dress the car's tires
- Polish silver
- Shovel snow

Seasonal chores for kids ages 14 to 17:

- Previous chores, plus:
- Mow the lawn
- Wash exterior windows
- Do yard work such as pruning
- Spring clean the garage
- Wash the car
- Wash the car's undercarriage each spring
- Clean the dryer exhaust vent
- Check the pool or hot-tub filter
- Maintain the compost pile
- Turn mattresses
- Vacuum drapes
- Clean out the fireplace and tools

yearly chores

These chores need to be done only once a year:

Yearly chores for kids ages 3 to 5:

- Wash or spot-clean baseboards

- Air-tumble throw pillows in dryer

Yearly chores for kids ages 6 to 9:

- Previous chores, plus:

- Clean all doormats

- Wash inside and outside of cabinets

Yearly chores for kids ages 10 to 13:

- Previous chores, plus:

- Wash screens and miniblinds

- Wash windows and wipe light fixtures

- Wash washable curtains

Yearly chores for kids ages 14 to 17:

- Previous chores, plus:

- Deep-clean carpet and upholstery (teens can make the call to the carpet cleaner for you)

- Scrub or strip and wax floors

- Wash and polish wood furniture

- Change furnace filters

- Dust and vacuum corners and crevices from high point to low

- Vacuum floors and carpets and move furniture to clean underneath

- Remove dust ruffles from beds to wash or dry-clean

Yearly chores for grownups:

- Check washing machine hoses. Replace if they're older than two years or you find bulges or cracks

- Vacuum heating vents and ducts

- Clean out the medicine cabinet by tossing expired medications

- Reseal wood floors

Mrs. Clean Jeans' Resources

I encourage you to check out these resources for more tips on cleaning and organizing—and doing both with kids without losing your mind. They offer far more information than could be squeezed between the covers of any book.

www.mrscleanjeans.com
My official Web site offers helpful information on cleaning, gardening, managing family life, organizing, planning family vacations, and scheduling—all with kids. Sign up for my Monday Update to get my latest tips.

www.mcjteens.com
My daughter, Lyndsay, and Mrs. Dirty Jeans' daughter, Marisa, created this cool place for kids to create their own cool decor. Get your tweens and teens into the home care scene.

Simplify Your Household. Pleasantville, NY: Reader's Digest, 1998.
My other book is a colorful guide to getting your household work done when you don't have time to do it—and conquering the clutter while you're at it.

Index

Boldface page references indicate illustrations. Underscored references indicate boxed text.

G